LIBERTY S

(RE

Æ

EASTERN ART.

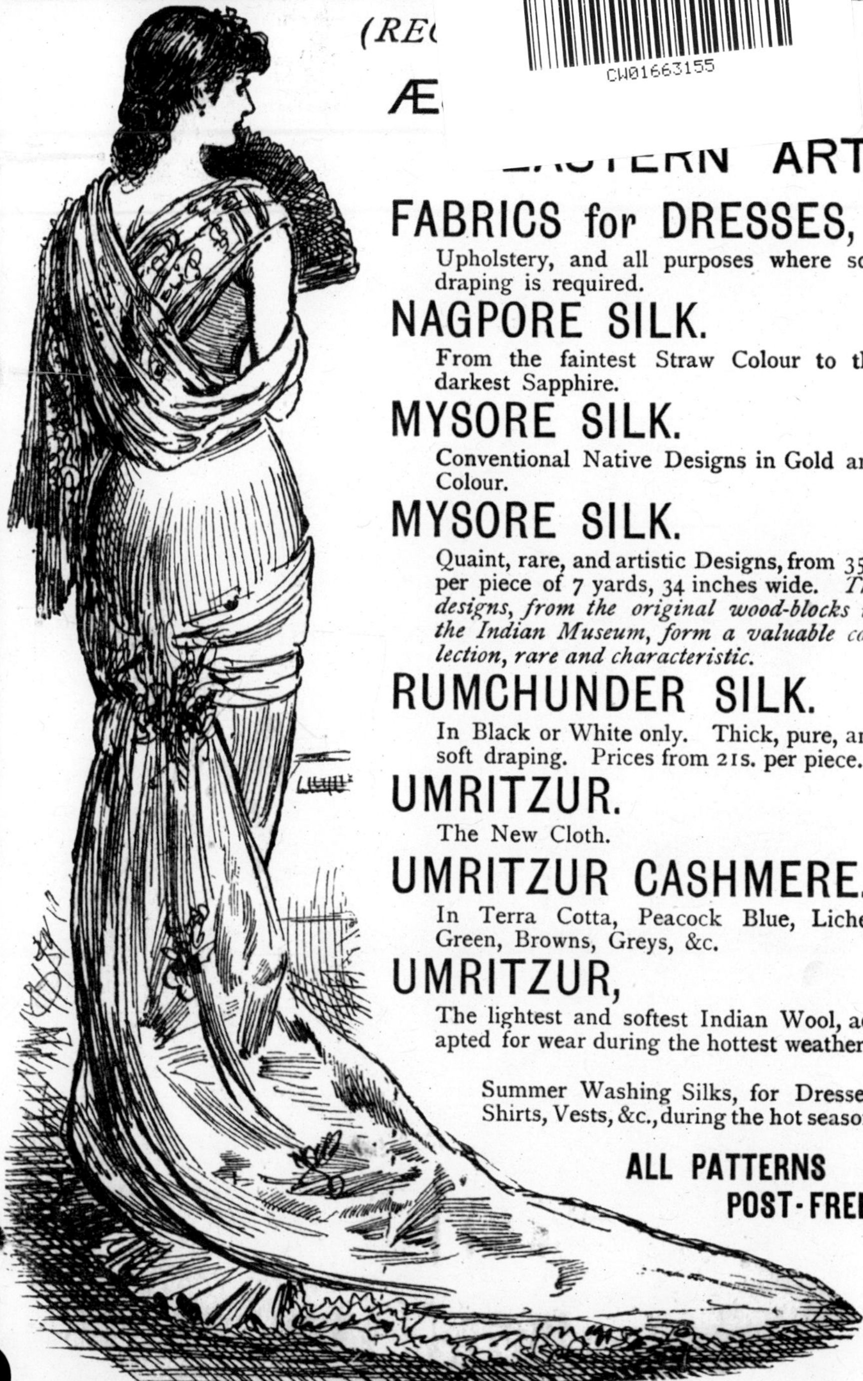

FABRICS for DRESSES,

Upholstery, and all purposes where soft draping is required.

NAGPORE SILK.

From the faintest Straw Colour to the darkest Sapphire.

MYSORE SILK.

Conventional Native Designs in Gold and Colour.

MYSORE SILK.

Quaint, rare, and artistic Designs, from 35s per piece of 7 yards, 34 inches wide. *The designs, from the original wood-blocks in the Indian Museum, form a valuable collection, rare and characteristic.*

RUMCHUNDER SILK.

In Black or White only. Thick, pure, and soft draping. Prices from 21s. per piece.

UMRITZUR.

The New Cloth.

UMRITZUR CASHMERE.

In Terra Cotta, Peacock Blue, Lichen Green, Browns, Greys, &c.

UMRITZUR,

The lightest and softest Indian Wool, adapted for wear during the hottest weather.

Summer Washing Silks, for Dresses, Shirts, Vests, &c., during the hot season.

ALL PATTERNS POST-FREE.

LIBERTY & CO.,

EASTERN ART STORES,
218 REGENT STREET.

THE GREATEST BLESSING THE HUMAN MIND CAN CONCEIVE.

A Royal and Noble Example!!!

"REFERRING to the continual manifestations of interest in sanitary science by members of the Royal Family—in short, in all matters affecting the health of the people—he remarked that if all the owners of cottages in the Empire exercised the same sanitary care that had been exercised in the cottages on Her Majesty's private estates, the general sickness and death-rate would be reduced one-third; in other words, it would be as if on every third year there were a jubilee, and no sickness, and no deaths"!!!—An Address by Dr. W. B. Richardson, F.R.S., &c., &c., at the Ladies' Sanitary Association.

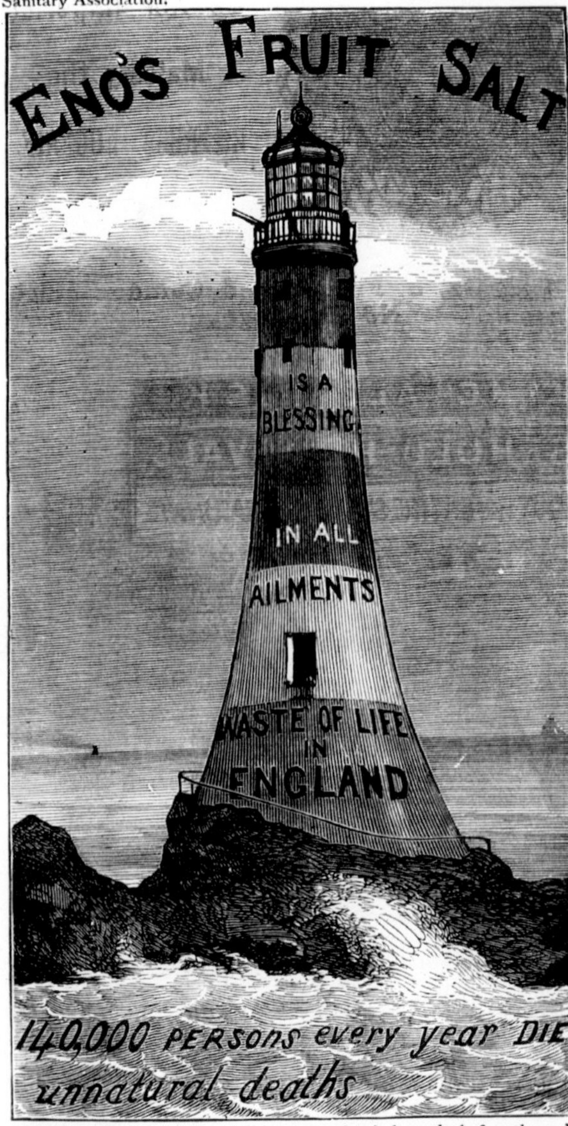

WITH each BOTTLE of FRUIT SALT is wrapped a large Illustrated Sheet, showing the best means of stamping out infectious diseases, Fevers, and Blood Poisons, &c. If this Invaluable Information was universally carried out, many forms of disease now producing such havoc would cease to exist, as Plague, Leprosy, &c., have done, when the true cause has become known.

ENO'S FRUIT SALT is particularly valuable. No traveller should leave home without a supply, for by its use the most dangerous forms of Fevers, Blood Poisons, &c., are prevented and cured. It is in truth a Family Medicine Chest in the simplest yet most potent form. Instead of being lowering to the system, this preparation is, in the highest degree, invigorating. Its effect in relieving thirst, giving tone to the system, and aiding digestion is most striking.

IMPORTANT TO TRAVELLERS.—"Clifton Down Hotel, Gloucestershire, Feb. 10th, 1881.—Sir,—having travelled a great deal in my life, and having suffered a great deal from poisoned blood and loss of appetite, I was induced by a friend to try your world-famed FRUIT SALT. I was immediately relieved, and am once more hale and healthy. I shall never be without a bottle again on my travels. I am too pleased to repay you in some way for your wonderful invention by giving you full use of my testimony to the above.—Sir, I am yours gratefully,

"DR. J. HANSON, M.A."

TORPID LIVER.—"Thornhill, Hampshire, March, 1881.—For three years I have suffered from an enlarged and torpid liver; could not sleep on either side, digestion bad: in fact, my whole system was out of repair. I tried all the German waters to no effect, and after great suffering for three years the use of ENO'S FRUIT SALT was suggested to me, and I am happy and thankful to be able to state that, after three months' use of your FRUIT SALT, at bed-time and in the morning, I am perfectly restored to my usual robust health. Again I thank you for your infallible discovery.

"H. M. DILLON, J.P."

SUCCESS IN LIFE.—"A new invention is brought before the public and commands success. A score of abominable imitations are immediately introduced by the unscrupulous, who, in copying the original closely enough to deceive the public, and yet not so exactly as to infringe upon legal rights, exercise an ingenuity that, employed in an original channel, could not fail to secure reputation and profit."—*Adams.*

CAUTION.—Legal Rights are Protected in every Civilised Country. Examine each Bottle, and see the Capsule is marked "ENO'S FRUIT SALT." Without it you hav been imposed on by worthless imitations. SOLD BY ALL CHEMISTS. Price 2s. 9d. an 4s. 6d. Directions in Sixteen Languages, How to Prevent Disease.

Prepared only at ENO'S Fruit Salt Works, Hatcham, London, S.E., by J. C. ENO'S Patent.

BRICHTON AQUARIUM

THE LARGEST AND MOST COMPLETE AQUARIUM IN THE WORLD,

And contains an unrivalled Collection of Fishes and Marine Animals, including, the SEA LIONS, Seals, Snapping Turtle, GIGANTIC STURGEON, ALLIGATORS, OCTOPODS, GUILLEMOTS, Shoals of Herring and Mackerel, and other interesting and rare specimens not seen elsewhere.

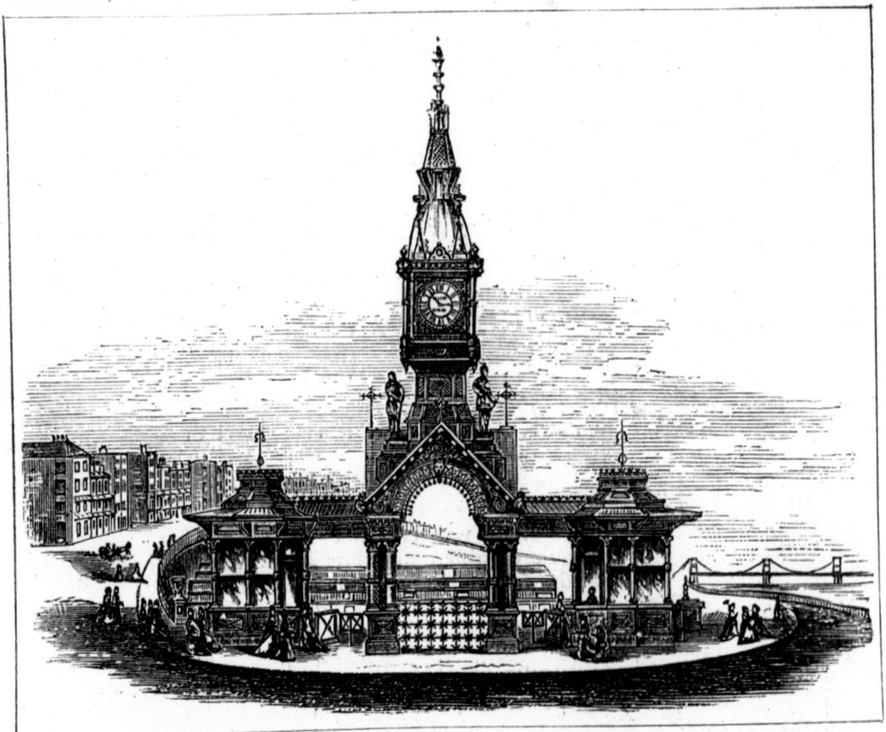

Instrumental Concert at 3 Daily. Varied Musical and other Entertainments every Evening at 8. Special Vocal and Instrumental Concerts, with the Leading Artistes, every Saturday Afternoon at 3. The Aquarium Band—*Conductor*, Mr. F. CORDER.

The Reading Rooms are supplied with all the London and Provincial Papers, Periodicals, and Latest Telegrams.

Well arranged Café and Restaurant. Luncheons and Dinners at fixed prices, or à la Carte.

Open Air Concerts on the Terrace during the Summer Months.

OPEN EVERY WEEK DAY FROM 10 TILL 10. SUNDAYS 1 TILL DUSK.

ADMISSION ONE SHILLING.

SEASON TICKETS—MONTHLY, 7s. 6d.; THREE MONTHS, 10s. 6d.; ANNUAL, 21s.

I. WILKINSON, *Manager.*

EVERYONE HIS OWN PRINTER WITH THE

"MODEL"

PATENTED SELF-INKING

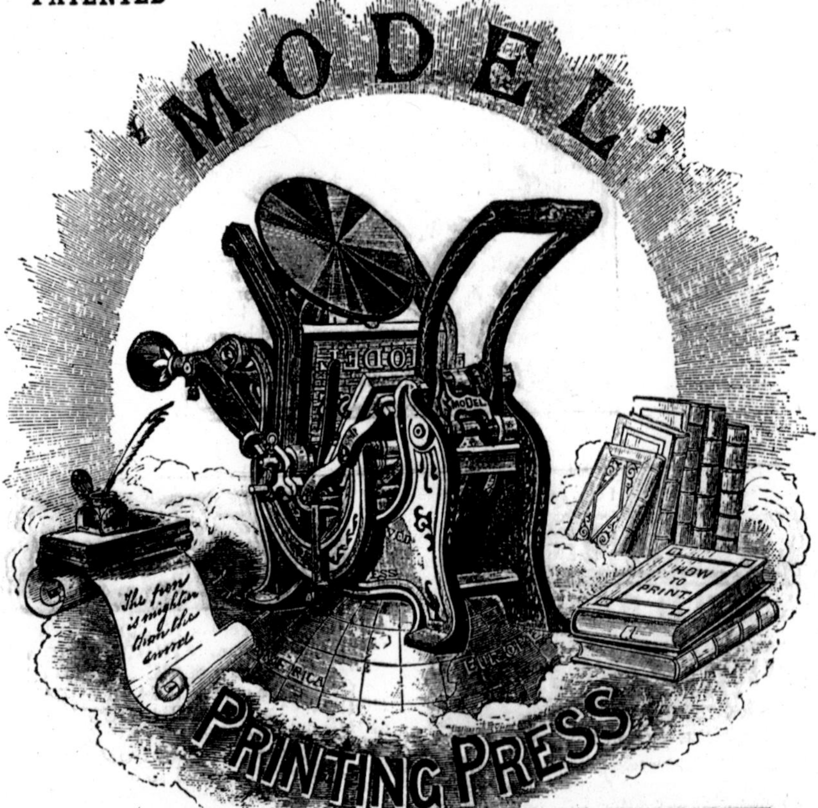

WHITE

HAND, FOOT & STEAM POWER.

PRINTING PRESS

DESCRIPTION.

The sheet to be printed is brought in contact with the type by the downward motion of the handle. As the handle is raised the platen returns to its former position, the left hand removes the printed paper whilst the right replaces a fresh sheet. The inking is effected automatically as the handle is lowered and raised. Hence extreme cleanliness and speed.

It prints from 500 to 1000 copies per hour, according to the skill of the operator and the size of the forme.

All the Hand Presses are now made from entirely New Patterns just completed, further Improvements having been introduced. New tools have been specially constructed, so that every part is guaranteed interchangeable. The Machines are beautifully japanned black and gold, the other parts being bright.

The "Model" has proved to all who possess it a great source of interest and recreation, and to many a profitable investment.

CAN BE WORKED BY A CHILD OF 10.

SIMPLICITY, DURABILITY, ELEGANCE AND PERFECTION OF WORK.

COMPLETE OUTFITS from £5 5 0

PATENTEES & MANUFACTURERS:

C. G. SQUINTANI & CO.

3, Ludgate Circus Buildings,
LONDON, E.C.

PRICES.

(The Presses complete only)

No. 1,	Size of Chase	3 × 5 ..	£3 10 0
,, 2,	,,	5 × 7 ..	6 10 0
,, 3,	,,	6 × 9 ..	9 10 0
,, 4,	,,	7 × 10..	12 10 0
,, 5,	,,	7 × 11 ..	22 0 0
,, 6,	,,	13 × 9 ..	32 0 0

Send for our Illustrated Pamphlet "HOW TO PRINT," containing an abridged history of the Art of Printing, Instructions in Printing, Catalogue of Type, &c. Post free, 7d.

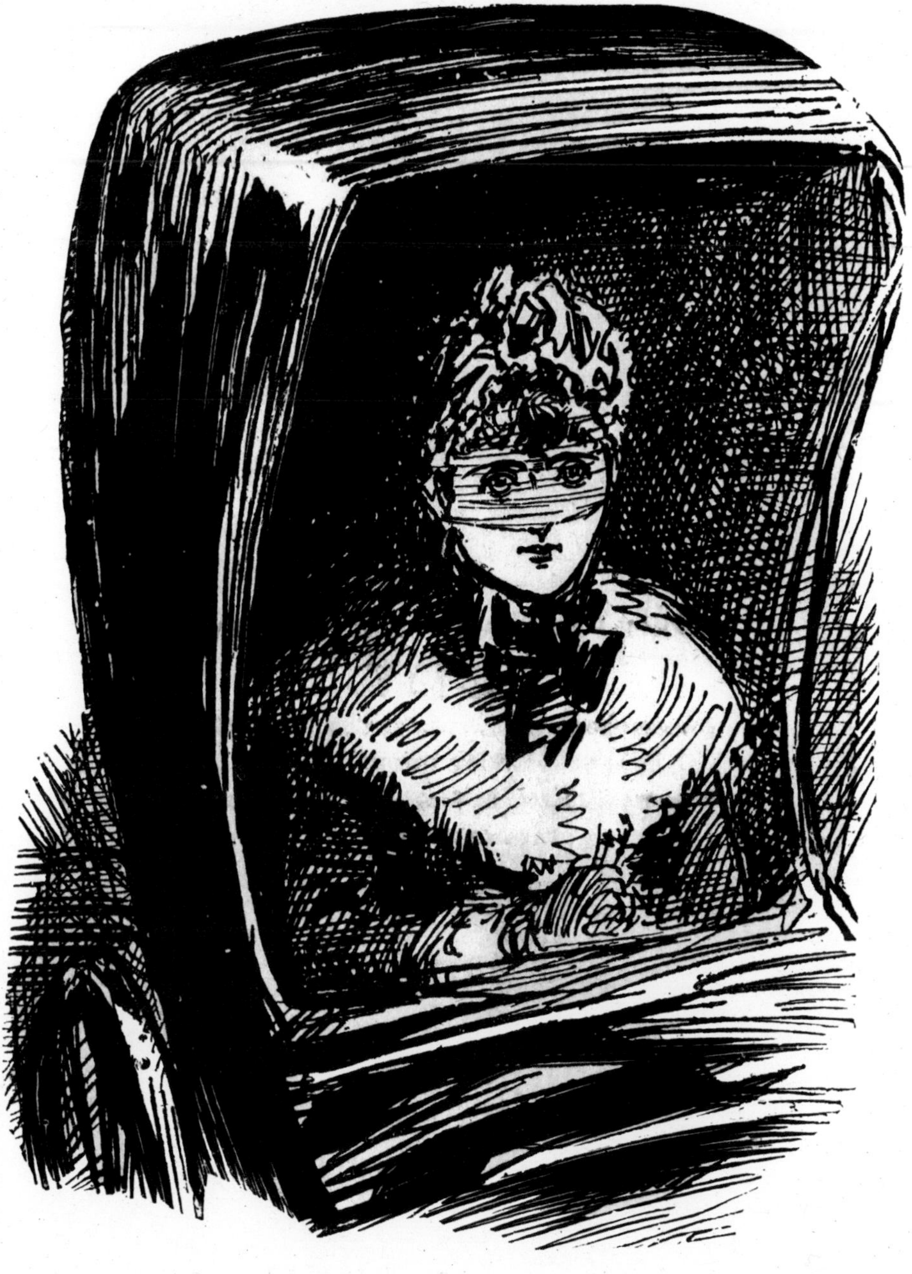

THE MOST INTERESTING OF ALL THE INTERESTING INVALIDS.

* * * And then one said, "What ails her, think you? And the other said, "I don't knew." And nobody ever did know. * * *

THE BOOK

OF

BRIGHTON,

AS IT WAS AND AS IT IS.

WITH SCENERY AND FIGURES

BY JUDY'S ARTISTS.

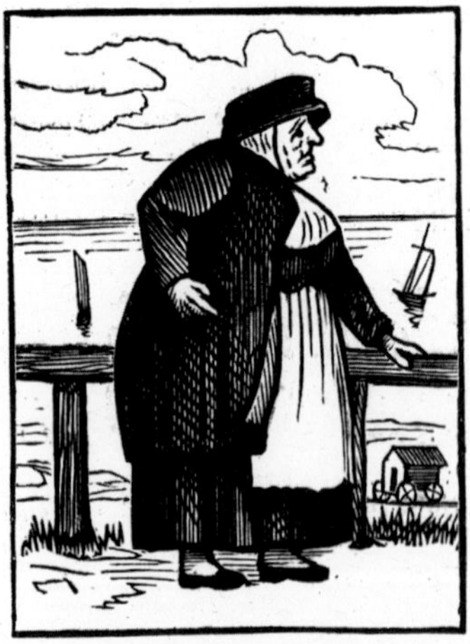

Martha Gunn, Dipper to the Royal Family (by Appointment).

AND TALKEE-TALKEE

BY CHARLES H. ROSS.

"JUDY" OFFICE, 99 SHOE LANE,

FLEET STREET, LONDON, E.C.

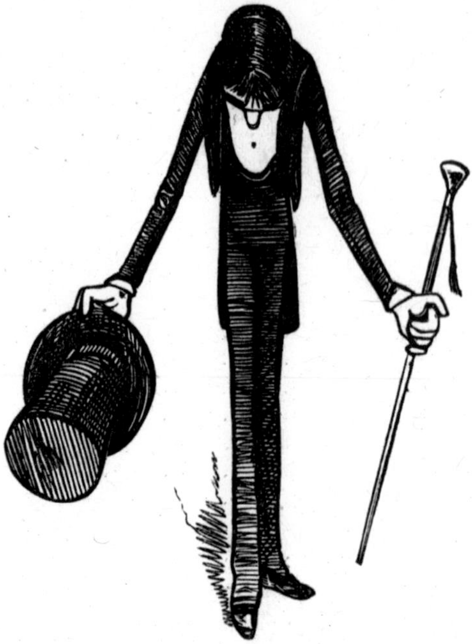

A CARD.

TO THE RESIDENTS AND VISITORS TO BRIGHTON.

LADIES AND GENTLEMEN,—*In the deeply regretted absence of the late* CAPTAIN WILLIAM WADE, LIEUTENANT-COLONEL JOHN ELD, *and* WILLIAM FORTH, ESQUIRE, *at present elsewhere, I beg most respectfully to offer myself as a candidate for the situation of* MASTER OF THE CEREMONIES; *and if you think me sufficiently worthy of your confidence to honour me with your support, I will do all in my power to deserve it.*

I have the honour to remain,
Ladies and Gentlemen,
Your obedient humble servant,
THE AUTHOR.

Palatial Premises,
Shoe Lane, London.

NOTE.

This book is not intended to be quite exactly a Guide to Brighton, nor a history of the First Gentleman in Europe and the only woman (or two) he ever loved, yet a little history and some useful information may be found here and there. Almost all that can be said of Old Brighton has been much better and more fully by Percy Fitzgerald in his fascinating Life of George IV., by Mr. John George Bishop in his most comprehensive and entertaining "Peep into the Past," and in Mr. Erredge's admirable work, which you should lose no time in procuring. I can hardly tell what my book is supposed to be, but of one thing I do feel quite certain,—you ought to buy it. This is the truth.

C. H. R.

CONTENTS.

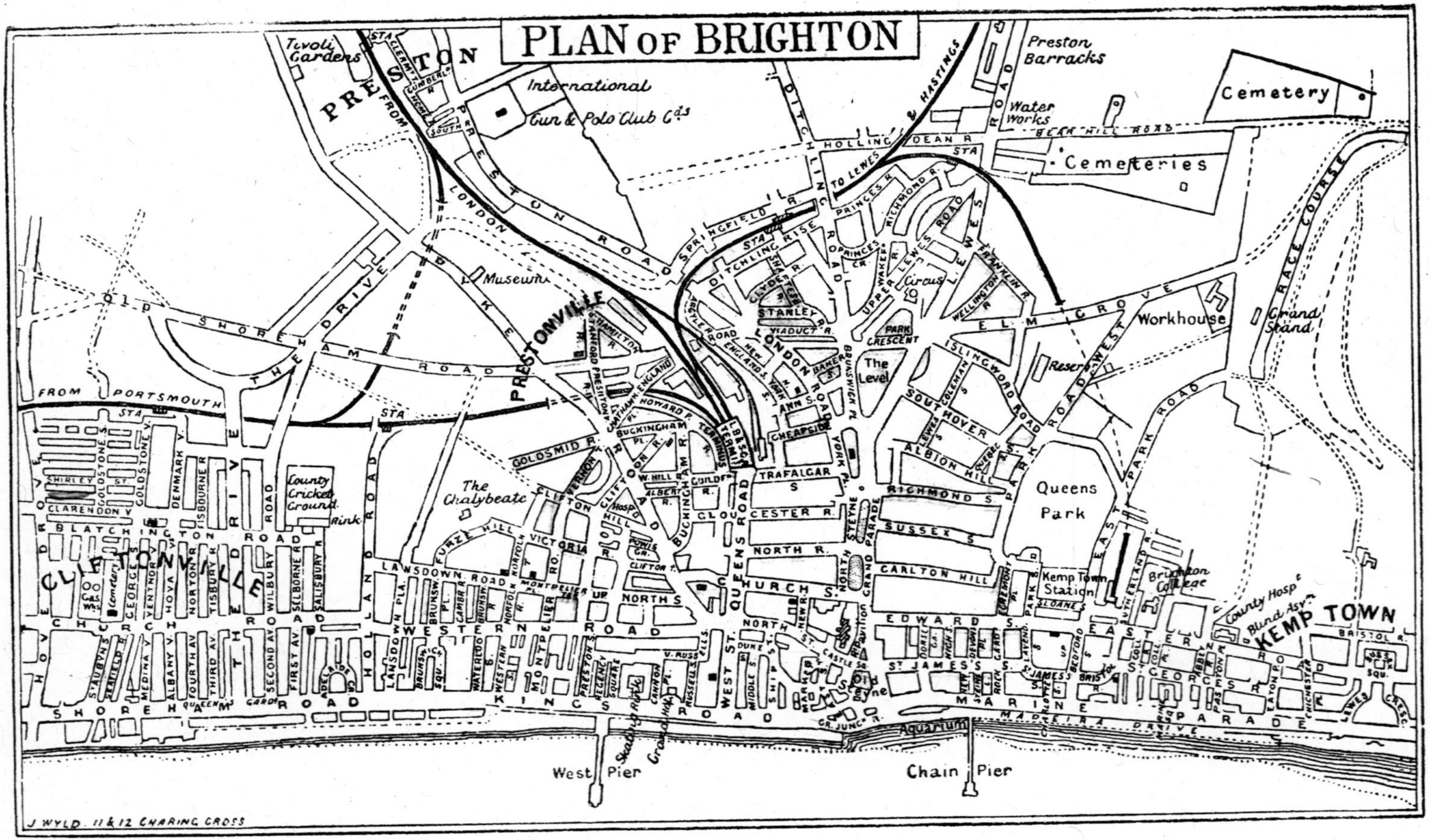
PLAN OF BRIGHTON
Preston
Tivoli Gardens
International Gun & Polo Club Gds
Preston Barracks
Water Works
Cemetery
Cemeteries
Preston Road
Ditchling Road
To Lewes & Hastings
Lewes Road
Race Course
Grand Stand
Workhouse
Elm Grove
Museum
Dyke Road
Prestonville
Old Shoreham Road
The Drive
From Portsmouth
London Road
The Level
Park Crescent
Queens Park
Park Road
Kemp Town Station
Brighton College
County Hospl
Blind Asyn
Kemp Town
The Chalybeate
County Cricket Ground
Rink
Cliftonville
Queens Road
North St.
West St.
Church St.
Western Road
Kings Road
Marine Parade
Madeira Drive
Aquarium
West Pier
Chain Pier
Skating Rink
Grand Hotl
Old Steyne
Pavilion
Edward St.
Eastern Road
St. James's St.
Shoreham Road
Church Road
Holland Road
Lansdown Road
Montpelier
Trafalgar S
Richmond S
Sussex S
Carlton Hill
Grand Parade
North Steyne
LB&SCR Termini
J WYLD 11 & 12 CHARING CROSS

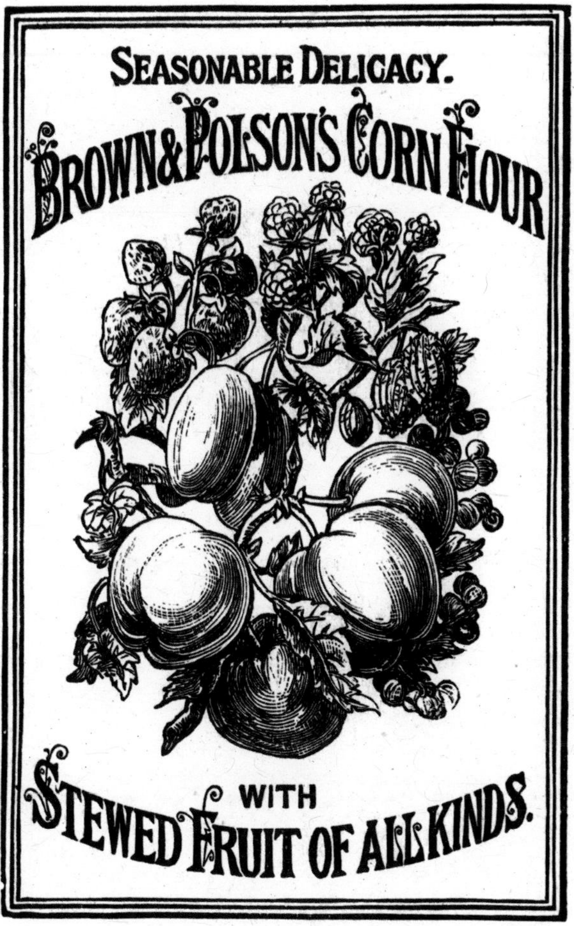
SEASONABLE DELICACY.
BROWN & POLSON'S CORN FLOUR
WITH
STEWED FRUIT OF ALL KINDS.

THE BOOK OF BRIGHTON.

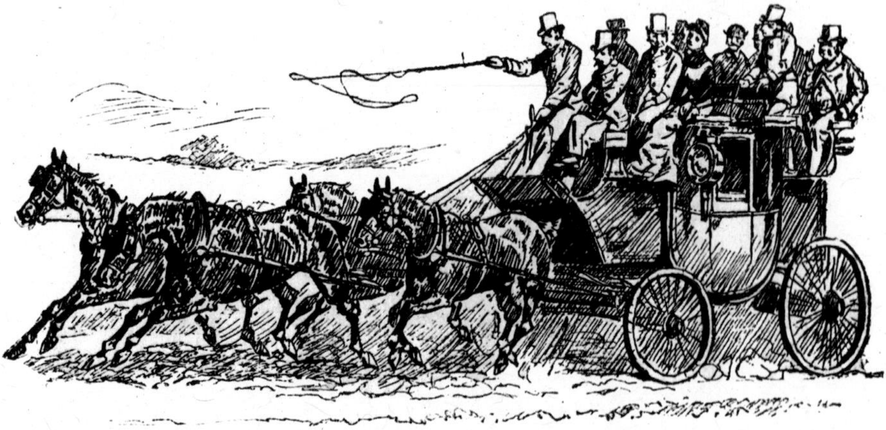

TO BRIGHTON BY COACH.

IT seems incredible, but it is nevertheless a fact, that unhappy mortals a hundred years ago, whose means only enabled them to travel to Brighthelmstone by waggon, were three days and two nights upon the road. Even by the "flying machines"—"the Lewes and Brighthelmstone machines will BEGIN TO FLY," says the advertisement—they took from six in the morning until midnight to do the journey. As to the dangers the passengers ran, you may read, in Mr. Bishop's account of Brighton in the olden days, how they were from time to time upset, blown over, frost-bitten, and robbed by highwaymen; and he quotes an account from Mr. Shergold's "Recollections of a Coach Journey from Brighton to London," in which the miseries of an ordinary journey are graphically described. How the coachman stopped at all the public houses. How, upon the least excuse, he compelled all the passengers, women as well as men, to get down and walk, so that, according to the writer—of the thirty-two miles that lie between Brighton and Reigate, he did twenty on foot. How at the place where they were expected to dine, the waiter, having laid the table, announced that they had just two minutes to eat their dinner in. How the coachman had to be bribed to stay a while by a tumbler of sherry and a shilling a head all round; and finally, how when at length, weary and worn-out, he reached London, his friends were astonished to see him so soon, exclaiming, "Only eleven hours from Brighton to London—wonder what we shall arrive at next!"

A writer in a newspaper some months ago, describing the journey, thus concluded a glowing description of the road to Tunbridge Wells:—"As for us,

 2

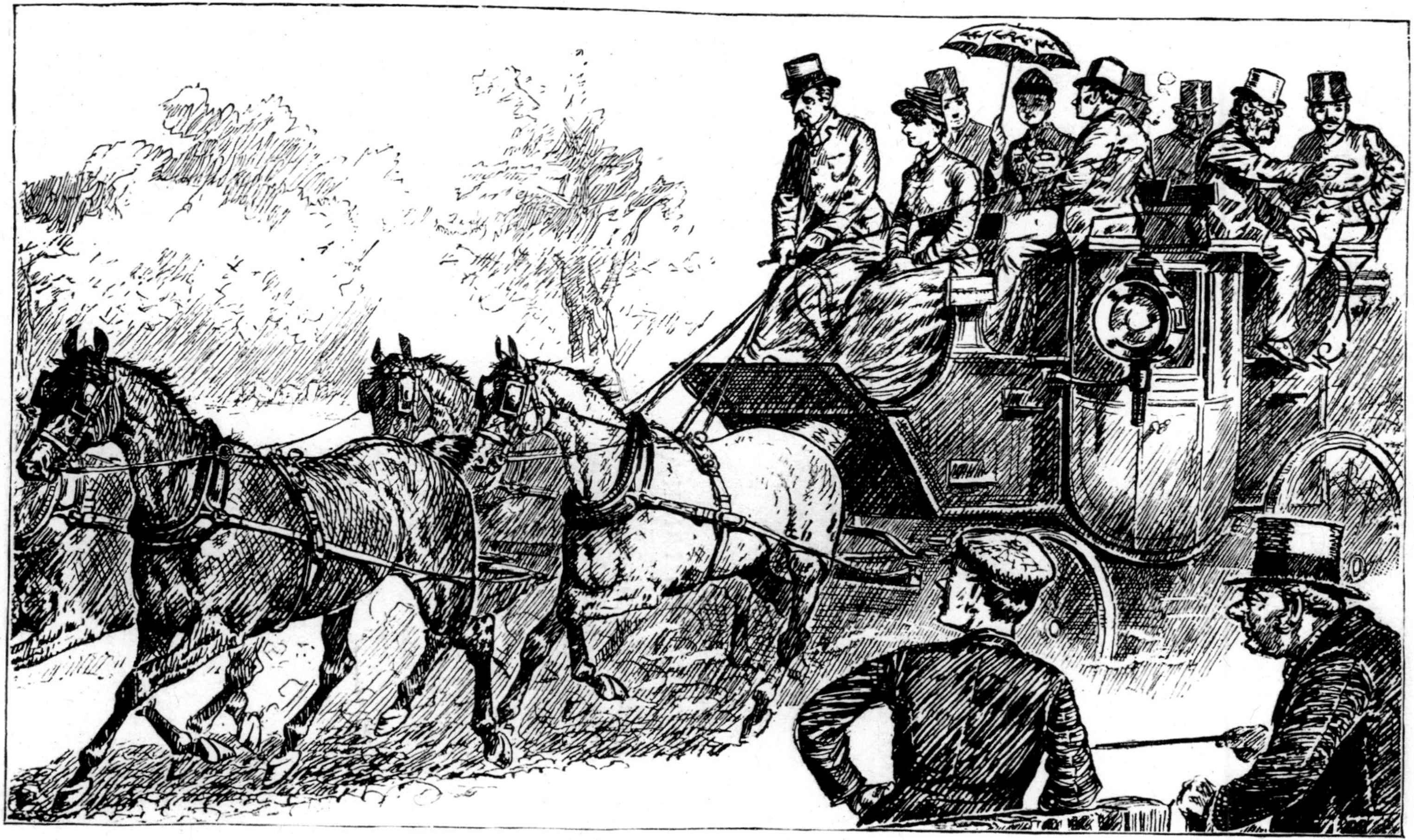

GOING DOWN.

we may be thirsty, dusty, and just a trifle stiff about the knees; but what do we care for that, when we have seen more of the charms of English country life in our thirty-odd miles' drive than we could see in a week of railway travelling, and when our air-bath has given us an appetite such as we have not revelled in since our last coach drive last year?"

Coach travelling was a serious business then; now it is a pleasure, and, given a fine day, I know nothing more pleasant than a ride on the Brighton coach-top, and, should the whole distance seem too long, the traveller might do worse than break the journey at Tunbridge Wells, and pass a day there, and go on by rail.

———o———

BY RAIL.

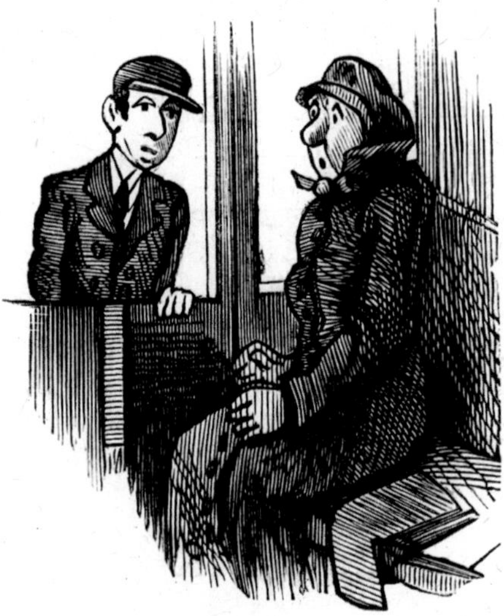

EXPRESS.
"When are we going to start?"
"Where to, sir? Back again?"

WONDERFUL thing, steam!—though that, I believe, has been observed before. A wonderful line, the London and Brighton! I was at London Bridge an hour and a half ago, and now am standing on the West Pier looking down upon the sea. When I say looking down, pray do not suppose there is anything disrespectful or contemptuous in the attitude I have assumed, or that I suppose it, except literally, in any way beneath me. I don't bathe in it except when warmed by my Hobden, my Brill, or my Buggins, but I am down upon it (with the flooring of the pier between) as often as possible, though not unkindly.

The journey to Brighton has been described as part of the pleasure of the outing, and so it is, for it is so soon performed. With Mr. Philp's amusing "Panoramic Guide" in my hand, I find that there are many places of interest we pass on the road, and I, for one, do not complain that we pass them quickly. The journey down, when performed with pleasant companions in a Pullman's car, is actually no journey at all, for you are at your journey's end before your chat is over.

It was prophesied when Royalty abandoned the Pavilion as a residence that Brighton was doomed. It was prophesied that when the railway opened its gentility was gone for ever; and when they ran the first common, vulgar, wicked infamous excursion train there and back for three shillings, everybody knew for a fact that all was over and the fate of Brighton sealed. Anarchy was expected, and 'Arry, in all his horror, would bring it about. 'Tilda Jane, with her tormentor, would range abroad, and squirt in the eye of the oldest inhabitant. There would be feathers and paper wreaths, chaos and kiss-in-the-ring. George the Fourth and Dr. Russel, according to the guide books, pretty equally divide the gratitude of loyal Brightonians for making the place. Nonsense! what kind of a place did they leave it when they left off the making process? The railway made Brighton, and transformed a shabby straggling town into a City of Palaces upon the Sea.

The average cost of laying the line, when the railway was first started, was £16,400 per mile, and the cost of the works, up to December, 1841, amounted to £269,359. In 1841 the capital of the Company was £2,250,000; in 1879 it amounted to £22,620,432. The returns of passenger traffic, exclusive of season-ticket holders, was, in 1848, 2,485,778, and in 1879, 32,525,341. In 1879, 3,663 calves, 70,211 sheep, and 5,442 pigs travelled to Brighton to be killed and cooked.

FOR 1881.—*Not responsible for any Alterations.*

VICTORIA AND BRIGHTON.

DOWN.—WEEK DAYS.	Parl 1 2	Exp 1 Cl	Parl 1 2	Fst 1 2	Exp 1 2	Parl 1 2	Exp 1 2	1 2	Fst 1 2	Parl 1 2	Parl 1 2	Parl 1 2				
	a m	a m	a m	a m	p m	p m	p m	p m	p m	p m	p m	p m				
Victoria ....dep.	7 35	10 0	10 55	11 50	1 50	2 40	4 30	5 0	5 43	5 55	7 8	10 5	..	..	..	..
Brighton ....arr.	10 3	11 25	1 15	1 40	3 15	4 40	5 45	7 3	7 15	8 28	9 10	11 55	..	..	..	..

DOWN.—SUNDAYS.	Parl 1 2	Chp 3	1 Cl	Parl 1 2	Parl 1 2	Parl 1 2										
	a m	a m	a m	p m	p m	p m										
Victoria ....dep.	6 50	8 50	10 45	1 10	5 50	8 5	..	..	..	..	..	..	..	..	..	..
Brighton ....arr.	9 18	10 45	12 15	3 5	8 18	10 8	..	..	..	..	..	..	..	..	..	..

UP.—WEEK DAYS.	Parl 1 2	C 1 2 P	Exp 1 Cl	1 2	Exp 1 2	D 1 & 3	Parl 1 2	1 2	Parl 1 2	1 2	1 2	1 2	Exp 1 Cl	Parl 1 2	Parl 1 2	
	a m	a m	a m	a m	a m	a m	a m	a m	a m	p m	p m	p m	p m	p m	p m	
Brighton ....dep.	6 10	7 35	8 45	8 55	9 45	9 55	10 3	11 0	11 30	1 35	3 45	5 0	5 45	6 10	8 40	..
Victoria ....arr.	8 30	9 11	10 5	10 52	11 7	11 30	12 15	12 32	1 55	3 22	5 58	6 31	7 2	8 25	10 38	..

UP.—SUNDAYS.	Parl 1 2	Parl 1 2	Parl 1 2	Chp 3	1 Cl	Parl 1 2										
	a m	p m	p m	p m	p m	p m										
Brighton ....dep.	8 30	3 10	6 0	7 10	8 30	9 30	..	..	..	..	..	..	..	..	..	..
Victoria ....arr.	10 56	5 6	8 16	8 53	9 56	11 22	..	..	..	..	..	..	..	..	..	..

C Mondays only. D Cheap Fast Train, run on Fridays only (1 and 3 Class). Day Return Tickets, 10s. 6d. and 5s.

LONDON BRIDGE AND BRIGHTON.

DOWN.—WEEK DAYS.	Parl 1 2	Parl 1 2	Parl 1 2	Fast 1 2	Fast 1 2	Exp 1 2	Parl 1 2	Exp 1 2	Exp 1 Cl	1 2	Fast 1 2	Parl 1 2	Parl 1 2	Mail 1 2 P	Parl 1 2	
	a m	a m	a m	a m	noon	p m	p m	p m	p m	p m	p m	p m	p m	p m	p m	
London Bridge............dep.	5 45	6 40	7 40	9 30	12 0	2 0	2 50	4 0	5 0	5 8	6 0	6 5	7 20	9 10	10 20	..
Brighton ....arr.	8 0	8 27	10 3	10 53	1 40	3 20	4 40	5 15	6 10	7 3	7 15	8 28	9 10	10 44	11 55	..

DOWN.—SUNDAYS.	Parl 1 2	Chp 3 Cl	1 Cl	Parl 1 2	Parl 1 2	Parl 1 2	Mail 1 2 P									
	a m	a m	a m	p m	p m	p m	p m									
London Bridge............dep.	7 0	8 55	10 35	1 20	6 0	8 10	9 10	..	..	..	..	..	..	..	..	..
Brighton ....arr.	9 18	10 45	11 58	3 5	8 18	10 8	10 50	..	..	..	..	..	..	..	..	..

UP.—WEEK DAYS.	Parl 1 2	Parl 1 2	Parl 1 2	Exp 1 Cl	1 2	Exp 1 2	Parl 1 2	1 2	1 2	1 2	1 2	Parl 1 2	Parl 1 2	Mail 1 2 P		
	a m	a m	a m	a m	a m	a m	a m	a m	p m	p m	p m	p m	p m	p m		
Brighton ....dep.	6 10	7 35	7 50	8 45	8 55	9 55	10 3	11 0	1 35	3 45	5 0	6 10	8 40	10 35	..	..
London Bridge............arr.	8 20	9 0	9 45	9 55	10 43	11 5	12 5	12 27	3 17	5 49	6 28	8 23	10 31	12 8	..	..

UP.—SUNDAYS.	Parl 1 2	Parl 1 2	Parl 1 2	Chp 3 Cl	1 Cl	Parl 1 2	Mail 1 2 P									
	a m	p m	p m	p m	p m	p m	p m									
Brighton ....dep.	8 30	3 10	6 0	7 10	8 20	9 30	10 35	..	..	..	..	..	..	..	..	..
London Bridge............arr.	10 43	4 55	8 12	8 50	9 40	11 15	12 8	..	..	..	..	..	..	..	..	..

EVERY SATURDAY, First Class Cheap Day Return Tickets will be issued as under, including Admission to the Grand Aquarium and the Royal Pavilion:—From VICTORIA, 10.55 a.m. and 11.50 a.m.; from LONDON BRIDGE, 9.30 a.m. and 12.0 noon; RETURNING from BRIGHTON by any Train the same day, except the 5.45 p.m. Pullman Drawing Room Car Train. FARE THERE AND BACK, First Class, including Admission to the Grand Aquarium and the Royal Pavilion, Palace and Grounds, HALF-A-GUINEA from all the above Stations.

ON TEN TOES.

HAD any one told me, as I walked along the King's Road one autumn day seven and twenty years ago, that the time would come when I should write a book about Brighton, I expect I would have been considerably surprised.

I was somewhat younger then, and considerably slimmer and more eager and energetic ; the world full seven and twenty degrees more directly in front of me. My ambition was to be an actor, and I had also literary aspirations, which, hitherto, I had found some difficulty in persuading the publishers to encourage. I had, however, been printed once. I had by chance been let loose upon the criticism of a pantomime for a great daily paper, and I had treated the subject exhaustively, omitting nothing and nobody set down in the playbill. The article was afterwards a good deal edited, but some of it next day appeared in print. I had literary aspirations certainly, and intended, I well remember, to write plays and novels, and much more conscientious and scathing criticism. Since then I have done a little in all three ways, though, as a rule, I don't scath—it is not worth while. Never, however, until a couple of months ago, among the many projects I have formed for book-making, had it entered into my head to choose the Queen of Watering-places as my theme, and when you come to hear how first I visited Brighton, you will say, I think, that it did seem rather unlikely I should at any future time turn up as its historian.

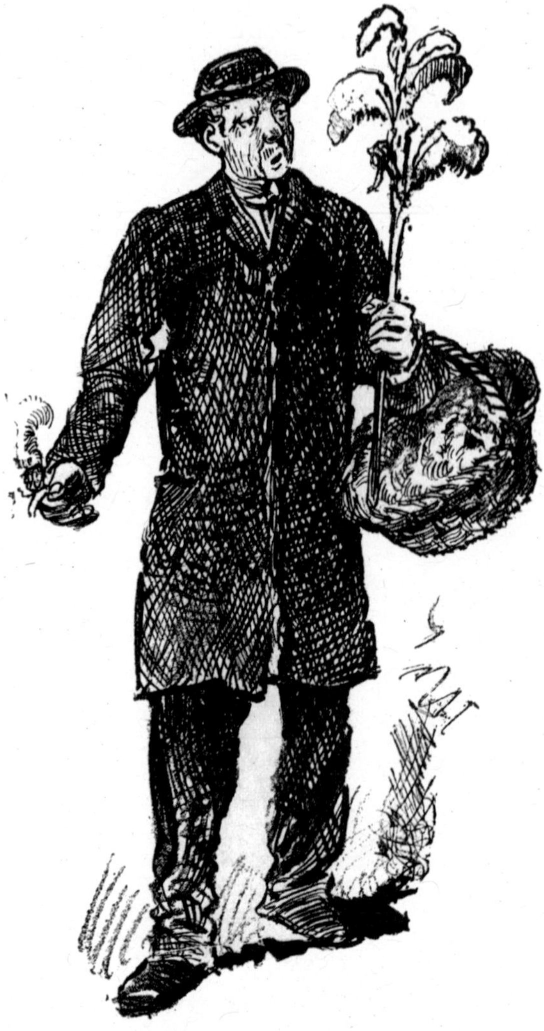

The fiend with the feathers.

Towards the close of a glorious August day in the year eighteen hundred and fifty-five, when the last rays of the setting sun were reflected from the rippling waves at the exact spot now occupied by the West Pier, a slender youth, dusty and travel-stained, and carrying strapped upon his back a battered knapsack, might, had anybody had time to waste on him, have been observed slowly wending his way upon the sea-side of the King's Road, Brighton, now directing his wistful gaze upon the stately rows of houses on his right, and anon casting his eyes pensively towards the ocean. Past him countless equipages whirled, and brilliantly attired pedestrians jostled him unceremoniously. What was he about, this wayworn pilgrim? Whence had he come? Whither was he going? No one knew—not even himself; and nobody asked, because nobody felt particularly interested. He had tramped into Brighton from Rottingdean, having started early in the day from Seaford, tarrying an hour here and there where he listed, and he had got as far as the site of the Grand Hotel without pausing since he entered the town, and now, though with evident weariness and regret, he still pursued his onward course, and presently leaving Hove behind him, and pausing only at Shoreham for a tankard of foaming shandy-gaff, he at length reached Lancing, where, exhausted by his exertions, he engaged a bed, ordered ham and eggs, and took that preposterous knapsack off his shoulders.

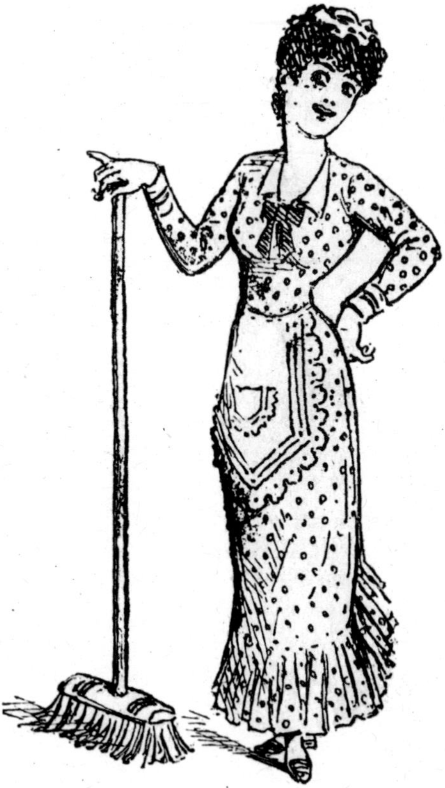

"Lawks a me! where can he be going to in such a hurry?"

"What line may you be travelling in?" asked the landlady, whose curiosity the knapsack had naturally excited; and the thin young man, heartily ashamed of himself, as well he might be, said, "Chemicals," hoping thus to stay further inquiries. But he was no commercial traveller, that young man. The absurd occupation in which he was engaged was, if you please, a walking tour; and the reason, the first time in his life he had ever been in Brighton, he plodded through it just as a sheep might have done with a drover and a drover's dog at its heels, was because, before starting, a certain route had been marked out by himself and some one else equally sapient, and to that route and its allotted stopping-places he was adhering to the best of his ability.

And the friend? Well, he was far ahead, and this was why:—They had started together fairly. They had made a map of the route. They had registered vows and bought thick boots. The idea was to walk from Gravesend to Stonehenge and back to London through Basingstoke, Chertsey, and Richmond. They walked the first afternoon from Gravesend to Rochester, one of the young men's boots troubling him a good deal. Next day they walked from Rochester to

Canterbury, the same young man's boots troubling him much more; and when, next day, the other young man arose at an early hour and urged on his blistered brother to resume the tramp, there was reluctancy, then angry words arose and they quarrelled and parted —and I was left behind.

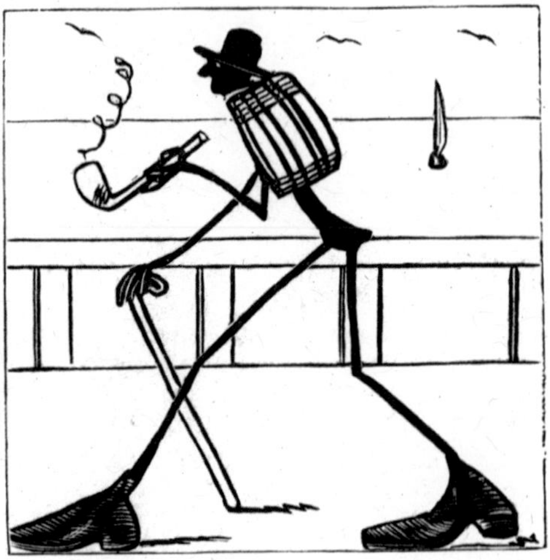

Hard at it.

And I never reached Stonehenge, as it happened, but, struggling on in some undecided fashion, finally subsided at Bognor, where I very happily basked in the sun until my leave was exhausted (I was at the time a Government clerk), and then made my way back to town as quickly as I could.

And there you have the particulars of my first visit to Brighton, possibly unique in their way. The next time, though, I paid Brighton a visit, I stopped rather longer in the King's Road; I lay ill in bed there on a second floor for ten days.

Since then I have been many times to Brighton, and have been as happy there at times, and at others much more miserable, than anywhere I know. And now for a fresh page of paper, a new pen, and another dip of ink, and I'll write about Brighton.

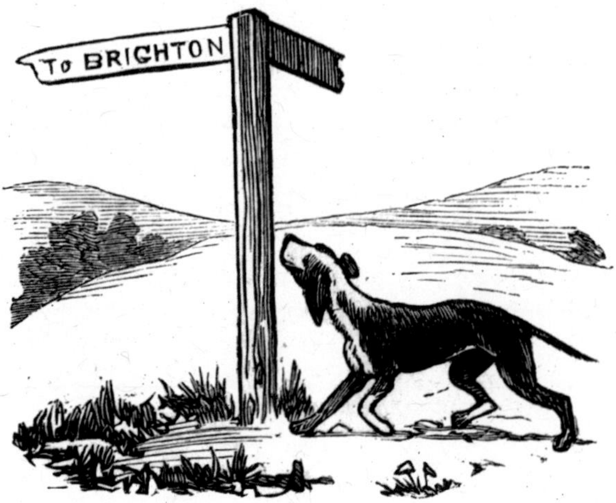

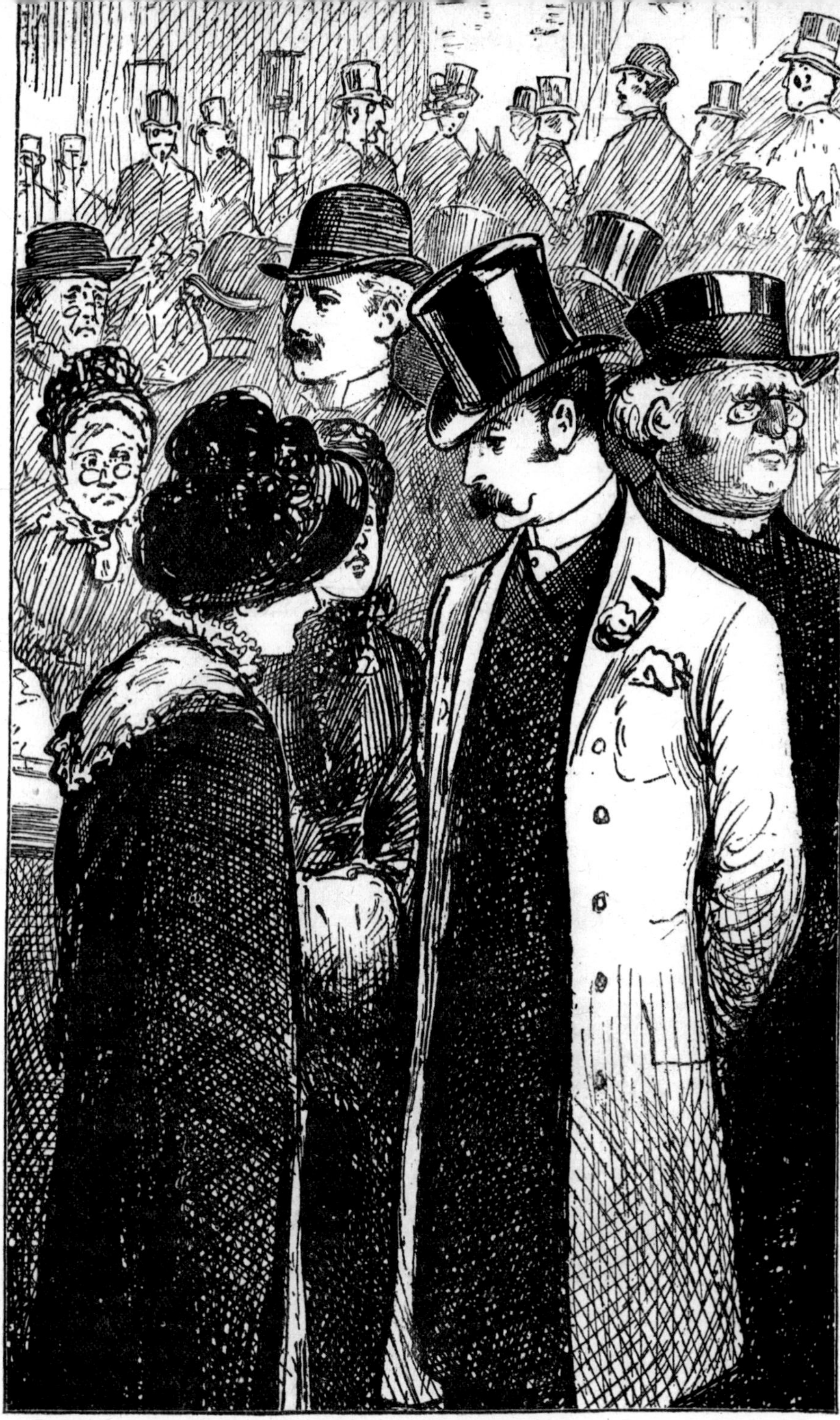

A BIT OF THE KING'S ROAD.

THE KING'S ROAD.

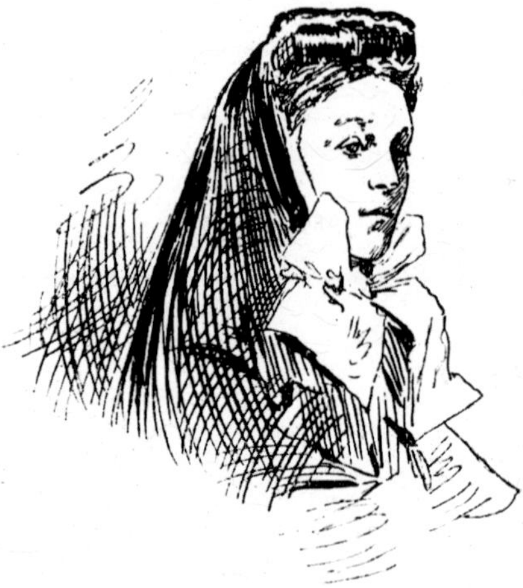

A great and good lady.

CAN you believe it possible that there was once a time when the King's Road, Brighton, was not in existence? It is the truth, though. I would deceive no one willingly, whatever other guide book writers may do. It was not until about two years after the accession of George the Fourth that the road was formally opened, "amid the acclamations of 10,000 people" and a "royal salute from the 42-pounder at the Battery." The King was in an open landau, accompanied by the Duke of York and the Iron Duke and the Duke of Dorset, and, according to an ancient custom, the spectators showered sweetmeats upon the royal and distinguished personages, who were not a little alarmed upon receiving, unexpectedly, these strange missiles upon their august noses. Casks of beer followed, not thrown like the sugarplums, of course, but tapped on the beach, and great were the rejoicings. Previous to this, although for many years Brighton had been the resort of fashion, the sea front of the town for carriages went no farther westward than a tumble-down public house called The Ship in Distress, at the corner of Middle Street. The houses lining the road before 1822 would seem to have been of small value, and even a year after the road was opened the lease of No. 53 was sold for £150. When the lease next ran out, Mr. Bishop says it was bought for £2,300.

The Brighton of the Regency was, after all, but a poor, shabby, shambling sort of place, as you may see for yourself any day you like to look at the pictures in the Pavilion. But it is not of the past I would just now speak, but of the incomparable King's Road, at the present time the grandest promenade in all the world. I cannot forgive my ancestors, the Ancient Britons, for one thing. What were they muddling about when they chose the site for London where they did, and how was it Julius Cæsar and the other Roman gentlemen who dropped in uninvited and stayed to a tea or two did not set things right? Of course Brighton ought to have been the capital, and the JUDY Office in the King's Road.

There is one thing, though, that tends somewhat to console me. If this amazing thoroughfare be not actually in London at the present moment, all London seems to be promenading in it. Why, this gloriously bright afternoon you cannot walk five yards, if you keep your eyes open, without seeing some notability. Look! that's a lord, though he is not much, and that a lawyer, only too awfully eminent. There goes an elderly duchess; here comes a *danseuse*, very distinctly white and pink. That is a great artist with the long hair, and this a great actor with longer. There's a slim general, and there's a general practitioner, plump and fat. A white-haired Prime Minister stands there, and that little, round, red-nosed man is—don't you know? can't you guess?—a poet. See what a study he is making of the window of that shop where they sell the foreign comestibles. How greedily he reads the labels, and, see, now he is feeling in his pocket. Ah! he enters!

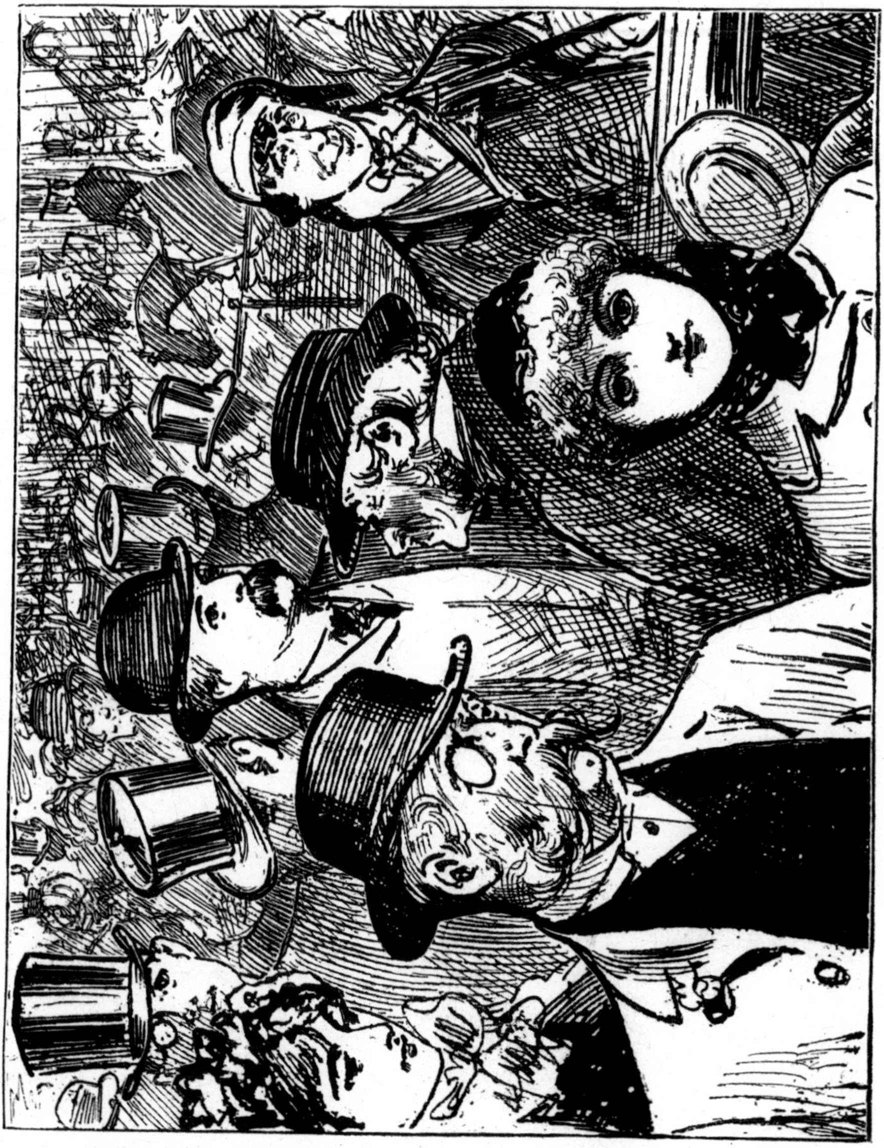

ANOTHER BIT OF THE KING'S ROAD.

We will pass on and return. He is still there! What a tuck-out he will have when he gets home! Why not? Poets must eat like other people.

Hither comes a lady in a dress that somewhat resembles the garb worn by a sister of mercy. She is Lady Bountiful, and scores upon scores, grateful for her great generosity and tender sympathy, murmur her name in their prayers. Yonder is a tall figure every one here knows by sight. Its owner is also the owner of a coronet, but he wears a billycock, and carries a walking-stick for the most part tucked up under his arm. All the pretty little children seem to know him, and smile shyly as he pats their fair heads.

But, oh, the never-ceasing stream of carriages in the roadway! It is, I am told, the annual custom, on or about the 15th of November, at four o'clock in the afternoon, to count the number of carriages passing in one direction at a certain point near to the Grand Hotel within the space of ten minutes. The number has been found to vary but little, the average being two hundred and seventy-five.

And the pretty pedestrians—heavens! I nearly omitted to mention them. "How beautiful they are!" as the poet says—not the fat poet,—another.

To be yet young and lovely, and wear delightful frocks as tight as tight, and break men's hearts, and smile with cold disdain, and have brass tips to your heels, must be a heavenly existence. I put on that suit you may remember me in last summer, and bought a flower for my buttonhole, and went forth with an elastic step, and found, a few hundred yards farther on, that the flower had broken off at the stalk without my noticing it, and that I had muddied the toe of my right boot when crossing Ship Street trying to get out of the way of somebody's confounded carriage. Then a sadness oppressed my soul, and I hid me in the smoking-room at the Old Ship, and a friend of my youth, who is now here, too—hang him!—came and said kind things to comfort me, and mentioned that my necktie had rucked up at the back above my collar.

THE WICKED PAVILION.

THIS odd jumble of mixed architecture, originally called the "Marine Pavilion," has been fantastically likened by the "London Spy" to a banquet-table grandly laid out. "The centre dome, a water magnum; the pointed towers, champagne-bottles; the square compartments, liqueur-stands; and the glass roof of the riding-house, a dessert-dish." And Mr. Sala calls it "this pot-bellied palace, this minareted mushroom, this gilded dirt pie, this congeries of bulbous excrescences, as gaudy and as expensive as Dutch tulips, and as useless." Bless me! The building of George's pleasure palace began in 1784, and additions and alterations made until 1817, when it was partly pulled down, and greatly altered according to plans conceived by the Prince, and Mr. Nash his architect. It cost upwards of a million of money, and, on its final abandonment as a royal residence, was sold, in 1850, by the Commissioners of Woods and Forests, to the town of Brighton for the good round sum of £53,000. Says a guide book written in 1803: "In the court is a finely sculptured figure of a negro bearing a sun-dial, an appendage that is little wanted where pleasure leads the hours, but which may be applied to many moral purposes." Another guide book, published in 1865, says, "Our present excellent and amiable Queen visited it once, and once only. Doubtless her pure and pious heart revolted at the idea of retaining possession of a palace every room in which had been defiled by the infamous orgies and abominable debaucheries of that very unkingly King—her uncle George."

There was heavy drinking at times at the Pavilion, as is instanced in the tolerably familiar story of the Prince Regent and the Dukes of Clarence and York inviting the Duke of Norfolk, famed for his prowess at the mahogany, with the notable scheme concocted of making the old man very drunk. The Prince

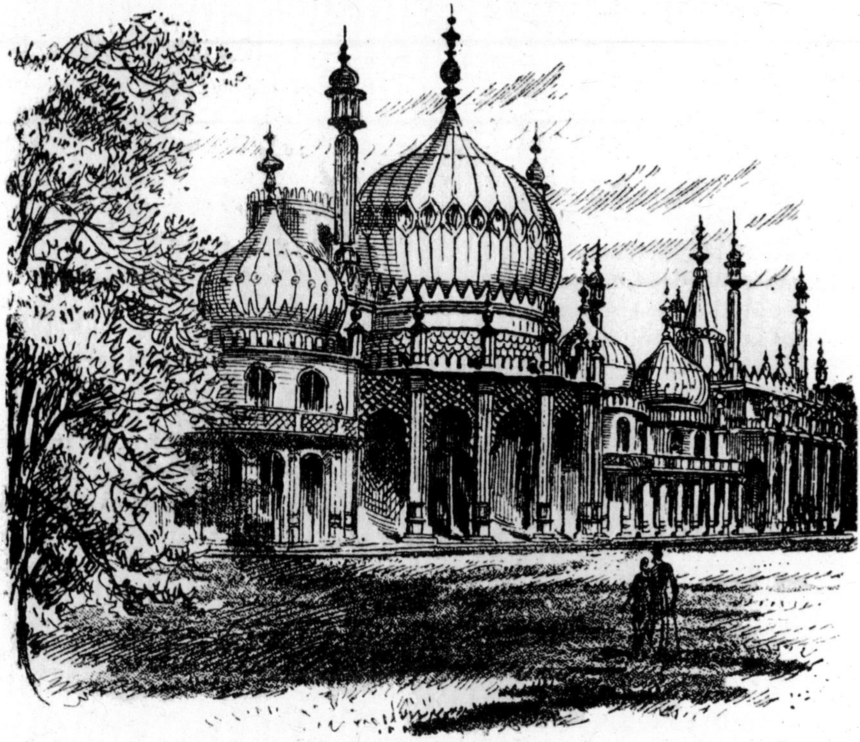

THE PAVILION.

wanted him to dine and sleep at the Pavilion, and Norfolk drove over from Arundel Castle with his famous four grey horses. Every person at table called upon the Duke to drink with them, a challenge which the old toper did not refuse; but, seeing that there was a conspiracy against him, he stipulated that all should drink glass by glass. Presently the hero began to totter, and the Prince, to hasten matters, proposed bumpers of brandy. One of the royal brothers filled a great glass for the Duke, and he stood up and tossed it off. "And now," he said, "I will have my carriage and go home." The Prince reminded him of his promise to stay and sleep under the roof where he had been so generously entertained. "Nc," he said; "he had had enough of such hospitality;" and left the place never to return again.

And other kinds of carryings-on were there, the recital of which would, I feel sure, make the gentle reader's hair stand on end. What jinks and junkettings were there—what woeful waste! In a room upstairs you will find a picture of the royal kitchen, in which thirteen cooks are seen all hard at work. I wonder William the Fourth's prim partner and the staid ladies of his household who worked Berlin wool monstrosities, drank tea and took snuff, could have sat composedly within walls which had echoed such mad revelries. I pay my sixpence and stroll through the fantastically-adorned apartments (by-the-bye, the artistic wall-paper designers might here get some splendid cribs), the "conservatory or music-room," the "rotunda or saloon," the "Egyptian gallery." They are having the guide book reprinted, the young person at the door informs me, but she lends me one upon my promising to return it. A man who takes my check points out the way I am to go, and I wander vaguely among the cold bare rooms, and strive to conjure up the gay company that once filled them, the rustle of silks whose owners are long since dead, light laughter the grave has closed upon, and old-fashioned jingling music long ago forgotten. Can it be fancy? Is there yet a faint odour of the attar of roses the Prince soaked his handkerchief in, and by which, when promenading on the Steyne, his progress might always be traced through the crowd? It is fancy, sure enough. There is but the musty, dusty smell coming from the curiosities in the singularly out-of-place museum of pots and pans and jars and dishes, instruments of torture, and poor Goo Man Jec's skull, "taken from the wall of a city" and "lent by Archdeacon Gray," who, I presume, somehow obtained a reversionary right in the upper portion of Goo Man Jec's anatomical arrangements. These and the sickening sketches of Chinese tortures, and a number of pictures which might be interesting were they catalogued or labelled, constitute the sixpennyworth.

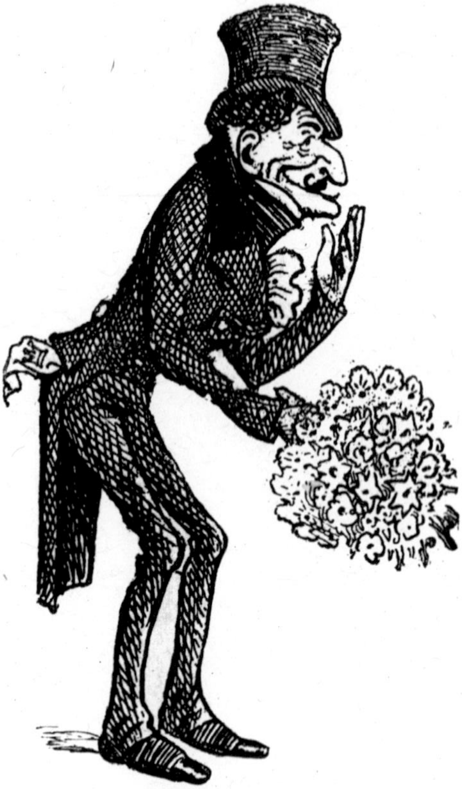

"Egad, sir, demme!"

At other times balls take place here, and public meetings, and all kinds of entertainments, serious and comic. There have even been exhibitions of dogs and monkeys and natural deformities. Poor played-out Pavilion!

In 1864 the Pavilion was entirely redecorated, and the suite of rooms used for balls, bazaars, concerts, &c., were restored to something like their original splendour. There is also a museum, Chinese collection, &c. Admission, *6d.* The rooms are open free to ratepayers on the first Monday in each month. A band usually plays on Wednesday and Saturday afternoons.

The entrance to the Brighton Free Public Library, Picture Gallery, and Museum is in Church Street. The Library contains 15,000 volumes. Open free from 10 a.m. to 5 p.m., and from 7 to 10. The Museum, containing collections illustrative of Geology, Zoology, Archæology, Botany, and Food Products; and the Picture Gallery, containing a collection of pictures in water-colours, are open free every Monday, Tuesday, and Wednesday; and on Thursday, Friday, and Saturday at a charge of *6d.*

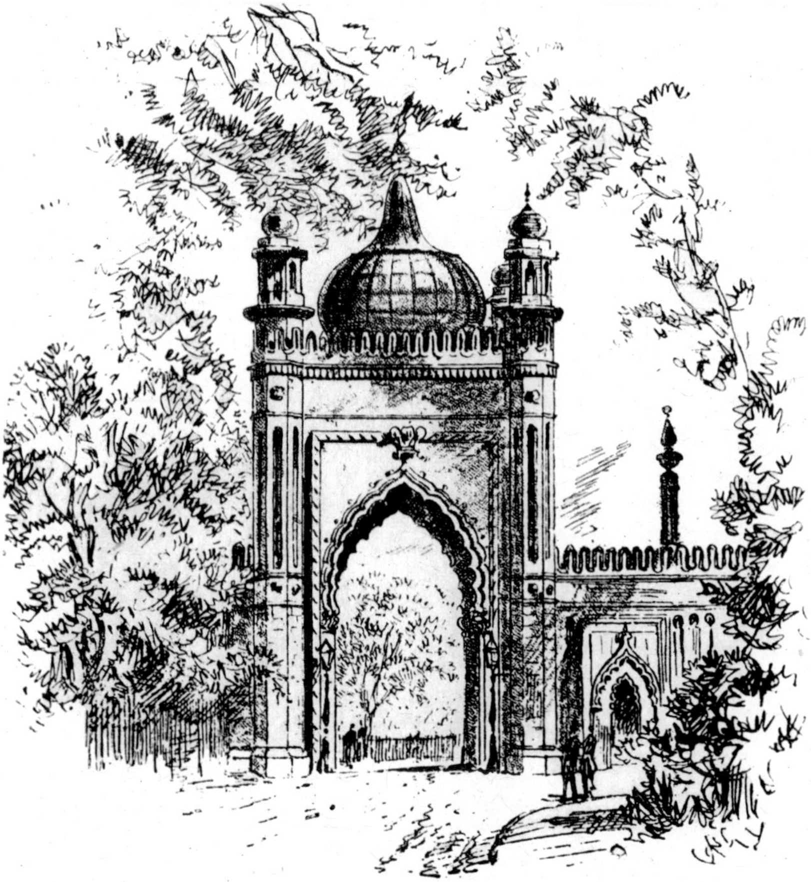

KING WILLIAM'S GATEWAY.

THE "CORPULENT GENTLEMAN."

To this Prince," says the amiable and erudite Miss Mangnall, "the western portion of the metropolis is indebted for many splendid improvements. The nation will look back with grateful pleasure to his regency, for the peace which terminated a sanguinary and ruinous war of more than twenty years' continuance against France and her dependencies. His reign was also honourably distinguished by important accessions to the religious liberty of the people."

"The Prince Regent," says the "Belle Assemblie" for 1819, "arrived at Buckingham House with an escort of Life Guards, amidst the loud huzzas of the populace as he passed, while the cannons were discharging a national salute in celebration of His Royal Highness's natal day, and the band playing *God save the King.*"

"Some years ago," the same authority tells us, "as the Prince was riding in the neighbourhood of Windsor, his horse flung a shoe. He alighted near the door of a cottage, where he saw a lad and girl talking together, and sent his servant away with his horse. The girl was pretty, and attracted his notice; she made a courtesy as he came towards her. 'Well, my pretty maid, what soft things does Colin say to you this fine morning?' She smiled, and the man coloured. 'When is the happy day to be?' 'I don't know,' said the girl. 'Father says we wants money,' said the lad; 'and, please, your honour——' 'How much?' asked the Prince, 'would satisfy him?' 'We ha' got ten pounds to buy things with, but we want as much more for expenses; and I owes a little money.' The Prince was charmed with the girl's beauty and modesty, and after looking at her some time, took her by the hand, and said, 'If you will make this good lad happy, I will give you ten pounds, but I must have a kiss into the bargain.' And putting his hand into his pocket, he took out ten guineas, and received thanks for it from the lips of the girl herself." History records not what the worthy lad said as he looked on.

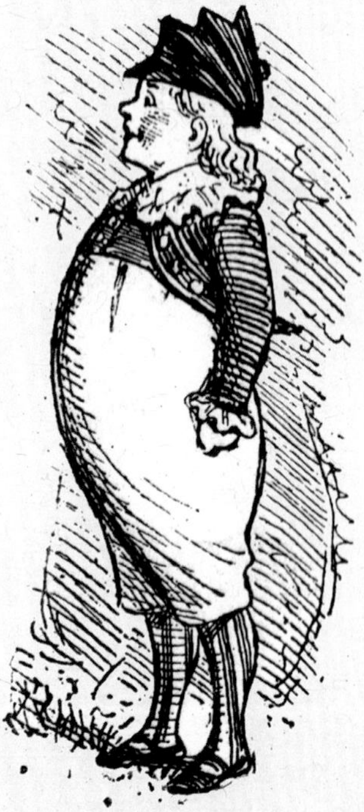

Georgy Porgy Princeps.

During the last years of the same George's life, another George (surnamed Cruikshank) caricatured him. "This," says a contemporary writer, speaking of the picture, "is the most *finished* gentleman in Europe. Look at the floor. His Majesty, *the King of Hearts*, has been *playing the Deuce*. The star has fallen, but the loose garter is ready with its excuse—*Honi soit*. . . . How very drunk His Majesty is, to be sure! There's a bonnet on the corner of the screen, and three or four bottles under the chair. The candles have not been snuffed lately—the royal hand became incapable about half an hour ago."

"It is the fashion," said Thackeray, "to run down George the Fourth;" and, in truth, it was a fashion with Thackeray to do so. He never missed an opportunity. He tackled the dead monarch again and again. He even wrote a lecture upon him, and stumped the country delivering it. Poor Georgius Rex! Though he might have been, and with cause too sometimes, somewhat shy of showing himself among his subjects, all was loyalty and enthusiasm in the seaside town that owed the beginning of its prosperity to His Gracious Majesty. Possibly the good folks knew but little of the goings on up there at the Pavilion during His Majesty's lifetime, or guessed at the relationship between him and pretty Mrs. Fitz, who lived in the Steyne hard by.

"His Royal Highness, to whom Brighton owes so much!" says the good guide book writer, during George's regency. To the Brightonians—they were all staunch Tories then—George was the greatest and grandest gentleman the world had ever seen. When first he went there he was, as he is in a portrait lying here before me, as handsome a prince as you could wish to see, with a curly head of hair, a loosely-tied white scarf round his neck, and a turn-down collar, and a star glittering upon his breast. I don't wonder so many women fell in love with him. He was only twenty years of age then, but even when he grew fat and unwieldy, bloated and dropsical, he was still a great monarch, for whom the Brightonians had a tender memory. As he rode by in his open carriage, in his plum-coloured coat, and raising his brown hat in real regal fashion, he looked every inch a King, and the Brighton tradesfolks, of whom he bought plenty of clothes and eatables and drinkables, afterwards at church asked Heaven's blessing on the "Benefactor of his people."

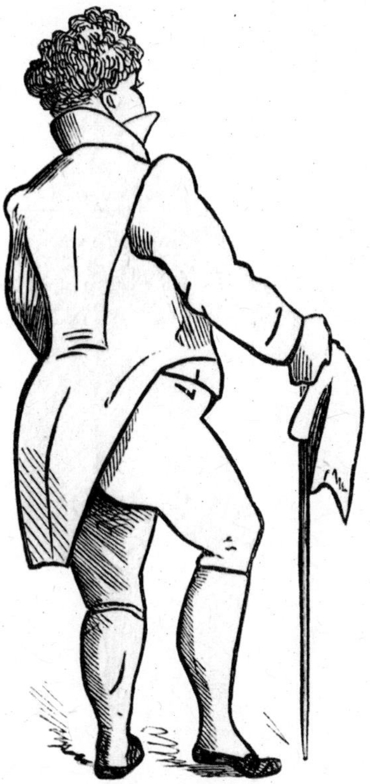

A Royal back view.

But it was not quite the same in London. Tom Moore writes in his Diary, *26th June*, 1830:—"Tempted out from my work by the fine day and the death of His Majesty, both of which events have set the whole town in motion. Never saw London so excited or so lively. Crowds everywhere, particularly in St. James's Street, from the proclamation of the new King being expected before the palace. The whole thing reminded me of a passage in an old comedy: 'What makes him so merry?' 'Don't you see he's in mourning?' Dined at the Lansdownes'; company: Duke of Grafton, the Jerseys, the Morleys, the Vernons, the Lord Chancellor, etc. Vernon told me that the first account he had of the King's death in the morning was from Botham, at Salt Hill," Botham saying to him when he came downstairs, "Well, sir, I have lost my *neighbour*."

"What is it to be a gentleman?" asks Thackeray in his "Book of Snobs." "Is it to be honest, to be gentle, to be brave, to be wise, and, possessing all these good qualities, to exercise them in the most graceful outward manner? Ought a gentleman to be a loyal son, a true husband, and an honest father? Ought his life to be decent, his bills to be paid, his tastes to be high and elegant, his aims in life lofty and noble? Out of court, out of court, fat old Florizel! Beadles, turn out that bloated, pimple-faced old man! If Georgius *must* have a statue in the new palace, it ought to be set up in the Flunkeys' Hall. He should be represented cutting out a coat, in which art he is said to have excelled. He also invented Maraschino punch, a shoe-buckle (this was in the vigour of his youth and the prime force of his invention), and a Chinese pavilion, the most hideous building in the world. He could drive a four-in-hand very nearly as well as the Brighton coachman; could fence ele-

could not say a few decent extempore words, if we are to judge, at least, from what he said to his regiment on its embarkation for Portugal! That this *Exciter of Desire*, this *Adonis in Loveliness*, was a corpulent gentleman of fifty! In short, that this *delightful*, *blissful*, *wise*, *pleasurable*, *honourable*, *virtuous*, *true*, *and immortal Prince* was a violater of his word, a libertine, over head and ears in debt and disgrace, a despiser of domestic ties, a companion of gamblers and demireps, a man who has just closed half a century without one single claim of the gratitude of his country or the respect of posterity!"

"Thackeray," says Percy Fitzgerald, "professed to see nothing but clothes when he looked through his life, and his judgment may be worth quoting as one of the most mistaken and superficial." Says Thackeray, "I try and take him to pieces, and find silk stockings, padding, stays, a coat with frogs and a fur collar, a star and blue ribbon, a pocket-handkerchief prodigiously scented, one of Truefitt's best nutty-brown wigs reeking with oil, a set of teeth and a huge black stock, under-waistcoats, more under-waistcoats, and then—nothing! I know of no sentiment that he ever distinctly uttered. Documents are published under his name, but people wrote them; private letters, but people spelt them. He put a great George P. or George R. at the bottom of the page, and fancied he had written the paper. Some bookseller's clerk, some poor author, some man did the work—saw to the spelling, cleared up the slovenly sentences, and gave the lax, maudlin slipslop a sort of consistency. He must have had an individuality: the dancing-master whom he emulated, nay, surpassed, the wig-maker who curled his *toupée* for him, the tailor who cut his coats, had that. But about George one can get at nothing actual. That outside, I am certain, is pad and tailor's work." Says Percy Fitzgerald, the best, the fairest, the most painstaking and conscientious writer who has attempted to sketch the much-abused King's life and character, "This view, founded on clothes, will be found to be a complete mistake. If he could devise these trifling things, he could turn his mind with effect to what was serious and important."

Mr. Fitzgerald thus sums him up:—"Jovial, epicurean, shifty, clever, and good-natured, he offers one more disastrous spectacle of a life wrecked by self-indulgence and an unbounded love of pleasure."

Chance has led me to read many hundreds upon hundreds of pages treating of George's character and intimate surroundings, and, upon my honour, I am half inclined to come to the conclusion that, altogether, his wickedest crime was being born an over-beloved Prince, and furthermore, his having lived to grow up into an over-eulogized Sovereign. All round him, all his life through, I find his most intimate associates speaking nothing but well of him. Poor people, to whom he was ever prodigally generous, with the generosity of a great, big, overgrown, over-fed, over-happy schoolboy, called down blessings on his head. Men of talent mixing with him and pitting their talent against his—instance Sir Walter Scott—came off only second best. Had he but been, instead of a Prince and King, an honest, good-natured-faced, cock-nosed country gentleman, with courteous manners and well-fitting clothes (as he had), he would assuredly have been well thought of and well loved, and, in due course of time,—wholly forgotten, as the best of us are, as a matter of course. But he lived a life where temptations of an extraordinary character beset his path at every turn, and all that was good in him has been allowed to slip out of memory, whilst all his follies—his almost unconscious and scarcely criminal criminality—have been most conscientiously noted down, retailed, and recorded *ad nauseam*. Oh, happy, thrice-happy nobodies, you who read and I who write, may the stones resting at the head and foot of our graves, when the time comes, be set up and engraven by loving hands, not cast recklessly and without other thought than the pastime of the hour by those who knew not, nor cared to know!

THE CHAIN PIER.

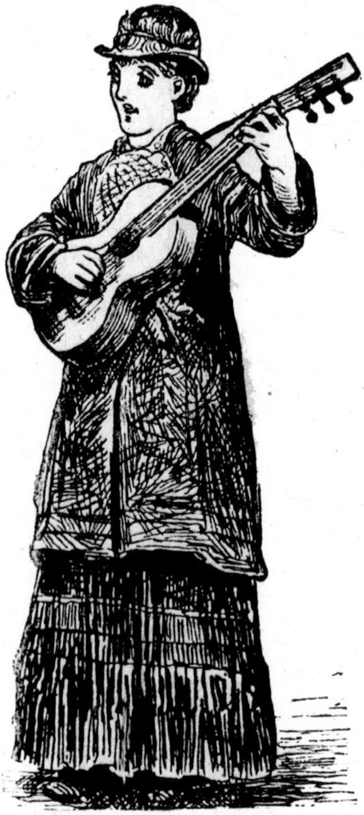

THE Chain Pier is a remarkable institution. It may be seen from the gallery overlooking the Aquarium Skating-Rink, and people living on the cliff above are said every now and then to go down in desperation with set teeth and look at it nearer.

There is, I have discovered, a modest charge for admission through the toll-gate, and when desirous of paying it, you tap your twopence upon a flat metal surface provided for that purpose, and after a time a small boy gives up a game of buttons somewhere a long way off on the beach, and passes you through the wicket. Your first impression doubtless is that you are the only living soul there beside an elderly lady, who appears prepared to do a brisk business in polished pebbles when a rush comes. But in this you are wrong. Whilst asking yourself why on earth any one comes there, you discover the answer by finding on a dreary kind of platform below the floor of the pier, exposed to wind and rain, an amateur fisherman, who asks you despairingly if you have got a vesuvian. Hearing you haven't, he pockets his pipe, draws up a line he has been dangling in the sea, puts fresh bait on it resignedly, and goes on fishing. By his side is an empty fish-basket. He has only been at work a few hours.

"This beautiful object of suspensive power," says a local Guide, "opposite Snelling's Grand Fancy Bazaar, was begun in 1822 from plans by Captain Sir Samuel Brown, under whose superintendence it was erected, and opened in 1829, at a cost of £30,000. It consists of a platform, about 13 feet wide and 1,000 feet long, suspended from eight chains passed over four towers. The towers are of cast iron, and each rests upon 20 piles driven into the bed of chalk. The last tower, and the platform forming the pier-head, rest upon 100 piles. Beneath are convenient stairs for landing from boats, and from which a steam packet for

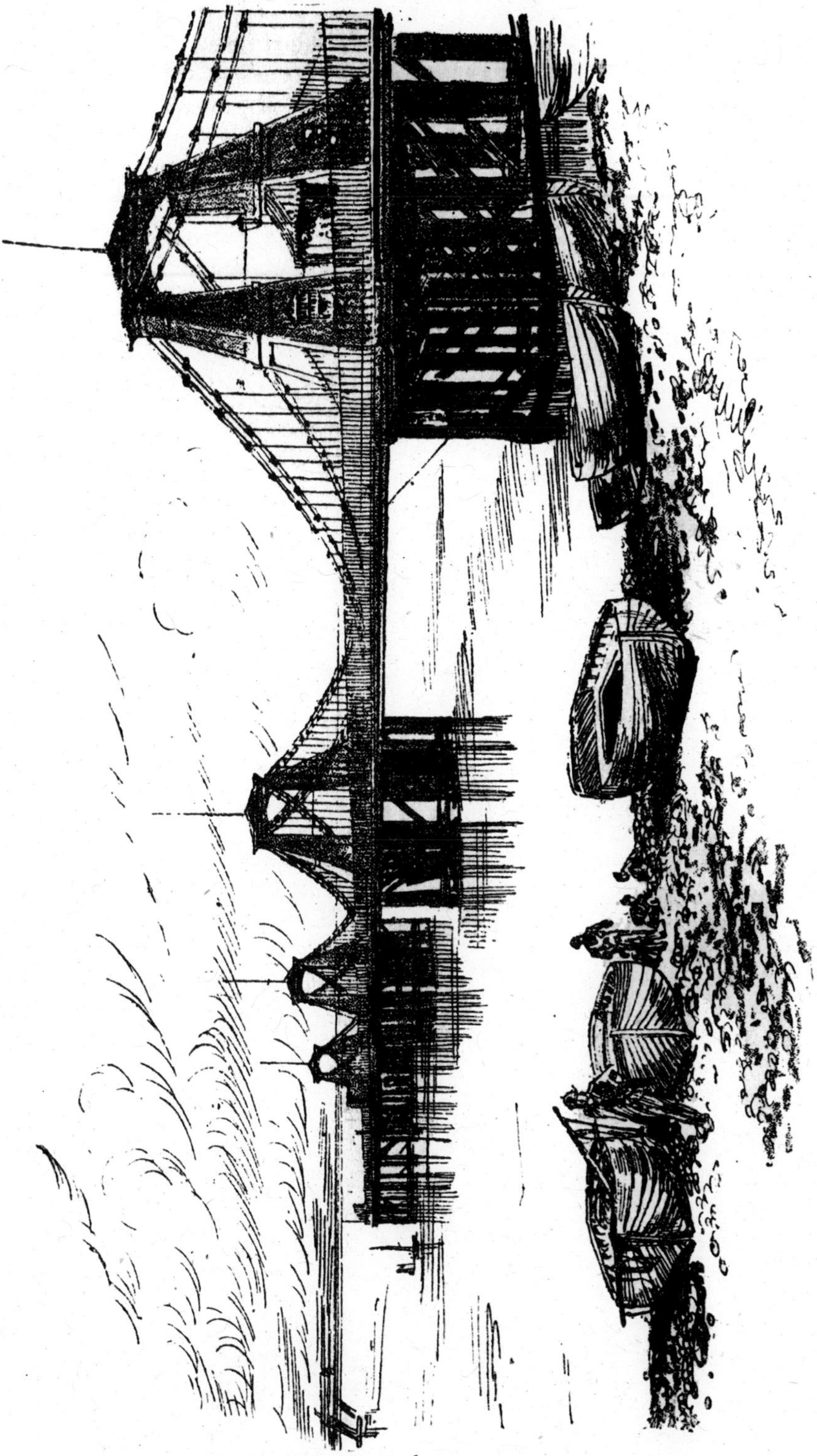

CHAIN PIER.

Dieppe formerly started. A grand view of the town, and also of a long line of the coast, is obtainable from the pier-head; and it is a beautiful promenade especially on summer evenings, about the time of sunset.

TERMS OF ADMISSION.

A Single Visit, each Person, 2*d.*

	1 *Year.* £ *s.* *d.*	6 *Months.* £ *s.* *d.*	3 *Months.* £ *s.* *d.*	1 *Month.* £ *s.* *d.*	1 *Week.* *s.* *d.*
One Person	1 1 0	0 15 0	0 9 0	0 4 0	1 6
Two Persons	1 10 0	1 1 0	0 13 0	0 6 0	2 0
Families not exceeding 4 in number	2 0 0	1 10 0	1 0 0	0 8 0	2 6
Ditto exceeding 4	2 10 0	1 15 0	1 5 0	0 10 0	3 0

Schools, not exceeding 25 in number, including the family of the Principal ... £3 per annum.
Exceeding 25 in number ... ... £4 ,,

Subscriptions do not include Servants unless in attendance on Subscribers, nor horses, carriages, or chairs.

They sell, when they can, pebbles and bottled porter upon the pier, and at stated times a band discourses music, to hear which, I presume, the subscribers assemble; and the young ladies' schools, with downcast eyes, drink in the dulcet strains. I am not absolutely positive sure that the Snelling's "Grand Fancy Bazaar" is a more conspicuous object to guide the stranger by than the pier itself. For instance, I myself only found the bazaar out quite by accident as I came off the pier, but when I did find it I straightway bought a toy, and went in wildly at the wheel of fortune. I had not time for the camera obscura.

———o———

THE WEST PIER.

THE Chain Pier was good enough for "the poor white-headed old gentleman in a blue body-coat and brass buttons, who used to potter about the beach and buy toy boats and cockles,"—"King Billy" and his Queen Adelaide, and the "homely old Royal Princesses" to land at and promenade upon; but Young Brighton will have none of it. I make a point, for I think it my duty, to go once, and once only, down the Chain Pier during each visit to Brighton, and to go every day, some time or other, upon the other. All the world and his wife, or, as a frivoller has put it, "the world and all his wives," his sisters also, and his cousins and his aunts—quite young things, too, some of the last named—are to be found upon the West Pier. According to the season the facial composition of the visitors may be found to vary, and the hooky nose follows the Bourbon, and anon is replaced by the snub and *retrousse.*

Architecturally considered, the West Pier is a noble structure, and, as a promenade, quite cheap at twopence. An annual ticket for one person is obtainable for 21*s.*; for six months, 12*s.*; three months, 7*s.* 6*d.* Twelve admission tickets, 1*s.* 6*d.*; 50 ditto, 6*s.*; 100 ditto, 10*s.*; and a Bath chair and attendant, 6*d.*; 12 tickets, 4*s.* 6*d.*

The Company's band perform at the pier-head, from May 1st to October 31st, twice a day, and from November 1st to April 30th once a day, weather permitting.

The pier is more than 1,100 feet long and 55 feet wide, except at the abutment and pier-head, both of which are 140 feet wide. The foundations are cast-iron and wrought-iron screws fixed in the bed of the sea, and these are surmounted

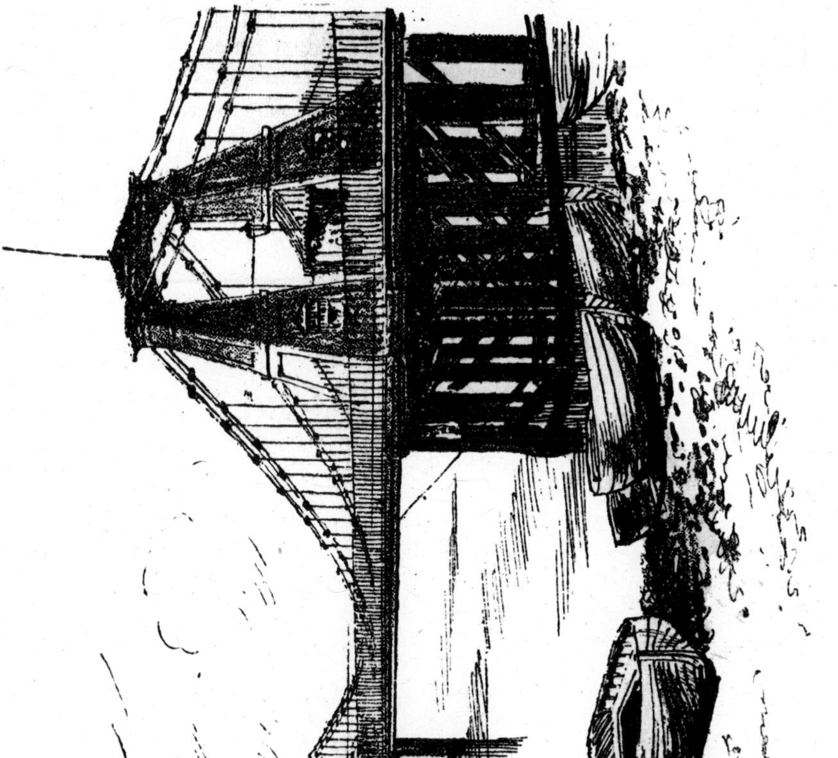

CHAIN PIER.

Dieppe formerly started. A grand view of the town, and also of a long line of the coast, is obtainable from the pier-head; and it is a beautiful promenade especially on summer evenings, about the time of sunset.

TERMS OF ADMISSION.

A Single Visit, each Person, 2*d.*

	1 Year.			*6 Months.*			*3 Months.*			*1 Month.*			*1 Week.*	
	£	*s.*	*d.*	*£*	*s.*	*d.*	*£*	*s.*	*d.*	*£*	*s.*	*d.*	*s.*	*d.*
One Person	1	1	0	0	15	0	0	9	0	0	4	0	1	6
Two Persons	1	10	0	1	1	0	0	13	0	0	6	0	2	0
Families not exceeding 4 in number	2	0	0	1	10	0	1	0	0	0	8	0	2	6
Ditto exceeding 4	2	10	0	1	15	0	1	5	0	0	10	0	3	0

Schools, not exceeding 25 in number, including the family of the Principal ... £3 per annum.
Exceeding 25 in number ... ... £4 ,,

Subscriptions do not include Servants unless in attendance on Subscribers, nor horses, carriages, or chairs.

They sell, when they can, pebbles and bottled porter upon the pier, and at stated times a band discourses music, to hear which, I presume, the subscribers assemble; and the young ladies' schools, with downcast eyes, drink in the dulcet strains. I am not absolutely positive sure that the Snelling's "Grand Fancy Bazaar" is a more conspicuous object to guide the stranger by than the pier itself. For instance, I myself only found the bazaar out quite by accident as I came off the pier, but when I did find it I straightway bought a toy, and went in wildly at the wheel of fortune. I had not time for the camera obscura.

———o———

THE WEST PIER.

THE Chain Pier was good enough for "the poor white-headed old gentleman in a blue body-coat and brass buttons, who used to potter about the beach and buy toy boats and cockles,"—"King Billy" and his Queen Adelaide, and the "homely old Royal Princesses" to land at and promenade upon; but Young Brighton will have none of it. I make a point, for I think it my duty, to go once, and once only, down the Chain Pier during each visit to Brighton, and to go every day, some time or other, upon the other. All the world and his wife, or, as a frivoller has put it, "the world and all his wives," his sisters also, and his cousins and his aunts—quite young things, too, some of the last named—are to be found upon the West Pier. According to the season the facial composition of the visitors may be found to vary, and the hooky nose follows the Bourbon, and anon is replaced by the snub and *retrousse.*

Architecturally considered, the West Pier is a noble structure, and, as a promenade, quite cheap at twopence. An annual ticket for one person is obtainable for 21*s.*; for six months, 12*s.*; three months, 7*s.* 6*d.* Twelve admission tickets, 1*s.* 6*d.*; 50 ditto, 6*s.*; 100 ditto, 10*s.*; and a Bath chair and attendant, 6*d.*; 12 tickets, 4*s.* 6*d.*

The Company's band perform at the pier-head, from May 1st to October 31st, twice a day, and from November 1st to April 30th once a day, weather permitting.

The pier is more than 1,100 feet long and 55 feet wide, except at the abutment and pier-head, both of which are 140 feet wide. The foundations are cast-iron and wrought-iron screws fixed in the bed of the sea, and these are surmounted by iron columns and piles, upon which the structure is placed. The entire length of the pier is lined with continuous seats for 3,000 persons, though I have never seen as many sitting down all at once. You may at all times buy toys upon the pier, and, now and again, a newspaper or railway book, when the party in charge of the stall happens to be about. There are also some penny or twopenny shows of an improving character, including a company of learned owls, to which a flippant yet amusing "Comic Guide to Brighton" has likened the local Town Council in respect to their gravity of demeanour and dignity of deportment. On Sunday evening a brisk business appears to be done in the refreshment-rooms.

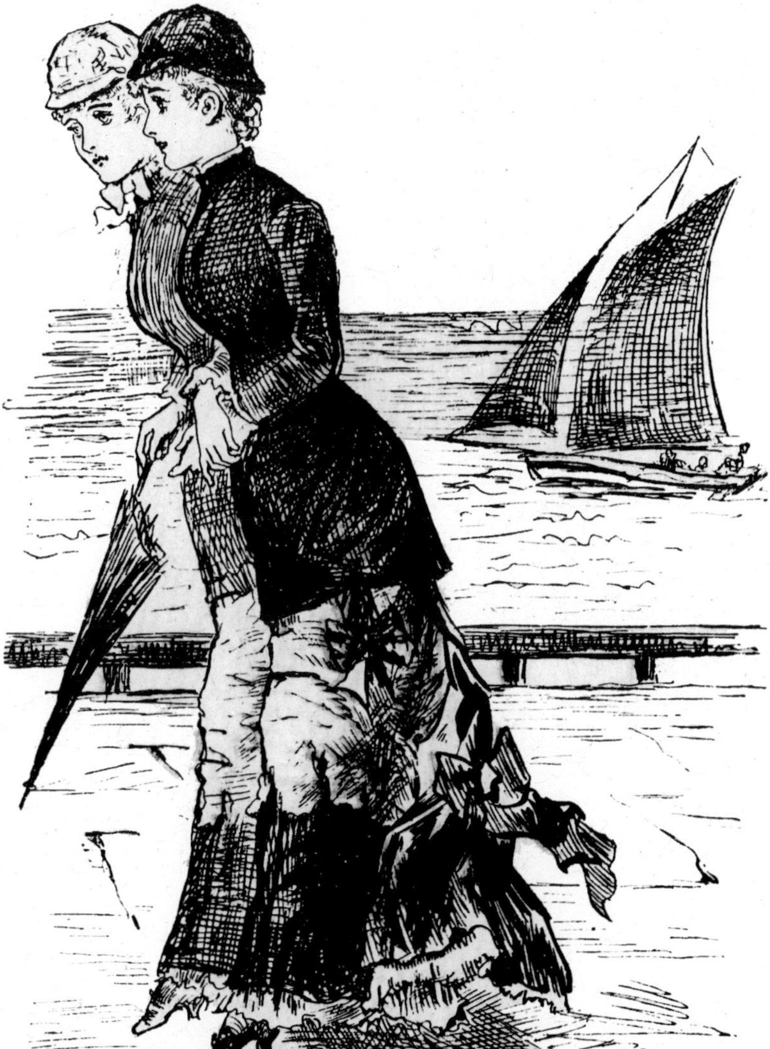

Two little Pier-esses in their own right.

As I glance back over the lines above written, I can't help thinking of the Bath chairs and their occupants, the interesting invalids. Some of them, it is easy to see, are ill enough, and pale from long sickness, but some, I must confess, are monstrously rosy. Can it be possible——No, I won't believe it!

TABLE OF TOLLS.

For every person passing on to the Pier upon each admission	2d.
For every Bath Chair and attendant	6d.
For every Perambulator and attendant	4d.
For every person landing at the Pier-head	2d.

THE AQUARIUM.

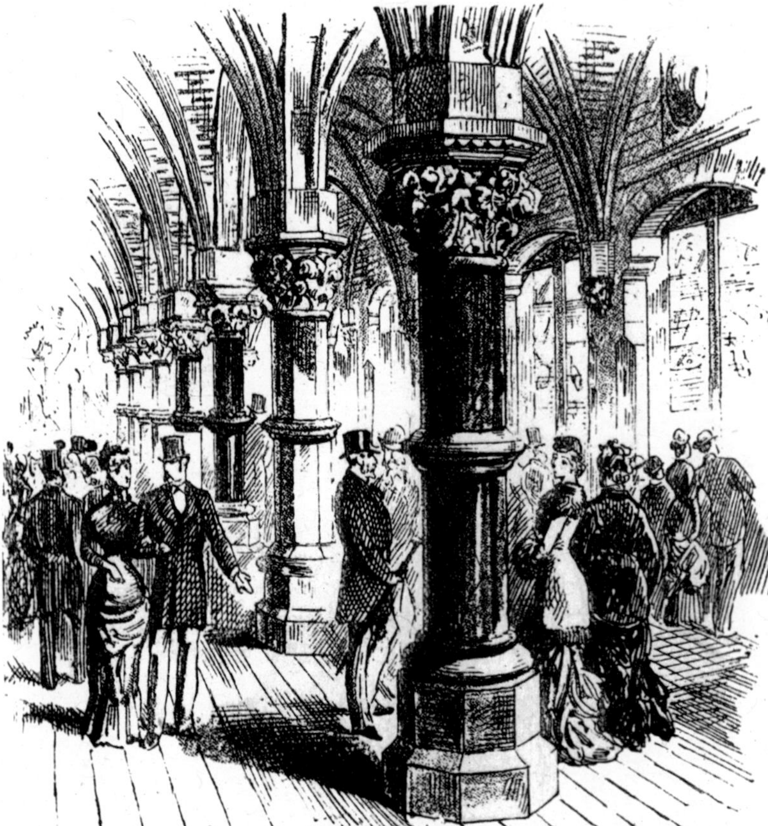

THE site of the Brighton Aquarium is close to the Chain Pier, immediately below the cliff; the building being protected from the waves by a strong sea-wall, formed of concrete and Portland stone. The principal entrance is opposite the east side of the Albion Hotel, near to the spot where for many years stood the Chain Pier Toll-house, well known as "Ratty's Tollhouse."

As long ago as 1867 the idea of an Aquarium at Brighton first occurred to

Mr. Birch, the engineer, and mainly through the co-operation of Mr. McMillan has that idea been carried out. The Act of Parliament was obtained in 1869, and in 1871 the structure was partially opened; but in August, 1872, on the occasion of the visit of the British Association to Brighton, the building was formally opened by Prince Alfred (Duke of Edinburgh) during the mayoralty of the late Sir Cordy Burrows. For some years following Mr. McMillan was a Director of the Company, and for the last four years Chairman, a post in itself

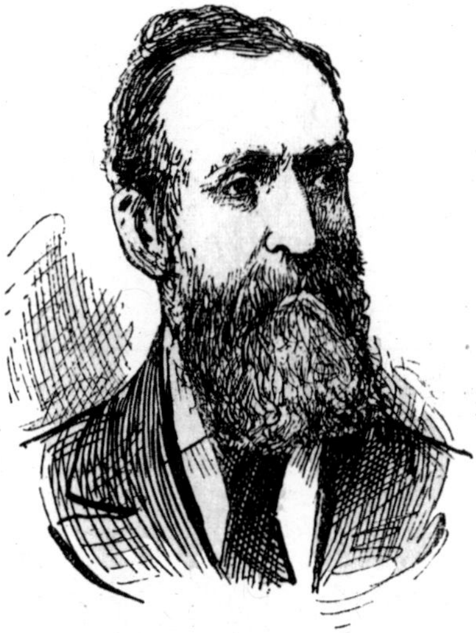

Mr. J. McMillan, Chairman of the Brighton Aquarium Co.

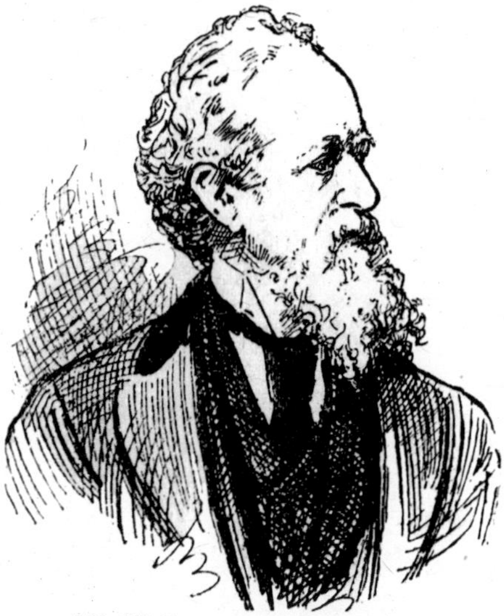

Mr. W. Stevens, late Chairman of Brighton Aquarium.

no sinecure, particularly following so able and energetic a Chairman as his predecessor, Mr. W. Stevens. Identified with all the varying fortunes of the institution, through his tact and skilful management many almost insuperable difficulties have been overcome. His ability and experience have had a beneficial effect upon all the important questions in connection with the management of the Aquarium.

On the northern side of the Entrance Court is the Restaurant, Buffet, and Dining-room. The Entrance Hall, which is 80 feet by 45 feet, is approached through three doors. This is furnished with reading-tables and supplied regularly with the serials, journals, and telegrams of the day. The largest tank, measuring over 100 feet in length, by 40 feet in width, and holding 110,000 gallons of sea-water, is devoted to the exhibition of Porpoises, Sharks, Turtles, and other animals of large dimensions.

Concerts are given every day by the Aquarium Band, and every evening there are performances by well-known and popular entertainers. Every Saturday afternoon there is given a concert of special attractiveness, at which some of the best *artistes* of the day appear. Admission, daily, 1*s.*; evening, 6*d.*

The salt water is pumped by engine power direct from the sea into reservoirs under the floors of the corridors, and is thence conveyed into the tanks by the same means. These reservoirs are capable of holding 500,000 gallons of water, which quantity can be pumped from the sea in about ten hours. The water in the tanks is constantly aërated and kept in circulation by a stream of compressed

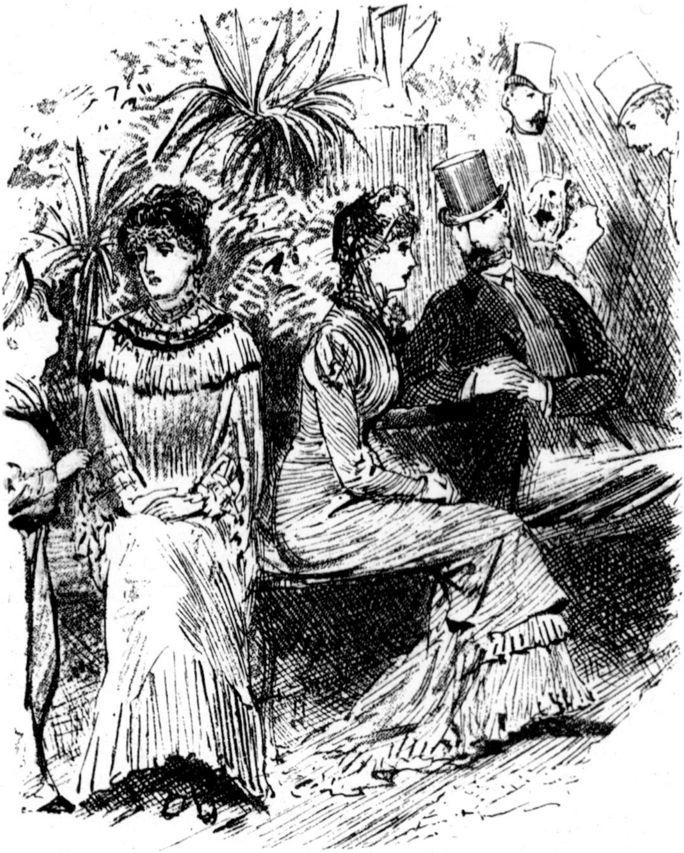

The Concert-Room.

air, supplied to the lower part of the tanks. This also keeps down the temperature and oxidizes any organic impurity which the water may contain.

The Café and Smoking Saloon are placed on a balcony raised above the terraces, from which a magnificent sea view in obtained.

In the water the strength and agility of the Sea-Lions are best seen, and a most interesting spectacle is that afforded at feeding-time, when their food, consisting principally of herrings, being thrown into the water, they plunge in and swim to it with wonderful grace and speed.

The average length of the Common Skate is from two to four feet; a specimen, however, taken on the Suffolk coast, and now in the British Museum, measured from its nose to the extremity of the tail sixfeet ten inches, across its pectoral fins five feet three inches, and it weighed over a hundredweight.

One of the Sturgeons exhibited in the Aquarium, a splendid fish, more than seven feet long, was captured at Bognor; and another, six feet in length, in a "kettle net" in Rye Bay. The flesh of the Sturgeon is white and firm, and when well cooked, which is a difficult process, is excellent.

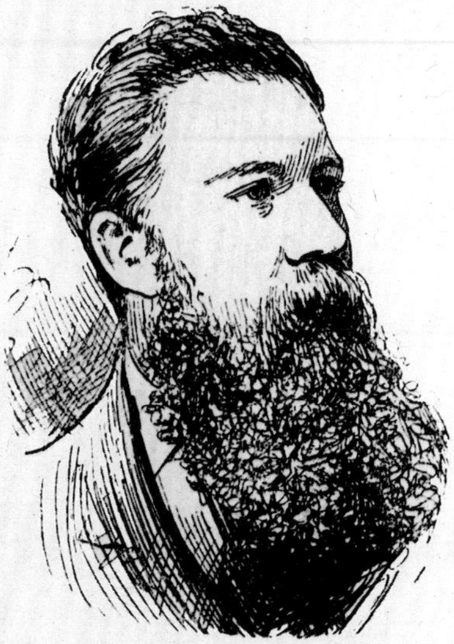

Mr. Taylor, the Secretary.

The most extravagant prices were paid for Surmullet by the ancient Romans, who regarded it as one of the greatest luxuries. It was scarcely valued, however, unless it had been obtained alive and had died in the presence of the guests. Juvenel writes of a single Surmullet as having realized the almost incredible price of fifty pounds.

Such is the impatience of confinement of the Mackerel, on first finding itself restricted in its movements by artificial boundaries, that one specimen beat its head so severely against the glass of the tank that the anterior facial bones were forced in so that the contour of the snout was rendered perfectly obtuse, and became strongly and immovably fixed in a strong curve towards the left shoulder. Notwithstanding those severe injuries, the fish outlived the accident many weeks.

The great abundance of Cod is accounted for by its extreme prolificness, an instance being given by Mr. Frank Buckland in which the removed roe from one fish weighed seven and three-quarter pounds, and, on careful calculation, was found to contain no fewer than 6,876,000 eggs.

ROUND ABOUT.

It must have struck the visitor to many popular pleasure resorts as being rather an odd thing that he should, immediately upon his arrival at a place where he had determined to make a stay of some duration, find himself surrounded by hoarse and energetic men, who clamour for his body, eager to convey it, without a moment's loss of time, to some distant spot. The exhausted traveller by water, at length, after long suffering, setting foot, with an intense sense of relief, on the dry land at Margate, is instantaneously urged, by the noisy throng surrounding him, either to take a car to Ramsgate, or, failing that, a boat out to sea for a sail. Is it not so? I do remember me, too, when once, after much vacillation and innumerable puttings off, I made a journey to Windsor for the purpose of seeing the interior of the Castle and buying Windsor soap, neither of which actions, owing to the Castle not being open that day and Windsor soap not being kept by the three Windsor chemists I applied to, was I able to accomplish. But I might have gone elsewhere quite easily had I chosen, for at the first glimpse of me the fly-drivers assembled, yelled out "Virginia Water!" with one voice, made a fell swoop, and, bearing down upon and surrounding me, would have laid hands upon and hustled me into one vehicle or another had I not desperately resisted, when at length they allowed me to depart, amidst expressions of withering contempt.

It is not, however, thus at Brighton. Arriving by the train, there is no lack of cabs ready to take you anywhere you like in the town, but no rival attractions far distant are suggested. The Brightonians seem to me, and very properly, too, to be thoroughly impressed with the value of the attractions their town possesses. If you are obstinately determined to urge on your wild career, say to Lancing, or Worthing, or Lewes, or Newhaven, you are at liberty to do so, but there are no kidnappers lying in wait for you, and if you really think Brighton is not good enough, perhaps the sooner you leave it the better. Everybody is not of your opinion.

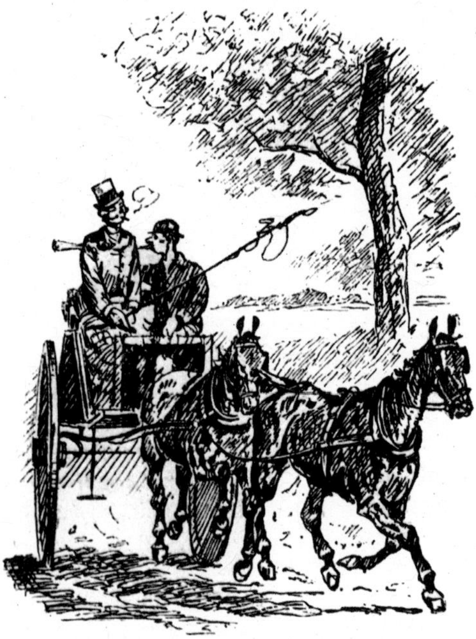

In the good guide book spread open before me I find, among the "places of interest *near* Brighton," Battle Abbey thirty-four miles away, and several others, respectively thirty-three, twenty-eight, and twenty-one. As, however, this little volume, in its quality of guide, only pretends to treat of Brighton itself, I think if I make some brief mention of the outlying places within a distance of fifteen miles, which it is possible to drive to, I shall have done all that can reasonably be expected of me.

I, of course, must begin with the Devil's Dyke.

"Revisiting the Devil's Dyke," says a writer in the *Cuckoo*, "it seemed to me to be much in the same place as it used to be. Several holes in the dyke, some three feet deep, were pointed out as the footprints of the august personage whose name it bears. 'The old gentleman must 'ave trod very heavy,' opined my informant—a local policeman. 'But why did he dig it?' 'Don't know, sir, I'm sure; unless that there was so much traffic between Brighton and his house, that he thought he would just dig a short cut to and fro.' That policeman was an intelligent man.

"A portrait of the great excavator hangs in the hotel on the summit—'reckoned a good likeness by those that know.' The implement he is represented as having used could not be called a spade by the most plain-spoken person; it seems a hybrid between a crutch-stick and an eel-spear."

THE DEVIL'S DYKE (5¼ miles N.W. of Brighton), by a pleasant, uphill road, commanding extensive views. The Dyke consists of a remarkable dip in the Downs, about 300 feet in depth. This sharp, steep declivity has all the look of a "trench cut by the hands of giant excavators.

"An old superstition," says a writer on the subject, "as its name implies, assigns the work to his Satanic Majesty, or, as he was sometimes called in Sussex, 'The Poor Man.' His Devilship's object was, it is supposed, to dig away right through the Down with a view of drowning all the churches in the Weald by bringing in the sea upon them ; but luckily a neighbouring old woman, roused from her sleep by the horrible noise made by the infernal workman, struck a light, and looked out of window, candle in hand, to ascertain the meaning of the clamour. His Majesty perceived the light, and, as he is not usually drawn as being overburdened with sense, but rather as being overreached in most of his bargains, mistook the old woman's light for sunrise, upon which he set off with a howl, leaving his work only half completed. His footprints, or rather *hoof*-prints, burnt in the turf, are still shown on the edge of the Dyke." A very fine panoramic view of the Weald of Sussex can be seen from the edge of the Downs, and portions of central Surrey and Hampshire, and even the Isle of Wight. On the brow of the hill beyond, traces may be found of an encampment. There is a commodious inn on the Dyke,

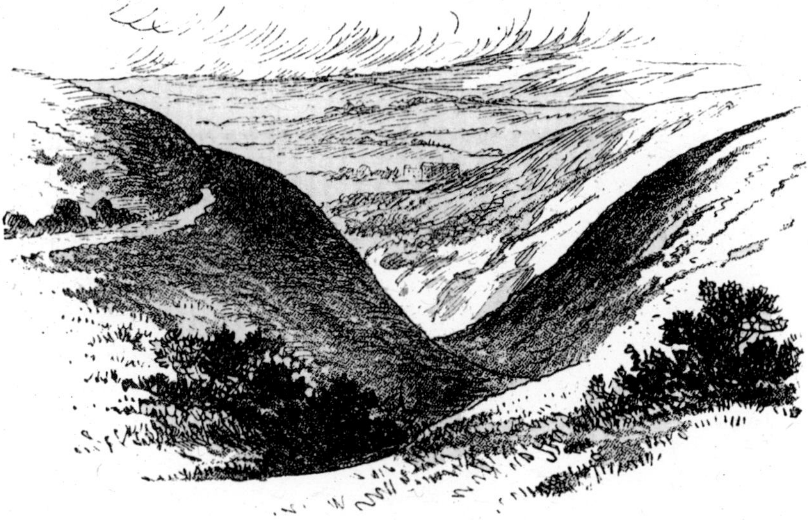

DEVIL'S DYKE.

where every comfort may be procured, Mr. William Thacker having been proprietor forty-six years. Waggonettes run daily during the season from King Charles II.'s Head, West Street ; return fare, 1*s.* 6*d.*

STANMER PARK affords a very pleasant drive for private carriages ; about four miles from Brighton on the Lewes Road, and a very short distance from Falmer Station. It is the seat of the Earl of Chichester ; the mansion, dating from 1724, is a plain stone building, enclosing a quadrangular court. Open daily.

ROTTINGDEAN (4 miles).—Rottingdean is a very quiet little watering-place, situated in a *dene* or valley, not four miles from the centre of Brighton, and may be reached by a pleasant carriage drive or a breezy walk along the greensward at the edge of the cliffs. Early in the reign of Richard II., the French landed here with the intention of sacking Lewes ; but the Prior of Lewes assembled his followers, and, with some neighbouring knights, marched to the Downs above Rottingdean. The unfortunate Prior was defeated and taken prisoner, the enemy, however, retiring without venturing farther inland. The Church is Early English. The Duke of Wellington, Archbishop Manning, and Lord Lytton received their early education here, under its late vicar, Dr. Hooker. Among the shingle, beautiful agates, known as the Rottingdean Pebbles, have been found from time to time.

NEWHAVEN (9 miles).—Newhaven, a most delightful drive along the sea-front, through Rottingdean, but the pedestrian will have the advantage of the best views, and can also take in Ovingdean, half a mile north of the carriage-road. The Church of Newhaven has a remarkable tower, supposed to be the earliest remaining Norman erection in England. The New Fort is well worth a visit. In the churchyard is noticed a weatherbeaten monument, erected to the memory of the officers and crew of the *Brazen* sloop-of-war, lost off here in 1800, when all but one man perished. Steamers leave daily for Dieppe.

DITCHLING BOSTEL (about 7 miles from Brighton, *viâ* London Road and Preston) is the highest point of the South Downs, being 858 feet above the level of the sea. The view is almost, if not quite, equal to that from the Devil's Dyke. A Roman road leads up the ascent, and on the summit are the remains of a Roman encampment.

LEWES (*viâ* Lewes Road, right hand of the Level) 8 miles from Brighton.—The county-town ot Sussex. The town is rich in antiquities. The most striking object of note is the Castle, a Norman edifice. Open daily, admission 6*d.* ; free to the Members of the Sussex Archæological Society, whose Museum, occupying the principal rooms, contains a collection of curiosities well worth inspecting. Tickets may be obtained here (4*d.* each) for admission to St. Pancras Priory. The Norman Chapel in Southover Church contains the tombs of William de Warrenne and Gundreda his wife, the daughter of William the Conqueror. Their remains rest in leaden coffins, which were discovered in the Priory Grounds in 1845. Near the town was the scene of a battle between Henry III. and Simon de Montfort.

PRESTON (2 miles from Brighton) is noted for the quiet beauty of its situation. The Church is well worth a visit, being very ancient, in the Early English style. On the wall of the nave, either side of the chancel arch, may be seen some very indistinct mural paintings, representing, on one side, the martyrdom of Thomas à Becket ; the other, St. Michael with his scales weighing souls. Douglas, the author of " Nenia Britannica," the first book which drew attention to the sepulchral wealth of Sussex and Kent, is buried in the churchyard. Withdean, a very pleasant little hamlet, is a little farther distant. Withdean Hall, a fine Elizabethan building, erected in 1861. Anne of Cleves, after her divorce, lived for some time at Preston House, but died at a convent at Falmer.

PRESTON PARK.—The International Gun and Polo Club hold their meetings here, and the Park is also thrown open to the public on Sundays during the summer months, by permission of Mr. Benett-Stanford.

PATCHAM (on the verge of the South Downs).—The Church of All Saints is situated on a rising ground, and presents a curious mixture of Early English and Perpendicular work, consisting of a chancel, nave, and tower with small spire. Patcham Place, a handsome building, erected in the reign of Queen Elizabeth.

HURSTPIERPOINT.—The Church is in the Decorative style, and is always open. Splendid views may be obtained from the churchyard. Danny, the seat of W. H. Campion, Esq., is a fine Elizabethan mansion close to the Downs, and dates from 1595. Some of the finest oaks in the county may be seen in the park.

ALDRINGTON CHURCH (near Portslade), until recently a ruin ; the only remains of a village long since swept into the sea, and which is supposed to have occupied the site of the Roman Portus Adurni. The Church is now rebuilt. Hangleton Church, 1 mile north. The remains of the late Dr. Kenealy were interred in the churchyard (1880).

PORTSLADE.—The Church of St. Nicholas is in the Early English style, and has the remains of an old Norman building, erected probably about the year 1150. A beautiful mortuary chapel is erected over the vault of the ancient family of Brackenbury.

SOUTHWICK.—A thriving business village, close to Shoreham Harbour. The Church is Norman; pulpit very handsome, of a Jacobean pattern. The village is celebrated as being the birthplace of John Peel, the eminent divine.

KINGSTON-BY-SEA.—A place of considerable trade, chiefly engaged in the shipping interest.

SHOREHAM (6 miles from Brighton).—Objects of interest are the Churches, which the archæologist should by no means neglect. Both were probably erected by the great Braose family, the early Lords of Shoreham. John landed here on his return to England as King after the death of the Cœur de Lion. The Swiss Gardens is a place of great resort during the summer months.

LANCING (2 miles beyond Shoreham) is a small and select bathing resort. Queen Caroline embarked here in 1822.

Two and a half miles beyond Lancing we reach WORTHING, once, like Brighton, a poor fishing village, but now a fashionable resort. It was a small fishing village until the commencement of the 19th century—"none of the houses exceeding 40*s.* rental, and an acre of ground might be bought for five gallons of rum." This is how it came into note:—In 1797 the Princess Amelia was advised by her physicians to reside here for the sake of her health. The presence of a Princess attracted fashionable visitors, and the modern Worthing rose as if by magic. The view from the Esplanade commands the English Channel, the Isle of Wight, Brighton, and the range of coast towards Beachy Head. The neighbourhood has many points of interest which should be visited, such as Bramber Castle (open daily, free), Highdown Hill, Broadwater, &c.

BRAMBER is situated on the river Adur, was formerly a borough, and, although could muster but twenty electors, sent two Members to Parliament. The Church was erected before the Norman accession, dedicated to St. Nicholas, has a nave with an embattled square tower. Bramber Castle was formerly the residence of the Kings of Wessex. It stands on an eminence, which is supposed to be artificial, and was, in Saxon times, a fortress of great strength. Only a small portion, however, of the ruins now remain, having been destroyed, it is supposed, by Oliver Cromwell. There is also a curious Museum about 200 yards east of the castle, which should be seen.

WEST GRINSTEAD (14 miles from Brighton on the Horsham Line).—Knepp Castle with ruins of the ancient Keep. West Grinstead Castle. Ruins of the ancient Priory of the Knights of St. John. Beautiful scenery.

WISTON.—A romantic village about 2 miles from Bramber. Wiston House, in the Park, belongs to the Goring family, and is a handsome Tudor structure, situate amidst stately trees. It was built in 1576.

HENFIELD, a picturesque village, situated on an eminence. Some old Sussex cottages here are well worth notice. The Church is Perpendicular, and contains two brasses of some interest.

CUCKFIELD (15 miles).—On the way notice the little Church of Clayton, with its Early English chancel. Clayton Hill commands a most extensive view to the north, and is pierced by a railway tunnel above one mile in length, which cost upwards of £90,000. On the main road, just as you ascend the hill leading into the village of Cuckfield, may be seen a fine Elizabethan mansion, the original of Harrison Ainsworth's "Rookwood Hall." The fatal tree, an enormous lime, from which a bough always fell on the approaching death of its owner, is still standing in the avenue that leads up to the house. The visitor will find good accommodation at the King's Head Hotel. The most picturesque little village of Lindfield should be visited, situated three miles east, passing through Hayward's Heath. Linfield, a very short distance; the Church of St. Peter is of great antiquity, and many old houses in the street should be noticed. Return to Brighton by another route, passing through Hayward's Heath and Wivelsfield. Ditchling Church is worth a visit.

IN THE CHURCHYARD.

IT is, I believe, generally agreed that the church, or, at any rate, the churchyard, of St. Nicholas should not be left unvisited. Climbing up a short but steepish hill, between the top of North Street and the bottom of Dyke Road, you come upon an edifice, the oldest part of which probably dates from the reign of Henry VII. Here the beautiful Mrs. Crouch lies buried. Here, too, is the grave of trusty Captain Tettersell; and a tombstone is erected to the memory of the worthy family of Gunns, the most illustrious of whom would appear to have been the Martha whose engraved portrait you may find in the Pavilion, the smoking-room of the Old Ship, and at several other places in the town. She is depicted in this plate nursing a remarkably well-fed boy, erroneously described, by some of the guide books, as the Prince Regent. The plump youngster undoubtedly looks more than seven, but he is under twenty, the age at which it has been settled George paid Brighton his first visit. "Martha," says her tombstone, "was peculiarly distinguished as a bather in this town;" and what there is certain about her is that in her latter days she was well cared for and respected. I do not, however, find any monument erected to Old Smoaker, the principal bathing man of that epoch—Old Smoaker who, one day when the Prince Regent had swum out too far and was evidently in great danger, dashed in, seized His Royal Highness by the ear, and lugged him to shore "without respect or pity," as the

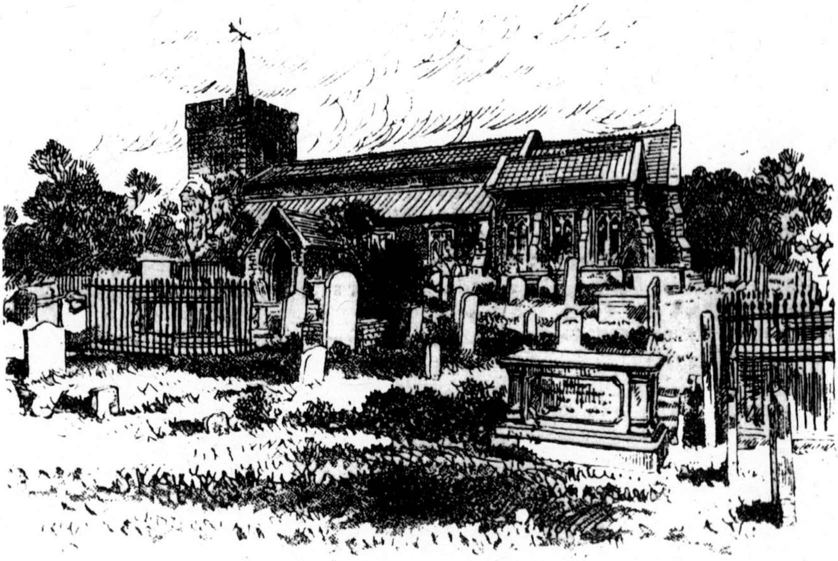

OLD PARISH CHURCH.

chronicler tells us, and possibly squealing like a pig. "How dare you handle me in such a fashion?" roared the Prince, purple and panting for breath. "Well," said Old Smoaker, "I didn't go for to hurt you, but I arn't a-goin' to let the King hang *me* for lettin' the Prince o' Wales drown hisself, to please *you!*" The Prince did not let good, rough Old Smoaker want. He did more, this much-abused "First Gentleman," among the poor folks of Brighton to cause his name to linger lovingly in their memories than many better or less quickly found-out persons have done before or since.

Among other things worth noting there is a quaint tombstone let into the wall at the entrance of a passage of the church to the memory of

"2 louving sisters who in this dust now ly,
That very day oune was bury[d]
Elizabeth did dy."

Ah, young lady reader, how few sisters of this pattern now exist! Look at the Robinson girls. How sweetly pretty are they in company, and with, oh! so dove-like a look in their tender blue eyes, and yet their maid told my man only yesterday they "slap and pinch each other awful" at times. Let us be sisterly and brotherly if we can be nothing else, and if we have no sisters or brothers of our own, let's be sisterly and brotherly to other fellows' sisters and other girls' brothers.

And you, sir, what have you to say, with your cynical smile and dyspeptic aspect? Are such sentiments out of place here in this churchyard, amongst the crumbling tombstones? If so, come inside and let us say our prayers. It will be a novelty for you, and I am told the hassocks are really not very hard to kneel upon.

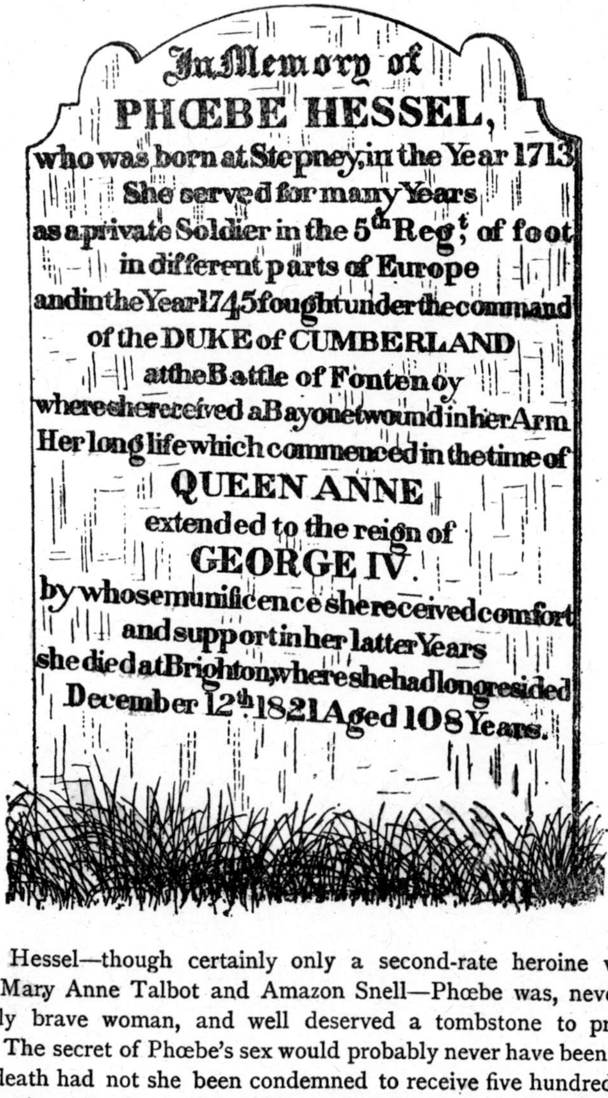

Phœbe Hessel—though certainly only a second-rate heroine when compared to Mary Anne Talbot and Amazon Snell—Phœbe was, nevertheless, a wonderfully brave woman, and well deserved a tombstone to preserve her memory. The secret of Phœbe's sex would probably never have been discovered until her death had not she been condemned to receive five hundred lashes for smoking a pipe when on guard. Then, refusing to strip, she owned up, and—became a heroine. It was not so with Amazon Snell, for, in the course of her extraordinary career, she was twice flogged, still keeping her secret, receiving on one occasion a hundred lashes, which she resolutely bore.

"HIS BLACK-WIGGED MAJESTY."

He was not very merry, I expect, that particular 14th of October in 1651, when, disguised as a footman, dusty and travel-stained, he took shelter with a few of his followers at a small tavern called the George, in West Street, Brighthelmstone (now called King Charles II.'s Head). It was kept by one Smith, who easily recognized his royal guest, but loyally kept the secret; and, next morning, the

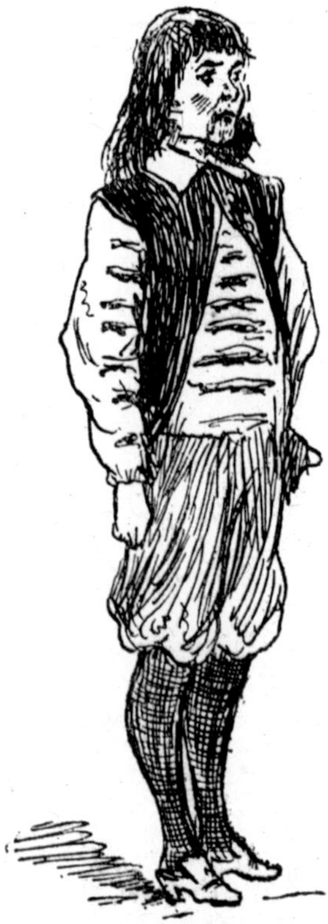

Mr. Smith, licensed to sell Beer and serve Princes.

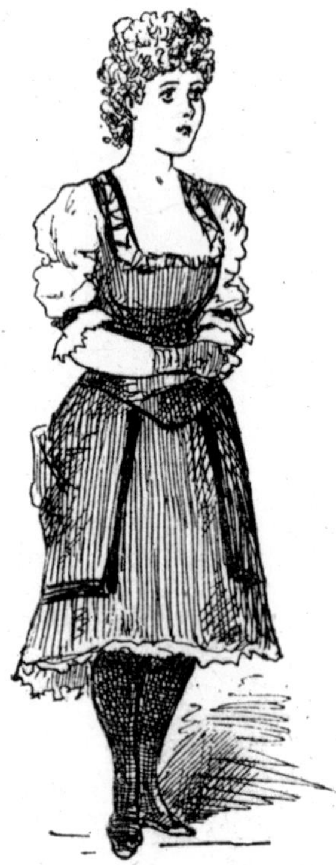

The little Barmaid—a fancy sketch.

future King was, at Shoreham, smuggled on board a coal-brig, owned by brave Captain Nicholas Tettersell, and safely landed a day later at Fecamp, near Havre-de-Grâce.

In the churchyard of St. Nicholas, near the chancel door, lie the old sailor's remains, covered with a slab of black marble bearing this inscription:—

"P.M.S.

"Captain Nicholas Tettersell, through whose prudence, valour, and loyalty, Charles II., King of England, after he had escaped the sword of his merciless rebels, and his forces received a fatal overthrow at Worcester, September 3, 1651, was faithfully preserved and conveyed to France, departed this life the 26th July, 1674.

> "Within this marble monument doth lie
> Approvèd faith, honour, and loyalty;
> In this cold clay he has now ta'en up his station,
> Who once preserved the Church, the croune, and nation.
> When Charles the Greate was nothing but a breath,
> This valiant soule stept 'tween him and death:
> Usurpers' threats, nor tyrant rebels' froune,
> Could not affright his duty to the croune;
> Which glorious act of his for Church and State,
> Eight princes in one day did gratulate—
> Professing all to him in debt to bee,
> As all the world are to his memory.
> Since earth could not reward the worth him given,
> He now receives it from the King of Heaven.
> In the same chest one jewel more you have,
> The partner of his virtues, bed, and grave.

"SUSANNAH, his wife, who deceased the 4th day of May, 1672, to whose pious memory and his oune.

"Honour NICHOLAS, their only son, a just inheritor of his father's vertues, hath paid his last duty in this monument. 1676.

"Here also lieth interred the body of CAPTAIN NICHOLAS TETTERSELL, his son, who departed this life the Fourth of the Calends of October, 1701, in the fifty-seventh year of his age."

Fine sentiments are those incorporated into the bit of poetry, and nobly are they expressed. The eight princes "gratulating" particularly strikes me, but they did not gratulate too precipitately, nor did the Merry One manifest any desire to do the Captain a good turn until the latter, by way of a gentle hint, brought the identical vessel, which had carried the King, up the Thames, moored her opposite Whitehall, and had the name of "The Royal Escape" painted in large capitals upon her. In consequence of this, an annuity of one hundred per annum was granted to Captain Tettersell for ever; but the claimants are extinct, or one of Mr. Bradlaugh's ancestors got the pension stopped, for it has for a long while been discontinued.

Mr. Bishop, in his *Peep into the Past*, says, "whatever merit may have been due to Tettersell in connection with the Royal escape, his conduct in after years was most despicable: he exercised his authority as High Constable of Brighton, in 1670, 'with the zeal of a bigot and the malign industry of a Ministerial spy.' Discovering a house in the town where a few Dissenters met, the door was broken open, under a warrant, and though there was no evidence against the inmates, except that it was asserted by Tettersell's minions 'that they had heard from within a voice in the elevated tone of prayer or instruction,' they were summoned before the Justices at Lewes, and fined in the full penalty allowed by the statute; and to enforce this Tettersell broke open William Beard's malthouse, and took thereout sixty-five bushel sacks of malt, which he sold to one of his partisans for *twelve shillings* a quarter. Verily Tettersell's memory deserves to be held in honour!"

The last of the Tettersells would appear to have been one Gabriel, better known as the "Doctor," a bathing man, who was accidentally drowned in 1806.

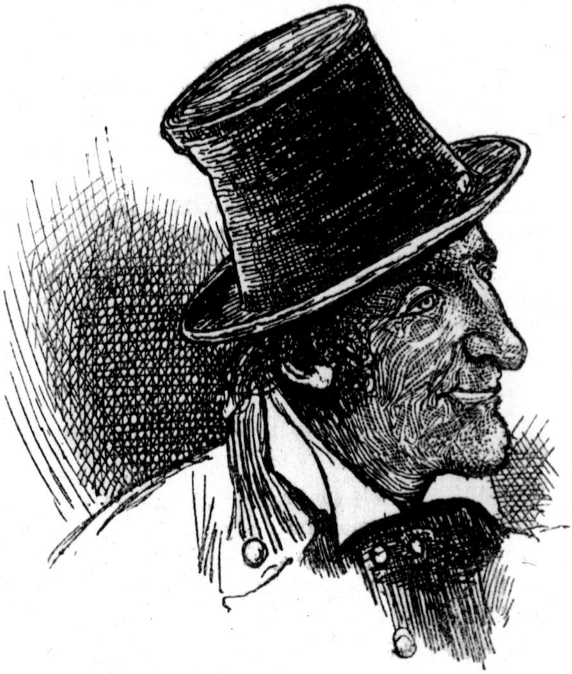

The Doctor.

SOMETHING WRONG IN WEST STREET.

HISTORICAL associations of old Brighton! Nonsense! there are none. There have never been, or, if there have, they have been so long forgotten, mixed and messed up, there is no getting at the rights of the case. Turning to my trusty guide book, I find that the house occupied by Mr. and Mrs. Thrale, and at which Doctor Johnson, Boswell, Foote, Sheridan, and a host of others were so frequently guests, is set down as No. 75 West Street, and is described as being "now stuccoed over." I go to West Street, and find one No. 75, up a passage, to be a modern warehouse, built on the site of a garden, and occupied by Messrs. Copestake, the lace warehousemen. I find a second No. 75, but there is no stucco. No. 74 is, however, stuccoed as described. What shall I do? Knock and ask for Doctor Johnson?

I have. He does not live there, the party who answered the door told me, but in Dyke Road.

* * * * * *

I turn once more to my trusty guide. I find that the house where Charles II.

sought refuge in is set down as the King's Head. I go for it. It does not exist, but there is a King Charles II.'s Head, "established 1646." There seems to be some sort of vagueness about this date, because it was in 1651 that Prince Charles slept there for the night, and the house was then called the George. However, let that pass. I enter and make inquiries. I read as much as I can of a weatherbeaten page, copied, perhaps, fifty or perhaps five years ago from a history of the Stuarts, and framed in the bar. I am also shown, in a back room, a portrait in oil of His Gracious Majesty, which, if it be like him, is most uncommonly unlike all his other portraits; and I learn that the bed-room where the King is supposed to have slept is now used as a lumber-room, and is despised and neglected. "Lots of people used to come and look at it once," says the young lady at the bar; and she adds that she cares nothing for old places herself, and thinks it would be much better to pull the house down and build a bigger one. Attached to it now is a booking-office for omnibuses to the Devil—his dyke.

After the old George took its new title another George would seem to have put in an appearance. In January, 1844, the foot-posts of the bedstead upon which Charles II. slept while at the King's Head were offered for sale at a furniture shop in the Western Road. Can any one of my readers say what became of them?

THE GHOSTS.

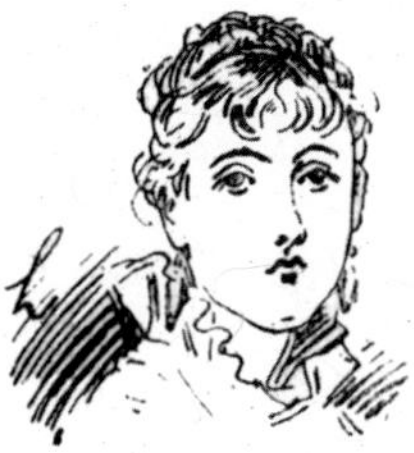

In one of his delightful essays, Mr. Ashby-Sterry tells us of Brighton Ghosts. "It is not," says he, "till long after the sun has set, and the Light Brigade have assumed their evening dresses, and the schoolgirls, clad in innocence and pretty frilled night-dresses, have retired to their warm white nests and taken a large instalment of beauty sleep; it is not even till the illuminations have become faint in the gigantic hotels, and the lamps along the Parade are burning pale, that the ghosts at Brighton begin to flit about. Then, when the streets are silent and deserted, when no sound is to be heard but the tramp of an occasional policeman and the moan of the wind, when the sea drawing back the shingle seems to speak clearly, and then breaks and runs up in a confused chorus, reminding one of the reading of Psalms by priest and congregation in some secluded country church, then, I can assure you, the ghosts come out very strong indeed."

Let us call by name a few of the ghosts of those who have walked, and talked, and fretted their little hour. Who comes first? Why, it is

THE DUKE OF CUMBERLAND,

if I mistake not, in all the pride of his hunting costume, with his hat tied on with a coloured pocket-handkerchief, secured under his chin to prevent its being blown away, followed by his famous dog "Turk." And this, the dramatist,

RICHARD CUMBERLAND,

with, Sir Egerton Brydges says, "a vast memory, and great facility of feeble verbiage; but his vanity, his self-conceit, and his supercilious airs offended everybody. He was a tall handsome man, with a fair regular-featured face, and the appearance of good birth. These are his staring daughters with him, who were once hissed out of a London theatre on account of the height of their feathers." And this,

ARTHUR MURPHY,

the actor, another handsome man, "tall and well made, with a very gentleman-like appearance." And this, as Cooke said, "is the nephew of the gentleman who was lately hung in chains for murdering his brother."

SAMUEL FOOTE.

He is a comical dog himself, and Doctor Johnson was obliged, the first time he was in company with him, to lay down his knife and fork, and throw himself back upon his chair, and roar with laughter. "Having no good opinion of the fellow, I was resolved not to be pleased," says the Doctor; "and I went on eating my dinner pretty sullenly, affecting not to mind him. Sir, he was irresistible." And here is

DOCTOR JOHNSON.

"Here Johnson comes, unblest with outward grace, with a lumber of learning, and some strong parts," says the amiable Horace Walpole. "Johnson was an odious and mean character; his manners were sordid, supercilious, and brutal; with all the pedantry he had all the gigantic littleness of a country schoolmaster." Poor Doctor! According to Curran, he is "a superstitious and brutish bigot." According to Adam Smith, "a brute." Miss Seward calls him a "literary despot;" Lord Auchinleck, "Ursa Major;" and Dr. Campbell, "a Hottentot." He was not, if the truth must be told, a pretty man, and, if we may believe the last-quoted authority, he had "the aspect of an idiot, without the faintest ray of sense gleaming from any one feature, with the most awkward garb, and unpowdered grey wig on one side only of his head; he is for ever dancing the devil's jig, and sometimes he makes the most drivelling effort to whistle some thought in his absent paroxysms." The great lexicographer rolls heavily along, until a rising mist hides his figure from our sight.

But Doctor Johnson is not alone. He has a lady with him, on whose praises he used to dwell with peculiar delight and a paternal fondness. It is

MRS. THRALE,

afterwards Mrs. Piozzi—"One of those clever, kind-hearted, engaging, vain, pert young women," says Macaulay, "who are perpetually saying or doing something that is not exactly right, but who, do or say what they may, are always agreeable." "She was, in truth," says her little friend, Fanny Burney, "a most wonderful character for talents and eccentricity, for wit, genius, generosity, spirit, and powers of entertainment." When she was eighty, Tom Moore spoke of her as "a wonderful old lady," and said "she yet possessed all the quickness and intelligence of a gay young woman."

And this with her is the future

MAID OF HONOUR,

who took the town by storm, in her twenty-seventh year, by her novel of "Evelina." Leslie says: "A novel, painting manners brief and pleasantly, with characters studied from life, and showing some range of social observation and humour, without licentiousness or coarseness, was at that time a phenomenon. Richardson, Fielding, and Smollett had passed away. The first was long-winded, and was beginning to be thought dull; the other two were voted low, and, above all, were 'taboo' to ladies who valued their reputation for propriety." Poor little Fanny Burney! Croker says of her novel: "It owed a great deal of its extraordinary success to the strange misrepresentation that had been somehow made of the author being ten years younger than she really was." "Evelina" is not as dull as "Pamela; or, Virtue Rewarded," but it is not very gay reading nowadays, and few like Sir Joshua Reynolds would sit up all night to read it, or, like Doctor Johnson, fall over it into "fits of admiration and laughter."

Yet one more figure is there in this notable group: "The incarnation of toadyism," Washington Irving calls him; "A jackanapes!" snarls Walpole; and Adam Smith dubs him

"BOZZY THE WIZARD."

Fanny Burney, who had good opportunities of studying the little Scotsman's peculiarities, tells us he had "an odd mock solemnity of tone and manner, that he had acquired imperceptibly from constantly thinking of and imitating Doctor Johnson. There was also something slouching in the gait and dress of Mr. Boswell, that wore an air, ridiculously enough, of purporting to personify the same model. His clothes were always too large for him, his hair, or wig, was constantly in a state of negligence, and he never for a moment sat still or upright on a chair. Every look and movement displayed intentional or involuntary imitation."

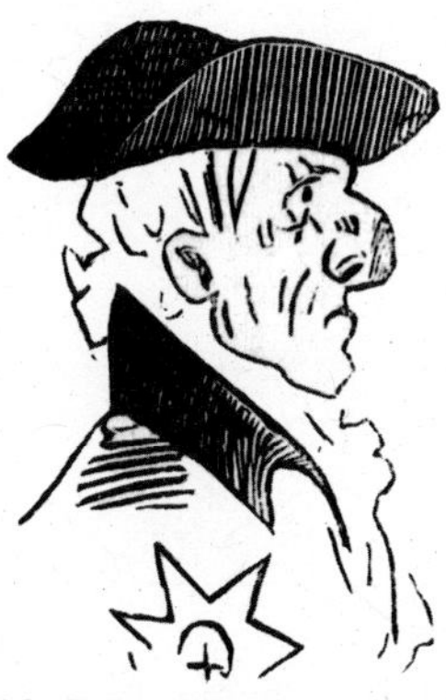

A noble Duke (His Grace of Grafton).

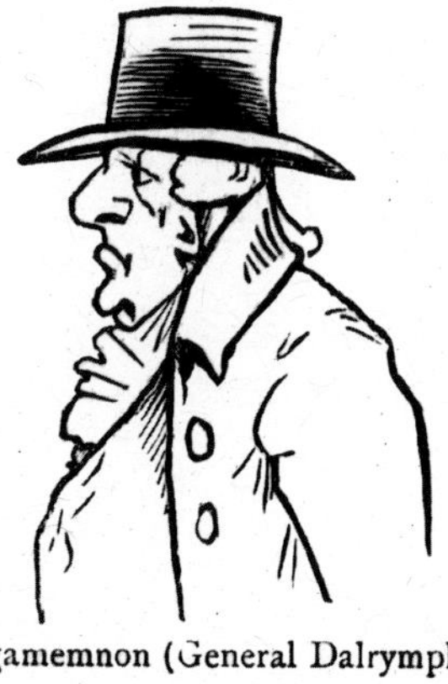

Agamemnon (General Dalrymple).

These pass away, and here comes another noble Duke, the Duke of Grafton Then comes "Agamemnon—a great general," plump General Dalrymple himself; and then

CHARLES JAMES FOX.

"About thirty-five years old—a brilliant debauched creature, the idol of his friends, already, too, a ruined gambler, and his health impaired by excess." "His features, in themselves harsh, dark, and saturnine, like those of Charles

II., from whom he descended in the maternal line, derived nevertheless a sort of majesty from the addition of two black and shaggy eyebrows."

THE BARRYMORES

follow him. Lord Barrymore's was but a short career, and he bore the nick-name of "Hellgate," possibly on account of his being the "warmest" of a very "warm" family. His brother, the Hon. Henry, was dubbed "Cripplegate," on account of his being club-footed. The Reverend Augustus was called "Newgate," because he was said to have been locked up in every other prison but that. Their sister the Prince dubbed "Billingsgate," because she swore more than most ladies of those times. It was Cripplegate who, for a wager, rode a horse upstairs to the garrets of Mrs. Fitzherbert's house. He also invented the smart boy-servant, "the Tiger." The eldest brother was accidentally shot dead by his own gun; the other two died in dire poverty; the sister swore hard all her life, that is all that is recorded of her. And then

SIR JOHN LADE,

who was, we are told, the Prince's tutor in the art of driving, in which, by the way, he acquired great efficiency; but Lady Lade excelled her husband, and her curricle and four excited the admiration of all. She was said to have been originally drawn from Saint Giles's under the favouring patronage of the too celebrated Mr. J. Rann, *alias* "Sixteen-string Jack," at whose execution, says the historian, "she secured the notice of persons of high degree." I know not whether this was the Eleanor Roche, "Rann's companion," mentioned in the trial, or her servant, Christian Stewart. Stewart, however, was acquitted, and Miss Roche sentenced to transportation for fourteen years. Mr. Rann took his trial in a new suit of pea-green clothes, his hat bound round with silver strings. He had "a bundle of flowers in the breast of his coat," says Captain Benson, "almost as large as a broom; and his irons were tied up with a number of blue ribands. He wore a ruffled shirt, and his behaviour evinced the utmost unconcern." The last Sunday before he died he had "seven girls to dine with him," so one of these may possibly have been her future ladyship. At his execution he "behaved with decent resignation, and surveyed the gallows with an eye of confidence."

I have but time in the crowd that follows to pick out witty Lord Alvanley, Mr. Sheridan, Mr. Mellish, and Mr. Crampton; Count D'Orsay, the beautiful Blessington, and Madame Vestris. We all become contemporaries when we become ghosts.

And who is this? "The glass of fashion, and the mould of form;" the "soul of his mess;" Prince Florizel's favourite; the pet Captain of the Tenth, that "did not dance;" the fastidious fine gentleman who broke off with one love because she ate cabbage, and another for asking twice for soup—the Other George!

BEAU BRUMMEL.

"Well fitted was he by nature," says Doctor Wm. Russell, "to be a distinguished clothes-peg." His face was not so handsome as the late Count d'Orsay's, but his elegant figure would show off a tailor's skill as well as could the Prince's own. Lord Byron, who knew him well, has said, with respect to his dress, that it was "only remarkable for its exquisite propriety."

Cannot you imagine him, this high priest of fashion and final Court of Appeal on neckcloths, strutting past in the Brighton sunshine, nodding affably right and left to the Dukes of Bedford and Argyll, Lords Jersey and Alvanley, and they but too eager to bow courteously in return?

Presently we read of him, bankrupt and ruined, broken in health, weak in mind, writing mad letters to Lord Palmerston from Caen, where, out of charity, he has been given a consulship, to the effect that there is no necessity for a consul there at all. A while after, the consulship taken away, the arms of England taken down rom the front of the house, he is dependent on the friendship of his last friend, worthy Mr. Armstrong, a grocer, who takes a journey to England to procure the help of the poor broken-down beau's rich friends. The journey is successful. He is released from prison, but for only a short time. His mind now gives way altogether, and he is carried, screaming with idiotic terror, to the madhouse of Le Bon Sauveur, fancying it another debtor's prison, and piteously praying Armstrong to raise more money to buy him out. And this

Lord Byron,

"the teeth-grinding, glass-eyed, lone Caloyer," as Carlyle called him; "The mystery in a winding-sheet, crowned with a halo," as Galt says. This "pale face," that was Lady Lamb's "fate," belongs to Lord Byron. Wonderful descriptions of the poet's manners and appearance have been left us by his contemporaries. Lockhart says, "his countenance is a thing to dream of;" Charles Mathews thought him the only man he had ever seen to whom he "felt disposed to apply the word beautiful;" Mrs. Opie said, "his voice was such a voice as the devil tempted Eve with;" and Blackwood describes the contour of his countenance as "noble and striking," and his forehead as "nearly as white as alabaster." When asked if he thought Lady Byron was in love with him when she married him, he said, "No. I was the fashion when she first came out: I had the character of being a great rake, and was a great dandy—both of which young ladies like. She married me from vanity, and the hope of reforming and fixing me." He was a dandy indeed, ever posing and ever self-conscious; although, the first time he appeared to the superb D'Orsay, he wore a faded nankeen jacket and a pair of green spectacles.

And who comes next? Let the lordly poet introduce him:—

> "And men unpractised in exchanging knocks
> Must go to Jackson ere they dare to box."——

Gentleman Jackson!

"Lord Byron's taste for boxing," says Galt, "brought him acquainted at an early period with this distinguished and, it is not too much to say, *respected* professor of the art, for whom, throughout life, he continued to entertain a sincere regard." In a foot-note to the eleventh canto of "Don Juan," the poet speaks of him as "my old friend and corporeal pastor and master, John Jackson, Esq., professor of pugilism, who, I trust, still retains the strength and symmetry of his model of a form, together with his good humour, and athletic as well as mental accomplishments."

High praise this sounds of a prize-fighter, now that the glories of the ring have gone for ever, yet I find nowhere anything but words of praise spoken of Gentleman Jackson's character. In some most graphic records of the prize ring, written by the late Sydney French, there is a lengthened description of his personal appearance, from which we may gather a few particulars. He had a somewhat low forehead, which appeared even lower from a peculiar mode he had of bringing his hair over it. His cheek-bones were rather high, while the lower jaw was narrower; and the ears were very prominent, though this may be due to the hair being cropped very short at the sides. His nose was slightly damaged; his mouth was decidedly well shaped, though large, and his eyes bright and piercing. He wore a well-fitting coat, tightly buttoned close around the chest, so as to display its ample proportions to the fullest advantage, and then cut away to reveal a satin vest, knee-breeches, silk stockings, and pumps. His chest was broad, being forty-four inches in circumference, his waist small, hips and calves very large, foot firm, and hand peculiarly diminutive for a prize-fighter; but his arm was his great beauty from an artistic point of view, and all the famous sculptors of the day, from Flaxman downwards, took models of it. And what brought him down to Brighton? It had been at the request of his noble patron; and on each occasion of his visits Lord Byron paid the chaise for him up and down. In speaking of his lordship's courage, Mr. Jackson said, "Nobody could be more fearless: he showed great spirit always in coming up to the blows."

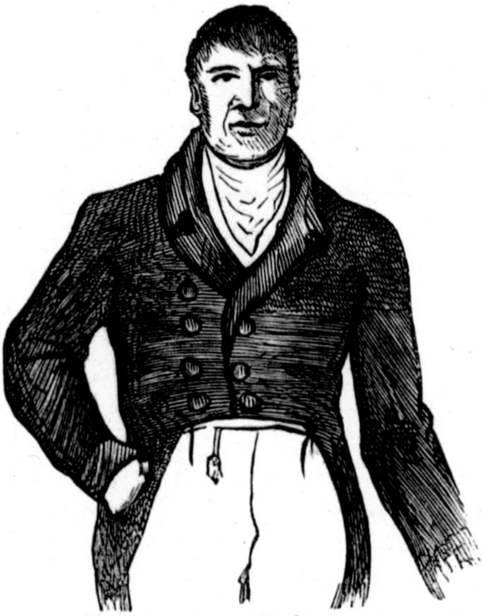

Gentleman Jackson.

But see, here comes

Tom Moore.

What says his Diary?

21st June, 1825.—Busy in my preparations for starting for Brighton to-morrow, where I am going to see a Mr. J——, who professes to tell me much about Sheridan. Edward Moore has offered to take me in his carriage.

22nd.—Set off between 11 and 12, and arrived to a late dinner at Brighton. Mr. J——, as I heard before I left town, gone to London on a consultation till Friday, so I shall have to stay all over to-morrow. Walked about.

23rd.—Sir Richard Phillips called, and bored me beyond measure. Heard that Lord Townsend was in Brighton. Went and sat some time with him; promised to drink tea with him and Lady John in the evening. Dined with Sir Richard (Edward and I), his daughter, fine woman, brought up entirely on vegetables, like himself, both telling well for this Pythagorean diet. Went to Lord John T——; had much talk with him about Sheridan.

24th.—Strolling about Brighton. Mr. —— was to arrive at 4. Conceived but little expectations from him—evidently a take-in. Dined in a hurry at the inn, and then set off with Edward to ——'s, who had claret, fruit, and Sir Richard Phillips laid out for us. Just as I thought: a good, vulgar, jolly, ignorant gentleman, whom Sheridan laid hold of in his latter days, and who was just as fit a recipient for his wit as a hog-trough would be for champagne. Got literally nothing out of him but a few glasses of wine, and escaped with Edward, as soon as I could, to a raffle at the Library. This is too bad—to come expressly, too, from London, for such a bubble!

25th.—Set off for town between 10 and 11. Dined at Richmond. Got to town at 7.

This would appear to have been Tom Little's only visit, and he does not seem to have enjoyed himself particularly.

Who come here? A lady's school—no, as I live, an army of elderly nuns, thirty-seven in number, who, expelled from their convent in Lisle, have come over by the packet boat. They seek shelter at a New Ship, and the first night celebrate High Mass. The Prince of Wales and Mrs. Fitzherbert visit them, and a subscription is got up on their behalf. The worthy landlord, it is said, has some difficulty in finding accommodation for them, for they cannot be prevailed upon to sleep two in a bed.

And who is this who has just passed, so bravely apparelled? A word in your ear—an intimate friend of his Royal Highness's—the Colonel—

Colonel Hanger.

He spent in clothes in one winter season nine hundred pounds, and for a ball-dress invented a satin coat, which was thenceforth (for ever so long) the rage. He once won three thousand on a race—Shark against Leviathan—and a short time afterwards we find him, when taxed with dulness at the Prince's table, producing three shillings and sixpence, with the words, "I've been reflecting, sir, upon the lofty independence of my present position. I've compromised with my creditors, paid my washerwoman in full, and have yet this balance left for the pleasures and necessities of life."

In course of time, however, the Colonel's "ship" came into port. By the death of his brother, Lord Coleraine, a coronet became his. By that time he had had enough of fashion. He took a small house at Somer's Town, and spent most of his leisure time at the nearest public house, where, "in acknowledgment of his rank, a large chair by the fireside was exclusively appropriated to the peer." Can you imagine him, his long pipe and long stories, his airs and graces, somewhat shabby and shambling, his position as umpire on all questions of taste and *haut ton*, and how he was listened to in mock seriousness by the small tradesmen who also used the house, and laughed in their sleeves at the poor old gentleman's bald talk when at a safe distance? His lordship died, unmarried, in 1824, at the age of seventy-three; "and with him the family honours became extinct."

* * * * * *

"Well, then, two more of the same, sir, please, since you're so pressing."

* * * * * *

"Hic!"

* * * * * *

THE ECCENTRICS.

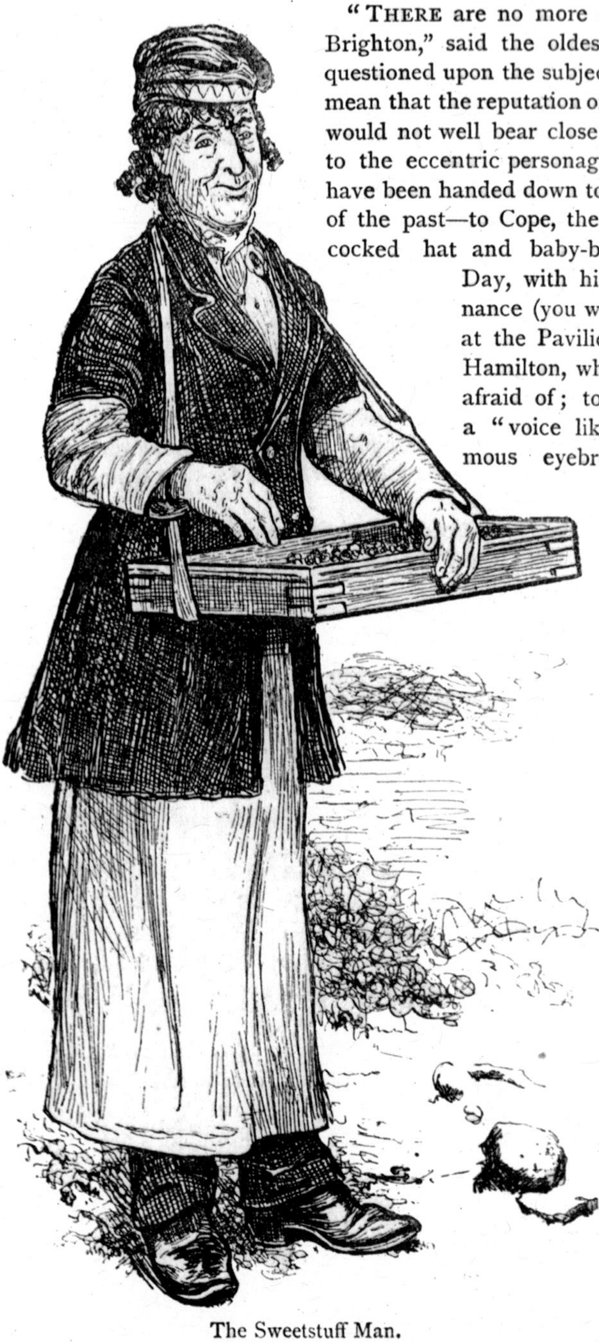

The Sweetstuff Man.

"THERE are no more characters now left in Brighton," said the oldest inhabitant whom I questioned upon the subject. He did not exactly mean that the reputation of the present company would not well bear close scrutiny; he alluded to the eccentric personages whose peculiarities have been handed down to us by the chroniclers of the past—to Cope, the green man, with his cocked hat and baby-boy face; to Gloomy Day, with his melancholy countenance (you will find their portraits at the Pavilion); to Single-Speech Hamilton, whom Miss Burney was afraid of; to Lord Thurlow, with a "voice like thunder and enormous eyebrows," refusing the Prince's invitation to dinner till his Royal Highness "keeps better company;" to Lord Onslow, *alias* "Tommy Titmouse," the famous whip; to Johnny Reeder, the poet-laureate; to Willis, the tailor, who, strutting on the Steyne, and bowing to a customer, was asked by him who he was. "Made your breeches, sir," curtly replied the dandy snip. "Major Bridges," repeated the other; "what regiment?" To Beach Roberts, the "Walking Newspaper;" to Captain Falkener; to "Cockie," the keeper of the King's privy purse; to mincing Madame Michau, *maîtresse de danse;* Captain Michelet, the fencing-master; "Protestant" Foskett; and old Mrs. Lawes and her lapdogs. "Clio" Rickman, the Quaker and friend of Tom Paine, who fled to France dressed in woman's petticoats, when the latter was convicted for the publication of the "Rights of Man;" Weston, the North Street smuggler, and "Master Wren;" and Dick Gregory, the librarian, with a laugh that is loud and clear, and toddling behind him the great Miss Widgett; and old Harricks, the hosier, who sold ladies' garters:

> "A present from Brighton:
> One for the left leg, and t'other for
> t' right-un."

These, and who shall say how many more, had I the space for them. And, in later times, the "Toddlers" at the brave, old, nonsensically impracticable Battery (the Grand Hotel now covers the site of that stupendous structure); the Star-Gazer, with a mania for shutting other people's gates; and the Hardened Sinner, lost to shame, sitting in his Bath chair in awfully public places, eating dozens of oysters, drinking pots of stout, and puffing churchwarden pipes in the face of outraged society. Why are there no more eccentrics? Here is the ringleted sweetstuff-seller, whose likeness to the *caricatures* of Lord Beaconsfield has so often been remarked upon; there is the blind

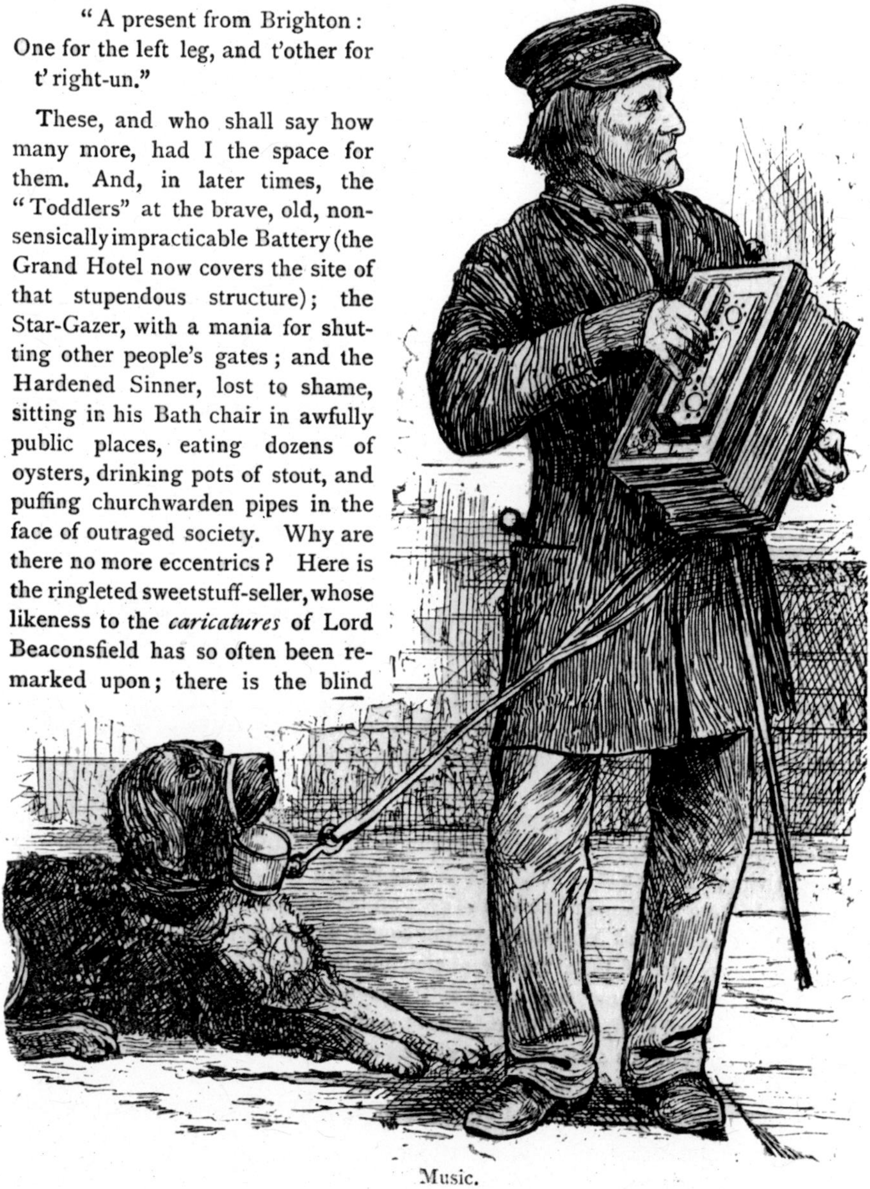

Music.

man, with a big dog and the musical instrument in a green-baize bag; there is also a musical-voiced vendor of watercresses, with a singularly docile donkey, who awakens the echoes in quiet bye-streets with his cry of "Oh, so fine to-day, ladies! so fresh! so nice! lovely!" which, without having tried them, I am quite prepared to believe those cresses are.

DANCING.

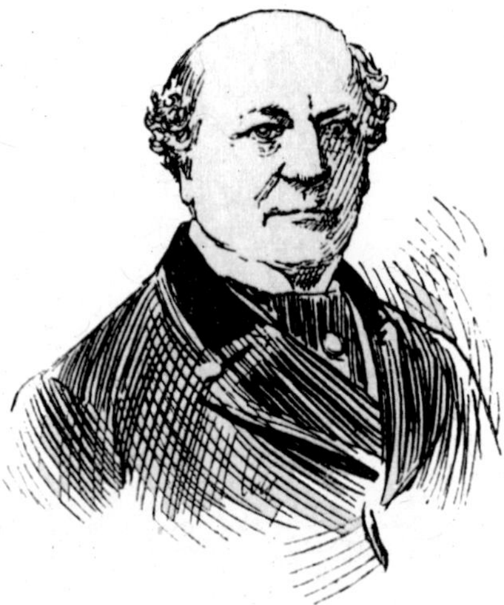

Ship ahoy!

"No event," says Mr. Raikes, "ever produced so great a sensation in English society as the introduction of the German waltz, in 1813."

In 1812 Lord Byron, then staying at Cheltenham, wrote his fierce "Apostrophic Hymn to the Waltz," —and published it anonymously in the spring of the following year. It was not very well received by the public, and the author was by no means anxious that it should be considered as his handiwork. "I hear," he says in a letter to a friend, "that a certain malicious publication on waltzing is attributed to me. This report, I suppose, you will take care to contradict, as the author, I am sure, will not like that I should wear his cap and bells."

His lordship was not the only person who, on its first introduction, objected to the Waltz, though one can understand how extra bitter the crippled poet felt sitting down and looking on. The words that, in an introductory letter, Byron puts into the mouth of the supposed author, honest, heavy-heeled Horace Hornem, pretty well expresses the popular sentiments at the time. "Judge my surprise on arriving," says he, "to find Mrs. Hornem with her arms half round a huge hussar-looking gentleman I never set eyes on before, and his, to say truth, rather more than half round her waist, turning round and round to a d——d seesaw, up-and-down sort of tune, that reminded me of the 'Black Joke,' only more *affetuoso*, till it made me quite giddy with wondering they were not so. By-and-bye they stopped a bit, and I thought they would sit or fall down. But no; with Mrs. H.'s hand on his shoulder, they walked about a minute, and then at it again like two cockchafers spitted on the same bodkin."

I stood a few days ago in the ball-room of the Old Ship, which time has changed into an auctioneer's sale-room, and conjured up the Ghost of William Wade, Esquire, M.C., and the ladies and gentlemen who frequented the inn "when this century was in its teens." The terms of admission to the balls, assemblies, and to tea and promenade, were, I find,

	s.	d.
Subscription for the season - - - - - - - -	10	6
For each ball - - - - - - - - - - - -	3	6
Tea and promenade - - - - - - - - -	1	0
Non-Subscribers for each ball - - - - - - - -	5	0
Sunday tea and promenade - - - - - - - -	2	0
Card assembly nights - - - - - - - -	1	0

And then the rules and regulations:—

"That the dress and fancy balls shall begin as soon as possible after seven o'clock, and conclude precisely at twelve, even in the middle of a dance.

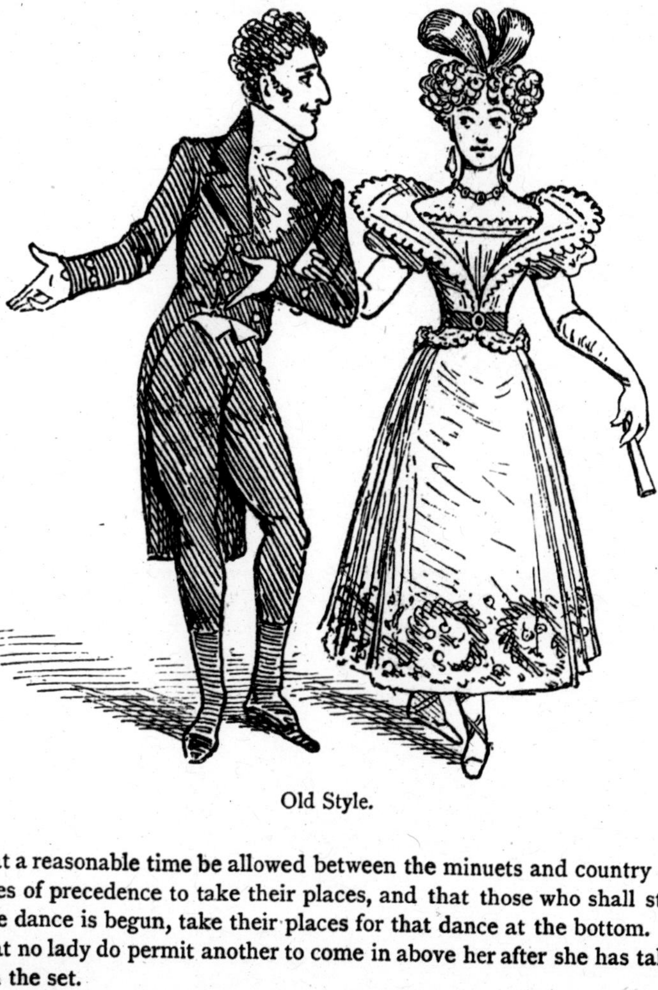

Old Style.

"That a reasonable time be allowed between the minuets and country dances, for ladies of precedence to take their places, and that those who shall stand up after the dance is begun, take their places for that dance at the bottom.

"That no lady do permit another to come in above her after she has taken her place in the set.

"That all ladies who go down a dance do continue in their places till the rest have done the same.

"That the three front seats at the upper end of the room be reserved for ladies of precedence, of the rank of peeresses of Great Britain or Ireland.

"That the musical band of these rooms do consist of twelve performers, including an harp, tabor, and pipe.

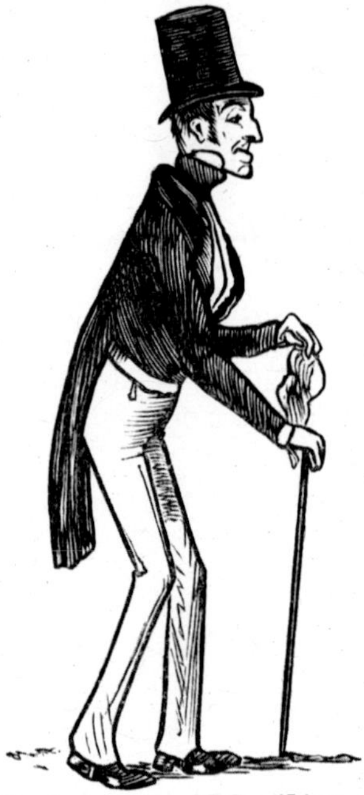

The last of the M.C.s (Lieut.-Colonel Eld).

"That no persons be permitted to play with cards left by another party.

"That no cards be allowed on Sunday.

"That ladies who intend dancing minuets do wear lappets; and it is requested that the rest of their dress be as comformable as possible to this distinction, regard being had to the prevailing fashion of the times. It is also hoped that gentlemen will accommodate their dress to the ladies.

"That no gentleman in boots or half-boots be admitted into any of these rooms on ball nights, or public card or concert nights.

"That on ball nights no ladies be admitted into the great room in habits, nor gentlemen in swords, boots, or pantaloons, military gentlemen excepted."

The "lappets" alluded to were, as well as I can make out, some scarf-like arrangement dangling from the fair wearer's head. At the same time "stiff starched stays" were not in much vogue, but were

> "Transferr'd to those ambiguous things that ape
> Goats in their visage, women in their shape."

Lord Byron also adds:—

> "Hoops are *no more*, and petticoats *not much*;
> Morals and minuets, virtue and her stays,
> And tell-tale powder—all have had their days."

It was the Waltz that had done all this, he said, but I fancy the minuet was not entirely a thing of the past at the time he wrote, and that it died hard. How fashions come and go and then return again! Within the last year or two I have seen ladies promenading with "petticoats not much," I have seen a minuet danced in a private house, I have seen "Swanbills" of alarming stiffness and incredible length in shop windows; and I know from personal observation that the "tell-tale powder" is in high favour, only it is no longer "tell-tale," because its owner, as a rule, carries it, and an emptied-out puff, about with her, and replaces the powder when occasion arises.

But, you see, then, as now, the male creatures were the first to object to any change in the ladies' dresses, and then once having got accustomed to the alteration, how they raise their voices against any fresh change, even if it be but a recurrence to a fashion of the past! I came by chance only yesterday upon a book by Mr. Sala, who, writing in 1859, places these words and sentiments in the mouth of one Lady Chesterfield—how far he himself agrees with her it is not for me to say: "When," says her apocryphal ladyship, "I look at the modern dress and bonnet of a friend pretty well advanced in years, I can scarcely realize the possibility of her, and of I, ever having worn the astonishing garments I can remember distinctly—in the days we wore no crinoline—a long while ago. Mrs. Lintot, with her hat and feathers, and her eternal amber satin pelisse ; the three Misses Hardy, with their coalscuttle bonnets, their lavender boots, their short sleeves, and their waists under the armpits. Look at her who was once Constance Sevignier, and is now poor old Lady Chesterfield, with a vandyked robe, a coral necklace, a little boa and muff, long gloves, and a sash. Till long after the Peace

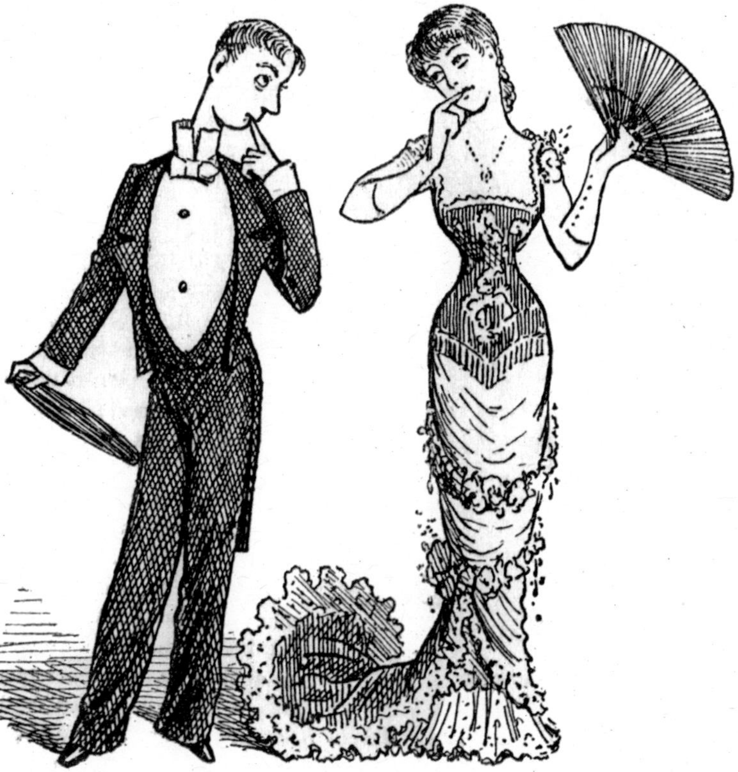

New Style.

of '15, we wore short waists, narrow skirts—were as flat laterally and otherwise. The crinoline, *pur et simple*, is an admirable supporter, amplifier, and draper, throwing the dress into those sharp, light, and shadow-giving folds that look so well in a picture. It has made in its time many appallingly awkward women look tolerable, and many handsome women more graceful still. Girls of fifteen or sixteen are all the better for a little crinoline ; their figures are generally as unformed as those of young colts or young heifers ; they seldom know how to walk, or how to carry their arms, or how to preserve their centres of gravity when standing still, and the sway and swell of the crinoline help and compensate for their undecided gait. A married woman is unquestionably benefited by crinoline in moderation. It tones down the sometimes too prominent self-assertion of her walk—many married ladies positively swagger—and by a reflex action it frequently lends her dignity and *pose*."

Well, every man has a right to his opinions. Merciful goodness! I think quite the opposite, and always did. As I closed my eyes in that desecrated drawing-room, I fancied I heard the gentle tum-tum and tootling of the musicians in the little tottering gallery overhead. I conjured up a host of thinly-clad and skimpetty loveliness, high-waisted, long-gloved, low-necked, and with clustering curls low down upon their foreheads, and eyes that gazed upwards into the eyes of plump and portly male royalty in tights and pumps, as they glided round the room. Where are they all now? "Going—going—gone!"

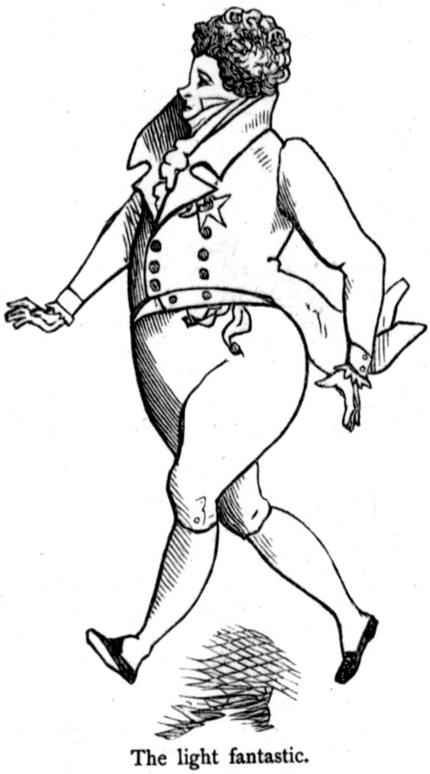

The light fantastic.

The auctioneer's hammer has fallen. A washhand-stand, with fittings complete, are mine. I must have nodded. * * *

There are at this present time, I find, seven professors of dancing in Brighton, male and female, without counting their assistants, doubtless highly qualified; and balls are among the most fashionable and best supported amusements of the greatest of the Brighton seasons. Robinson's "Popular Directory" enumerates not the M.C.s available, but I suppose they may be found on application at proper quarters. Dancing ever has been, and will, I daresay, continue to be, in high favour here, and numerous fancy balls are given every year, the whereabouts of which, with full particulars, are extensively advertised.

Going back again to the time of the Regency—one can't get far away somehow, try as hard as hard—it was to the balls at the Castle Inn, on the west side of the Steyne, that the Prince went most frequently—("every Monday," it says in one place); and one day, there being only thirteen persons assembled, His Royal Highness said, "We've a small party to-night, but that is no reason it should not be a merry one." And before he left he danced with every lady present, a circumstance which must have filled some half-dozen or so of hearts with ecstatic feelings.

A LITTLE MUSIC.

THE most fashionable concerts take place at the Dome Assembly Room, in the Pavilion grounds, originally the royal stables, built at the cost of £70,000. The room is capable of seating 3,000 persons. Height, 60 feet; diameter of dome—outer circle, 124 feet; inner circle, 80 feet. The grand organ is by Messrs. Wills and Co. The Concert Hall, in West Street, is 200 feet in length, 51 ft. 6 in. high, 46 ft. 6 in. wide. Entrances in West Street and Middle Street. It contains an orchestral organ, by Messrs. Bryceson and Co.

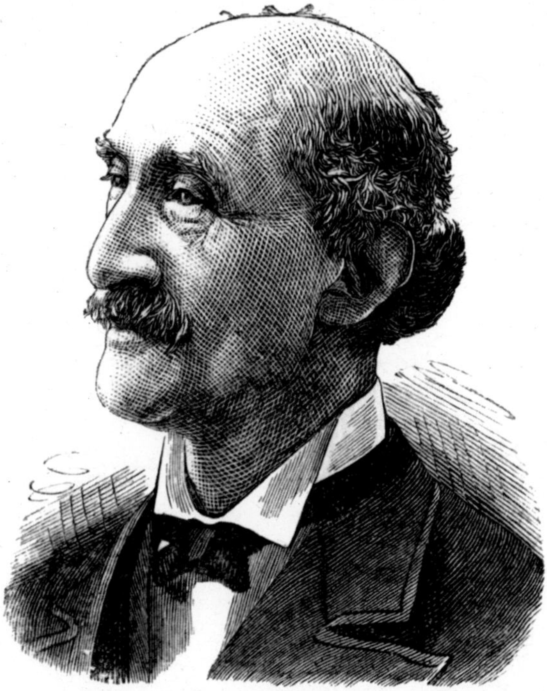

The Chevalier.

In the autumn of 1847 Mr. Kuhe came to Brighton, and commenced his local career as *entrepréneur*. He gave his first concert in the upper room of the Town Hall, for there was no Dome or Pavilion available for public use in those days; and he shortly afterwards gave his first three pianoforte recitals in the Newburgh Rooms in Cannon Place. In the year 1869 Mr. Kuhe inaugurated his annual festivals, under the denomination of "Orchestral Concerts," but in 1871 the term was judiciously altered into that of "Musical Festival." That the town recognizes this event is plainly shown in the wide local interest it evokes, and even more substantially in the testimonal presented to Mr. Kuhe by the inhabitants in 1871. Mr. Kuhe also had the distinguished honour in 1865 of being

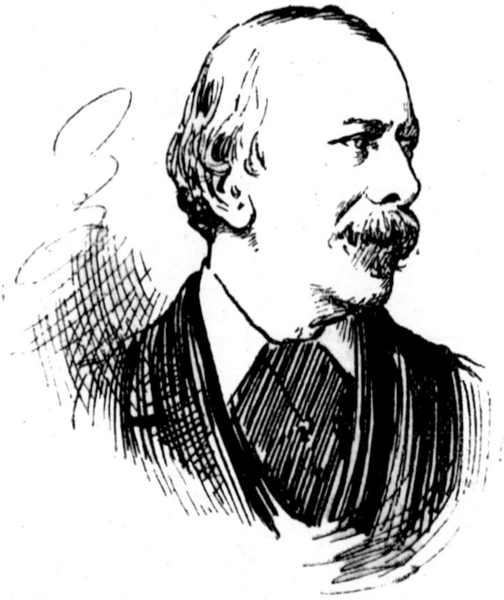

Another Musical Celebrity.

created a Chevalier of the Order of the Crown by the Emperor of Germany, then King of Prussia.

There are two Slopers. One is an Ally and the other a Lindsay. One causes moderate mirth, and the other makes no end of music. I am glad to say I find both of them very popular in Brighton.

THE SHOPS.

"It is," says Thackeray, "the fashion to run down George IV., but what myriads of Londoners ought to thank him for inventing Brighton! One of the best physicians our city has ever known is kind, cheerful, cheery, merry Doctor Brighton. Hail! thou purveyor of shrimps and honest prescriber of South Down mutton! There is no mutton so good as Brighton mutton; no flys so pleasant as Brighton flys; nor any cliff so pleasant to ride on; no shops so beautiful to look at as the Brighton gimcrack-shops, and the fruit-shops, and the market."

I am not quite sure about the flys (things upon wheels, you know, not wings), or the market either, which, after all is said and done, must take a very back seat in comparison with the markets of many provincial towns, but I quite agree with him with regard to the shops. Are not the shops in the King's Road—I appeal to you who know them—a joy for ever? Can you elsewhere find such a show of jewellery as is to be found in the windows of Messrs. Lewis and Son, "established 1790"? What a jolly window, too, is that of Heath's, in which there seems to me to be a "constant change and variety." Do you like toys? I myself love them, and would, did I dare, bring pounds' worth home to set up on shelves and play with when no one was looking. Can you imagine a more suitable name for a toy-shopkeeper than Child, and can you point me out a window fraught with interest more intense? Now I come to think of it, another toy-maker, still more famous, perhaps, once when I was down here lodged over the shop—Caleb Plummer—John L. Toole!

What is this? An emporium of foreign comestibles! And what a wondrous assortment of delicacies are here, from the choicest *bon-bons* to potted meats, and, by my troth now, *fricassée* of frogs!

And, hard by, at Hayward's, a veritable window of mysteries—frilled and embroidered, plaited and tucked, lace-edged and flounced. Before it the brain of a merely mortal male grows dizzy, and, asking himself what and why, wherefore and when? he hurriedly departs, feeling that he has no business there.

But stay, I am leaving out the photographers. Here's Signor Lombardi's show-case, with portraits of ladies and gentlemen in fancy ball costumes (buy "Stage Whispers" when you want anything of that kind again), and, among them, a plump gentleman with a white wig and whiskers, looking mighty well pleased with himself for not having been such a fool as to shave only just for the sake of being historically correct. And here are Messrs. Hennah and Kent's, and Lock and Whitfield's, and M. Boucher, who has turned out some excellent work, and to whose courtesy we are indebted for several portraits in this volume. I can recommend him to the mammas of pretty children whose portraits are to be taken. And here, at Monsieur Bertin's, nicey-nicey bright and beautiful photographs of Prettiness from the Theatres Royal.

Now, I don't like having my portrait taken. I can sit out much at the theatre and elsewhere, but, sitting for my portrait worries me beyond all patience. I never can make out when the business is going to begin, and exhaust myself unnecessarily in advance. Long before there is the least occasion, as I have found out afterwards, I have got into attitude, and have been re-arranged and adjusted, and told to look at something at an uncomfortable angle, doing which makes my eyes water; then the photographer, who has been away whistling tunes in a cupboard in a corner, comes out and nods approvingly, and goes back again and whistles more tunes, and at last, when I am on the point of succumbing altogether, he makes a sudden rush at me, and cries, "Now! quite steady!" and pulls my head off slowly, with a piteously agonized expression upon the front part of it that I never remember it, in all my troubles, to have worn before. But with the instantaneous process all this is changed.

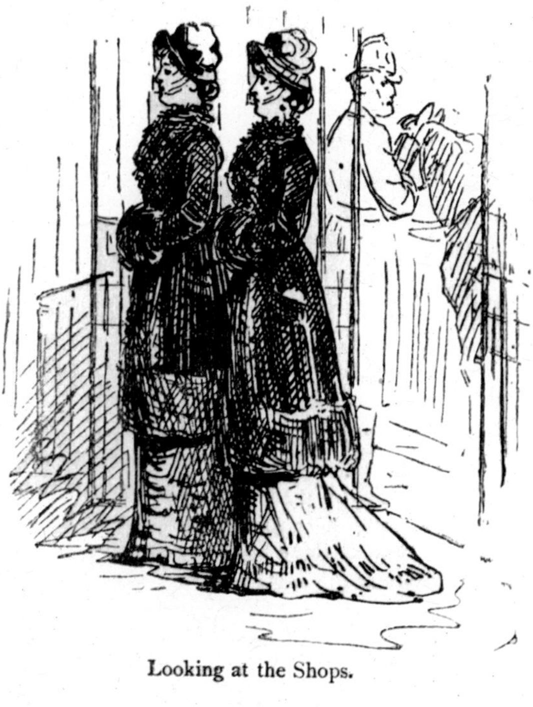

Looking at the Shops.

I am gazing, as I have said, on much Prettiness, long-stockinged, and secretly registering a vow not to keep a promise I made, last time I was down here, to give M. Bertin a sitting, when that artful person suddenly appearing before me, lures me in to see the process, and processes me before I can say, were I so willed, "Jack Robinson"—upon my word, I don't quite think there is quite time to say "Jack." "And now," he says, "you *must* see how I prepare my plates."

With this, he conducts me downstairs to the hall, and then down another flight, which is pitch dark, guiding me by the hand in mysterious fashion. Then he opens a door leading into what appears to me to be more pitchy darkness still, only presently, as he moves from in front of me, I find there is a paper lantern emitting a faint red glimmer. "This is all the light I have," says he, "to work in; you'll get used to it after awhile. Do you see the plates on the shelves?" I don't: I see nothing; but shortly afterwards I hear him close by me, and, according to his account, he is showing me a plate. I don't see it, but I say I do to make things comfortable, and, wicked story-teller that I am, I come up out of this cave of mystery once more as wise as when I went down. If there is much of that cave (several hours at a stretch, he told me), "take one little duty with another," a photographer's "lot" can hardly be "a happy one."

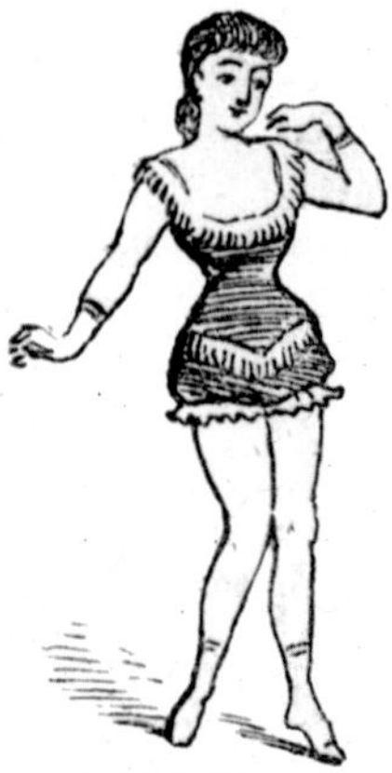

A little Photo.

But about the shops—the other shops—for there are shops elsewhere than in King George's Road. Give me your arm. As no doubt Dr. Johnson often said, "Let's take a walk up East Street."

What say you to the sweetstuff in Drogrez's window? Have you ever been inside with uncalculating Loveliness two or three in number? *I* have, but if *you* haven't, don't, but only look through the glass. And the coral jewellery at Montini's—surely never was a more charming show. And the toys at the Misses Kyte and Harris's fancy repository—bats, balls, battledores, baa-lambs, babies, and (in a whisper) birch rods. And the boots and shoes at Frampton's (they sell higher heels, ladies, here and at Chargois', of Western Road, than at any other shops in the town). And Beal, best of stationers and news-agents; and Hudson Brothers, for curious cheeses and relishes and tit-bits of all kinds.

Do you care for seltzer-water or for soda? Brighton is *par excellence* the fountain-head, and Ridge and Sons the favourite makers, and their offices are at 98 Queen's Road. Do you ache, and are you in pain? Let me recommend to your notice Hamilton's grasshopper couch, for which he obtained prize medals at the Paris and Sydney Exhibitions, to be met with in Ship Street: there is a springiness about the name that should do wonders. And if you would pack up your traps and leave the Queen of Watering-places, is there not Dell, who moved the furniture, writing-table, and various relics of Napoleon I. from the palace at Biarritz, and from Camden Place to Farnboro' Hill? "That great men rule the earth from their graves," says "that man P." in his journal, "is an acknowledged fact. George Robins still speaks through Dell of Brighton." To use the great Remover's own words when describing the Devil's Dyke, "from the flowerey Dell the sweet voice of the nightingale may be heard."

Are there shop-windows elsewhere in England as fascinating to the idler as those of Brighton? I will give you my beloved Strand—there won't be many shops left there soon, the theatres, restaurants, wines from the wood, and public houses will occupy all the space—I will willingly give you Fleet Street, with its old associations and modern shabbiness, Regent Street, beloved of foreign shopkeepers and old ladies from the country; *bourgeois* Oxford Street, which I don't seem to remember much about since those times when an elderly female relative used to take me to the Pantheon—there were toys, and parrots, and Bath buns, and the "Raising of Lazarus" there then, in the place now occupied by Messrs. Gilbey's gigantic storehouses—and regale me afterwards, either in the refreshment-room adjoining the aviary or at one of the many pastrycooks' shops outside, with the succulent yet pluggy bun of Bath; I will give you Bond Street, now more a street of shops than loungers, and Piccadilly, more a street of loungers than shops; I will even give you the Burlington Arcade, and right gladly throw in the poor, vulgar, cheap-Jacky Lowther, if you will give me in exchange long life and good health, and unimpaired eyesight, that I may enjoy the glorious Brighton shop-windows. I at all times love to look in shop-windows, but have not always leisure to do so. At Brighton it is a duty, and I make it a rule to do my duty when it is so agreeable.

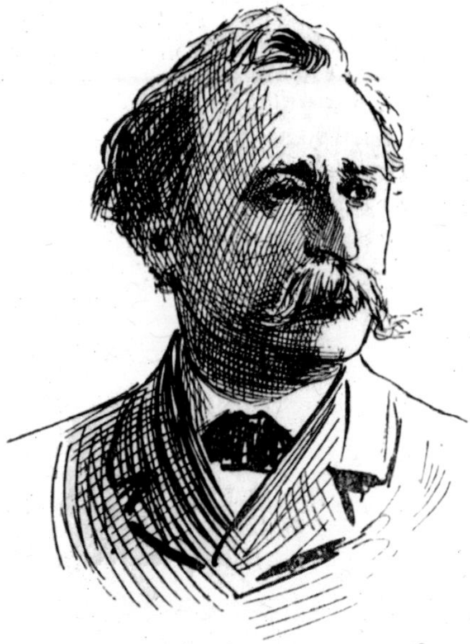

A popular Photographer.

THE FAIR EQUESTRIENNES.

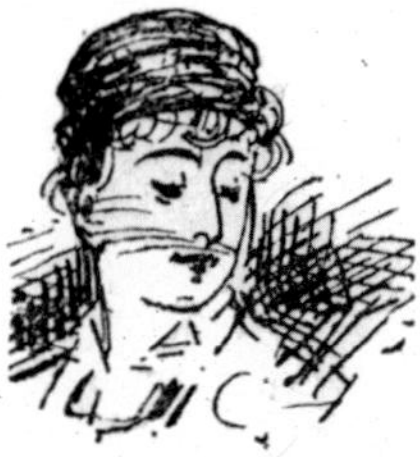

YOU may see and study a vast variety of "seats" among the girls who ride in the King's Road. All the girls are not young, nor are they all graceful, and the jog-trot is trying to most. It is only one in a thousand who is born a Gay Spanker.

"To sit erect upon your saddle," says Mrs. Power O'Donoghue in her advice to ladies, "is a point of great importance; if you acquire a habit of stooping it will grow upon you, and it is not only a great disfigurement, but not unfrequently a cause of serious accident, for if your horse suddenly throws up his head, he hits you bang upon the nose, and deprives you of more blood than you may be able to replace in a good while.

"As soon as you can feel yourself quite at home upon your mount, and have become accustomed to his walking motion, your attendant will urge him into a gentle trot. And now prepare yourself for the beginning of sorrows. Your first sensation will be that of being shaken to pieces. You are, of course, yet quite ignorant of the art of rising in your saddle, and the trot of the horse fairly churns you. Your hat shakes, your hair flaps, your elbows bang to your sides, you are altogether miserable. Still, you hold on bravely, though you are ready to cry from the horrors of the situation.

"Your attendant, by way of relieving you, changes the trot to a canter, and then you are suddenly transported to Elysium. The motion is heavenly. You have nothing to do but sit close to your saddle, and you are borne delightfully along. It is too ecstatic to last. Alas! it will never teach you to ride, and so you return to the trot and the shaking and the jogging, the horrors of which are worse than anything you have ever previously experienced. You try vainly to give yourself some ease, but fail utterly, and at length dismount—hot, tired, and disheartened."

When I think what the girl of my choice has most probably gone through before she learnt to ride as she rides now, my heart bleeds for her. That's the truth.

———o———

THE ROWING CLUB.

THE Brighton Rowing Club, on the beach, under the King's Road, which includes most of the best known men of Brighton among its members, and has Mr. James Ashbury for its president, is a social as well as an aquatic organization, and those who have experienced the fatherly care of, and partaken of the creature comforts provided by, the steward, always acknowledge that you might look a long way for more comfortable quarters than this little club-house.

The beach at Brighton is a little world all by itself, and little wotted of by the majority of Brighton's visitors and residents; but except when an excursion comes down, it is well worth visiting, and the quaint interior of the cabins where the good seafaring folks live are curious to see.

———o———

BOATING.

Boating is one of the most popular sources of amusement in Brighton, and every facility is provided. Sailing boats must be 18 feet in length, rowing boats 14 feet; an excursion steamer makes hourly trips from the pierhead, and several well-known pleasure yachts sail twice daily during the summer season.

FARES FOR BOATS, AND BATHING MACHINE CHARGES.

SAILING BOATS.

(The time to be computed from the time of starting to landing.)

	s.	d.
For a boat 30 feet or upwards in length, for any time not exceeding one hour	10	0
For a boat under 30 feet in length, for any time not exceeding one hour	5	0
For every additional half-hour or portion thereof, whatever the length of the boat ...	2	0
When the whole boat is not engaged, for each passenger, for any time not exceeding one hour	1	0
For every additional half-hour or portion thereof	0	6

ROWING BOATS.

	s.	d.
For a boat for any time not exceeding one hour	2	6
For every additional half-hour or portion thereof	1	0
When the whole boat shall not be taken, then for each passenger for any time not exceeding one hour	0	9
For every additional half-hour or portion thereof	0	3

But for further information I would refer you to Captain Collins, the gallant captain of the *Skylark;* you cannot be in better hands.

FISHING.

This favourite sport may be enjoyed within easy reach of the shore, as several attractive fishing-grounds, such as "Town Hall Rock," "South West Rock," "Black Rock," "Bee," and the Jenny ground, are well known to the Brighton fishermen.

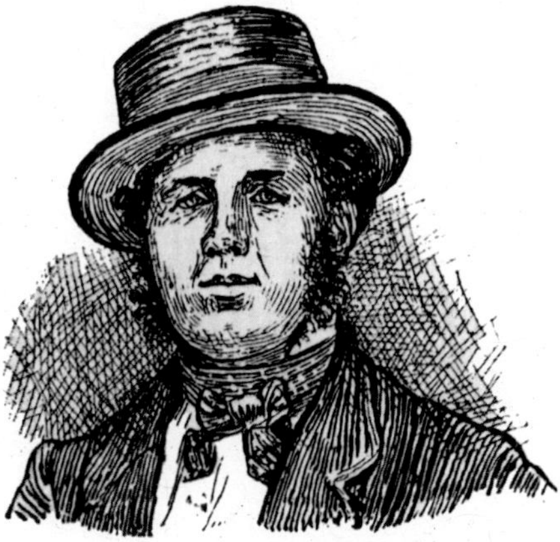

The Skylarky Skipper.

SUSSEX COUNTY CRICKET GROUND

is situated about a quarter of a mile north-west of Palmeira Square. Admission, *6d.*

Cricket has ever been a favourite game in Sussex, and we read of the "Maidens of the Green" taking up the bat in 1747. The old White Lion in North Street was a cricketers' house, and in 1765 there was a cricketers' "ordinary" there. The White Lion now-a-days is the only house the tavern part of which most resembles in construction the London public house. Of the portion used as an hotel I hear the best accounts from those who have stayed there. Its host is the Mr. Dale formerly manager at Messrs. Spiers and Pond's establishment at Ludgate Hill. I wondered what it was that suddenly recalled Fleet Street and Shoe Lane when one day I dropped my eyes upon him.

RACKETS, TENNIS, AND LAWN TENNIS.

The Racket Court, Middle Street, and the Tennis Court, Little Preston Street, where the Prince Consort was taught the noble game of tennis, and also where awn tennis is played.

CROQUET CLUB AND GERMAIN'S LAWN TENNIS.

The meetings of the Sussex County Croquet Club are held on the lawn of the Pavilion every Tuesday and Friday, for matches, and at other times for practice. Lawn tennis has been added. Subscriptions for the season, £1 1*s.*; two months, 10*s.* 6*d.*; one month, 7*s.* 6*d.*

THE WICKED RACE WEEK.

I WAS staying, a long while ago, in a sleepy little street at the back of the Grand Hotel, the fronts of the houses of which are studded with pebbles and its pavement composed of red bricks, hard at work at something I had come down to get through quietly and without interruption; and the first day, just as I dipped my pen in the ink—I had been playing during the morning and a great

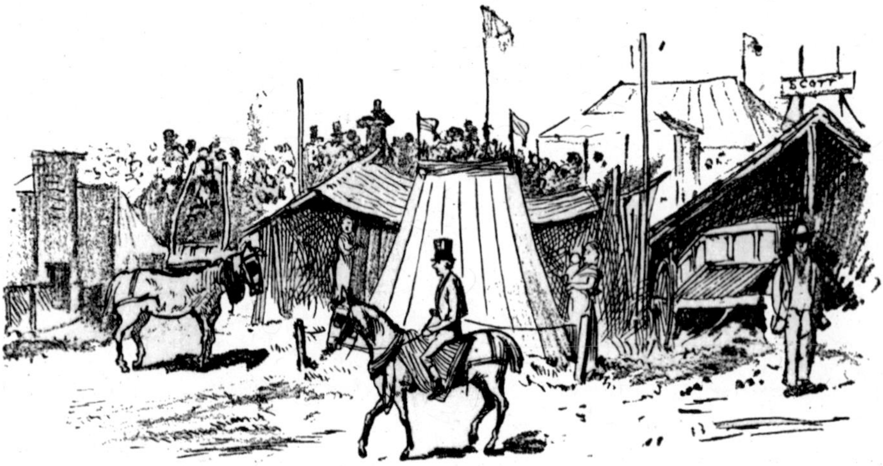

part of the afternoon—my landlady burst into the room, very rosy and radiant, and told me she had let the parlours. I thereupon laid down my pen, and asked for full particulars. She had let them, she said, for two days, and the gentleman had paid a pound on account for them in advance.

"He's a sporting gentleman," she said, "from what I can make out."

"Oh," said I, "what is he sporting about down here?"

"Bless you! don't you know, sir?" she said. "It's the race week."

It *was* the race week, and I had not known it. I had previously no notion, although I knew her well, that my landlady had a taste for the turf; but evidently I had lost caste by acknowledging my ignorance. Later on she had a lot to tell me about the sporting gentleman, the money he had made, and the money he was going to make, and of his wife—"a perfect lady." Next day, at lunch, I saw that something weighed upon her mind which she wished to communicate. "What is it?" I asked. "I've give the gentleman a pound to put upon the race," said she; "and I'm to make ten pounds if I win." I asked the name of the horse, but that she did not remember, though it was a favourite. I looked at the odds, but I could not see how the ten pounds were to be made if the quotations were correct. However, it would all be settled at dinner-time when the gentleman was to return to eat a dinner he had directed her to provide.

But when dinner-time came he did not turn up, nor the perfect lady either. Later on, though, some one else did, who was very red, and angry, and loud-voiced, and who swore he, too, had been swindled. That sporting gentleman got his lodgings, food, and little exes, on reasonable terms.

The Race-course is on the Downs to the N.E. of the town. The Grand Stand was erected at a cost of £4,000, and since much enlarged. The Races are held on the Tuesday, Wednesday, and Thursday following Goodwood Races. There is also an Autumn Meeting.

Next to the Easter Review there is nothing during the year which so thoroughly upsets Brighton as the races; but I don't suppose, as a rule, except where the landlady is sportively inclined, that the hotel keepers and the lodging-house keepers have much cause to regret it. Sporting men are large-hearted and liberal. Of all the nights in the year this is the one to drop in at the Gaiety Music Hall, a very well-conducted establishment, where a good entertainment is generally given, and where, on this occasion at least, the number of bottles of champagne consumed might, I should imagine, be counted by the gross.

Both theatres and music halls in Brighton close early, and—this in a whisper—so do the p*bl*c h**s*s, where they sell s*d* and B.'s; but come with me, I have the *open sesame*. Tap! tap!

Observe the fine-art gallery. Here are I don't know how many hundreds of cabinet-sized photographs of celebrities, and here is the genial host.

*   *   *   *   *

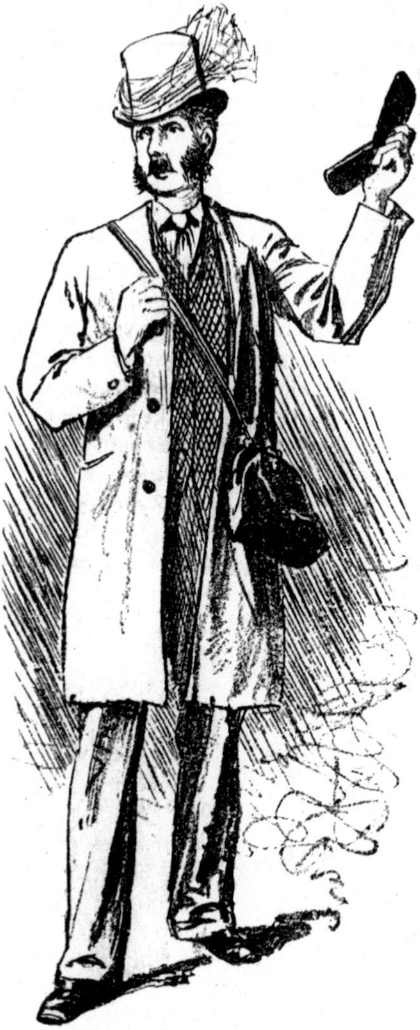

A Leviathan.

THE EASTER REVIEW.

WHEN I speak of Brighton being "thoroughly upset," it must be understood that I speak advisedly. A portion of the Brighton population is never upset, whatever may be going on elsewhere, in confirmation of which statement I quote from Mr. Sterry's account of the last sham battle:—

"Off the Downs, along the valley, past the Sussex County Hospital, and through sundry back streets, at last I gain the Marine Parade and descend the steps to the Madeira Road, and feel warm for the first time since I emerged from my chariot this morning. Here I find peace once more. The scene I have just quitted and the one I now behold are as great a contrast as Landseer's celebrated pictures of 'Peace' and 'War.' The sunshine is hot and brilliant. I am well screened from the wind, the sea is sleepy, it is lovely in colour, and flashes and glitters. A baby in a perambulator is waggling its head solemnly over a very large bun, and its attendant nursemaid is reading a novel, a disreputable-looking red retriever is playing at being a depraved doormat, and winks one eye at me, and gapes as though he would split his mouth at the hinges as I go by; an ancient mariner is dreamily leaning on a windlass and smoking a very short pipe, and has not even energy to suggest that it is 'a nice day for a sail;' the Chain Pier seems to be deserted altogether, and the good lady who takes your twopence is apparently enjoying forty winks in her glass case. The rush and ripple of the waves on the shingle still keep up its ceaseless music—a weird music, with an undercurrent of sadness about it, a quaint sea-song in a minor key, that it has been singing ever since I knew Brighton. A song fraught with many memories —a soothing song—a lullaby particularly refreshing at the present moment. And so I take my way homewards, listening half sadly to the rush and ripple of the waves on the shingle, and feel I am at peace."

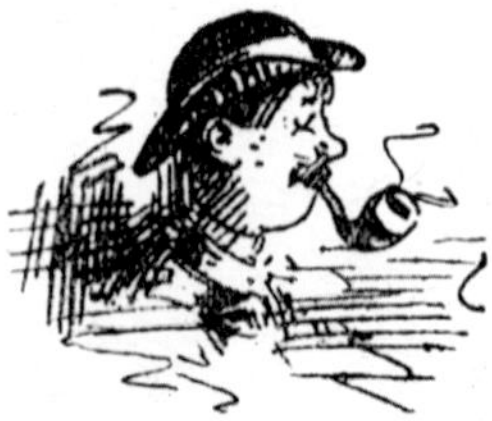

The piping time of peace.

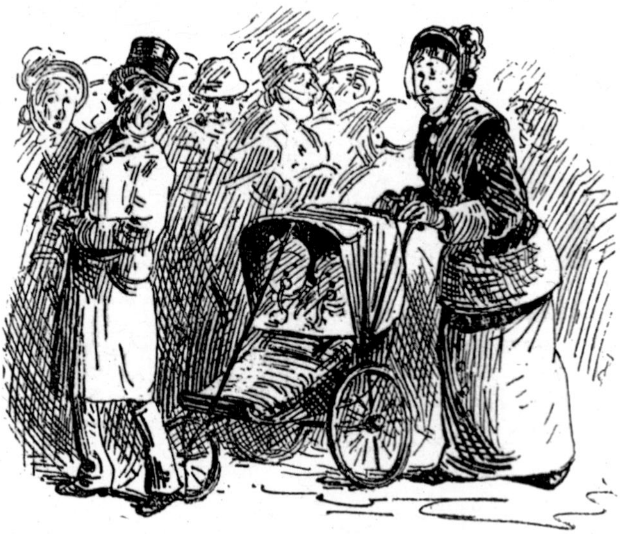

BRUTE.—"If you do it again I'll sit on 'em."

———o———

THE HARRIERS.

DOCTOR JOHNSON hunted the hare and rode like a young sportsman of twenty." In the records of the past you may have read how the Prince had a young deer turned out on the Steyne "for his and Mrs. Fitzherbert's diversion," a proceeding which, attempted now-a-days, would certainly cause a sensation. Lord Barrymore, too, had his stag-hunt; indeed, he hunted two the same day. The first started on the Race-ground, and, going seaward, jumped over the cliff and was killed. The second at first refused to move, then ran full butt into the crowd, then bolted to Patcham, and entered the house of a Mr. Paine, and, after knocking down a maid-servant who attempted to stop him, sought shelter in the pantry, and there was taken.

In the season the meets are on Wednesday and Saturday, at eleven o'clock, at the Dyke Inn. They afford a good excuse for a gallop over the wind-swept downs, and possibly the fact that there are no fences or ditches to be "flown over," does not detract from the attractiveness of the spot chosen, in the eyes of some of the noble sportsmen who patronize the hunt. I had no fault to find with the master or whips, or with some of the company, the day I looked on, but there were OTHERS—there were OTHERS!

THREE ROYAL FAVOURITES AND A QUEEN

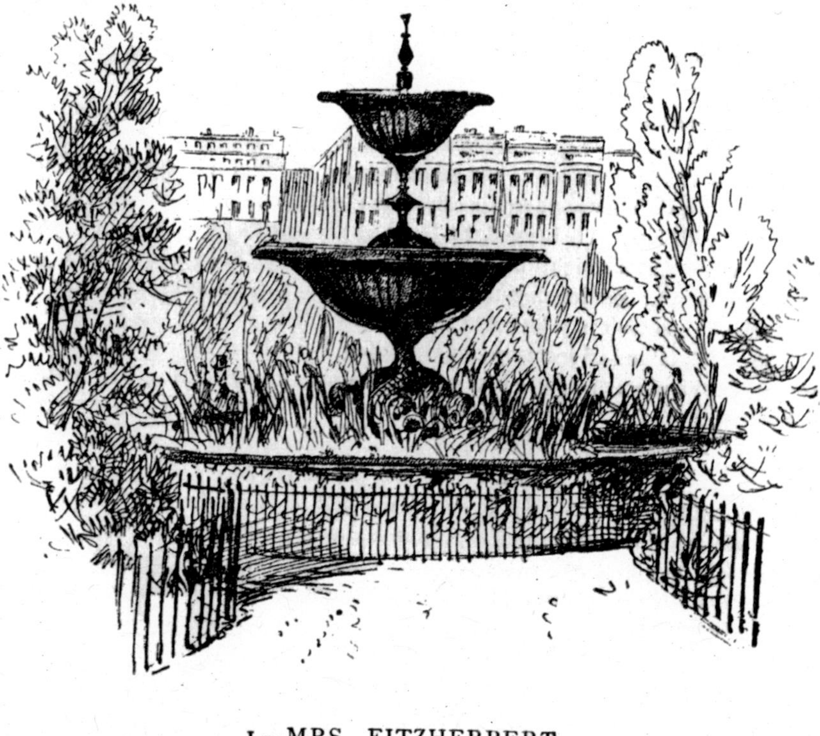

I.—MRS. FITZHERBERT.

ON searching the cabinets and drawers in the dead King's bed-room, the Duke of Wellington told Mr. Greville they found "a prodigious quantity of hair—women's hair—of all colours and lengths, some locks with the powder and pomatum still sticking to them; heaps of women's gloves, *gages d'amour* which he had got at balls, and with the perspiration still marked on the fingers; notes and letters. The whole were destroyed."

You may find opposite the club-house—unless it is being pulled down while I write—the house in which poor ill-used Mrs. Fitzherbert lived in the Steyne. The exterior remains almost unaltered, but the interior no longer resembles what it was when princes and nobles, statesmen, soldiers, authors and artists, and men and women of fashion, eagerly sought admission to the presence of its beautiful owner, whose natural grace and charm of manner fascinated all alike.

In 1828—when she was seventy-three years old—she gave a fancy dress ball, one of the most splendid ever given in Brighton, at which were present two hundred guests, including many persons of the highest rank—she, in "a rich dress of white satin, with white dress hat," playing the hostess "with that rare grace for which she was so pre-eminently distinguished, winning all hearts." Nine years later George's unacknowledged wife lay there dead, in her crimson velvet-covered coffin, the walls draped with black, tapers burning around. There is a monument erected to her memory by her ward, the Honourable Miss Seymour, in the Roman Catholic Church in Bristol Road: these words are inscribed upon its base:—"One, to whom she was more than a parent, has placed this monument to her revered and beloved memory, as a humble tribute of her gratitude and affection."

In 1838 the house was brought to the hammer by Mr. George Robins, and bought in by Mr. Harris, of Covent Garden Theatre.

During the last hours of the King's life a letter was brought to him from Mrs. Fitzherbert, offering to come and watch over and soothe him. She was told afterwards that this letter had given him much comfort. She cherished the belief that he always wore her miniature next his heart, and desired that it should be buried with him. He begged the Duke of Wellington that he might be buried as he lay, without his night-dress being disturbed; but Lord Albemarle says the Duke could not resist looking to see the reason of this request, and found Mrs. Fitzherbert's portrait in a locket, "attached to a dirty piece of black ribbon."

The much-talked-of secret passage leading from Mrs. Fitzherbert's mansion to the Pavilion was a myth, but is still generally believed in. The man who takes the checks at the Pavilion believes in it. He told me it had been closed some time. *It never was open.*

2.—FLORIZEL'S PERDITA.

"YESTERDAY," says Miss Hawkins, "she had been the dressed belle of Hyde Park, trimmed, powdered, patched, painted to the utmost power of rouge and white lead; to-morrow she would be the cravated Amazon of the riding-house. I saw her one day handed to her outrageously extravagant *vis-à-vis* by a man whom she pursued with a doating passion. All was still externally brilliant; she was fine and fashionable, and the men of the day in Bond Street still pirouetted as her carriage passed them—the next day the vehicle was claimed by the maker. The Adonis whom she courted fled her: she followed to no purpose. What was the next glimpse? On a table in one of the waiting rooms of the Opera House was seated a woman of fashionable appearance, still beautiful. She was not noticed except by the eye of pity. Two liveried servants took from their pockets long white sleeves, which they drew on their arms, then lifted her up and conveyed her to her carriage: she was then the helpless, paralytic *Perdita.*" It was the celebrated trooper, Colonel Tarleton, who, it appears, is here alluded to, and with whom she fell desperately in love on his return from the guerilla warfare in the backwoods of America. In a journey by night, undertaken to render him a great service, she caught a cold, followed by a severe fever, and lost the sinews of her knees at the age of twenty-two, never being able to stand upright or walk during the remainder of her life. A feverish life, full of mad pleasure and bitter misery: educated by Hannah More—a bad pupil, though,—married at sixteen, separated from her husband at nineteen, a popular actress, authoress, and a Prince's favourite. We find Florizel writing to her at the Old Ship, Brighton:—"I have received your letter, and it really quite overcomes me, the scene of distress you so pathetically paint. I will certainly wait upon you, but I am afraid it will be late before I can come to the Ship, as I have company with me."

She died aged only forty-two; and the lock of his Royal Highness's hair enclosed in a billet with the words, "To the ever-adorable Perdita—Florizel, to be redeemed," in the Prince's writing, was purchased by Sir Richard Phillips who published her Memoirs written by herself.

3.—FAIR ROSAMOND.

MISS Lucy Howard of the Prince's Dairy. At the dairy itself were rarely to be found more than two cows, but on the pastures were held many *fêtes champetres*, of which the traditions handed down are of a somewhat lively character. In connection with the Prince's intrigue with Miss Howard is one of the ugliest items I have come across in George's history.

A stable boy, set on by Lady Jersey to watch, and caught by the Prince, was thrashed by him so unmercifully he was rendered a cripple for life. After all, though, the blow which lamed the boy was struck in a moment of passion, and no doubt deeply regretted, for his parents were allowed enough money to support the victim until his death years later. And whence came the record of the worst of these scandals? From custodians and check-takers on the back stair—from lacqueys grown fat on the Prince's bounty!

4.—CAROLINE OF BRUNSWICK.

PRESENTLY to be "the unfortunate Queen Caroline"—a large-boned woman, given to corpulence, in a long narrow skirt, a pelisse, and a big hat and feathers. When Bluff King Hal's affianced bride, Anne of Cleves, came over to England, he posted privately to Rochester to get a peep at her. He pronounced her utterly destitute of beauty and grace, and very unlike the pictures he had had of her, and ended by swearing she was a great Flanders mare. It would seem that in the good old days, before the discovery of photography, princes were thus frequently imposed upon.

The first meeting between the Regent and the Princess Caroline lasted barely five minutes. "She," Lord Malmesbury tells us, "very properly, in consequence of my saying it was the right mode of proceeding, attempted to kneel to him." He raised her gracefully enough, and embraced her, said barely one word, turned round, retired to a distant part of the apartment, and, calling to me, said, 'I am not well, pray give me a glass of brandy.' I said, 'Sir, had you not better have a glass of water?' Upon which he said, with an oath, 'No. I will go directly to the Queen.' And away he went. '*Mon Dieu!*' exclaimed the

Princess, 'is he always like that? He is not at all like the picture sent me. I find him very fat." She herself, at that time, was "a rather ungraceful, hard-featured young woman, redeemed, however, by a certain air of coarse good humour."

Before they were married, the Prince found fault with her shoes, and she with his wig. At the wedding his eyes were continuously fixed on his then favourite, Lady Jersey, and in absence of mind he rose impatiently from his knees before the ceremony was half over. The Archbishop stopped short, but the old King stepped forward and recalled his son to the situation. The bride and bridegroom quarrelled driving away from church. In less than ten days we find her at the Prince's rural retreat at Kempshott, where she had but one female companion, her lady-in-waiting, and the men were the "blackguard companions of the Prince, who were constantly drunk and snoring in boots on the sofa." One night, over pipes and punch, when the lady-in-waiting had sipped a little, the Prince, in a marked way, took her glass, on which the Princess took Coleraine's pipe from his mouth and puffed the smoke from it in the Prince's face. Four months later the happy couple were present at the opening of the Chapel Royal, Brighton, the foundation-stone of which the Prince had laid in the company of Mrs. Fitzherbert. Four years later all friendship was over between them, and when they met they did not even bow. Four years again, and the poor half-demented woman was on her trial for adultery. "Her appearance," says Mr. Percy Fitzgerald, describing the scene, "was anything but prepossessing. She wore a black dress with a high ruff, an unbecoming gipsy-hat with a large bow in front, the whole surmounted with a plume of ostrich feathers. Nature had given her light hair, blue eyes, a fair complexion, and a good-humoured expression of countenance; but these characteristics were marred by painted eyebrows, and by a black wig with a profusion of curls, which overshadowed her cheeks, and gave a bold defiant air to her features." Within a year the soldiers were fighting over her coffin with a mob who, in the end, carried it triumphantly through Temple Bar in defiance of the King's wishes.

BRIGHTON BEAUTIES.

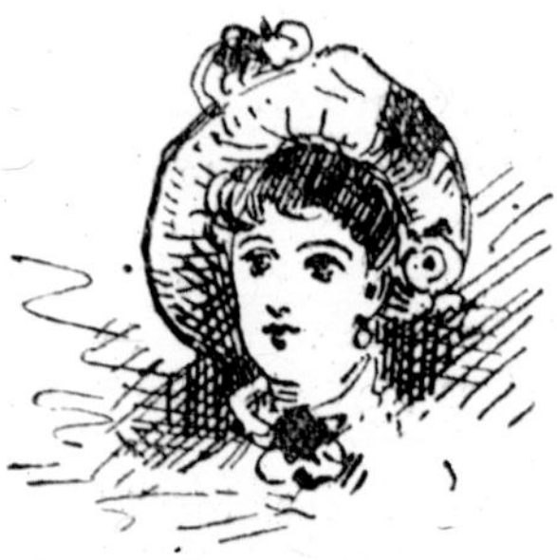

AH! my dear young ladies—I mean the Beauties of the Past, those whose roses have long ago faded, whose hair is as white as snow, who have, alas! for the most part gone over to the Great Majority. Gone! I should think so, indeed, for it is of the Beauties of 1780 and 1785 that I would speak. Here lies a list of them before me, and the ink in which it is printed is now a pale brown:—Mrs. Musters, "the reigning toast of the season," the mother of the man who married Byron's Mary Chaworth; "good and pretty" Lady Pembroke, lovely Lady Di Beauclerk, Lady Beauchamp, Lady Sefton, Lady Lisle, Lady Mary Bligh, Miss Streatfield, Miss Woodly, Miss Molesworth, Miss Shakespear, Miss Bingham, Mrs. Lawrel, the Honourable Miss Monckton, afterwards Countess of Cork; Miss Elliot, and Mrs. Sergeson, who drove four-in-hand. What became of them all? I myself have searched for hours, but to find some few

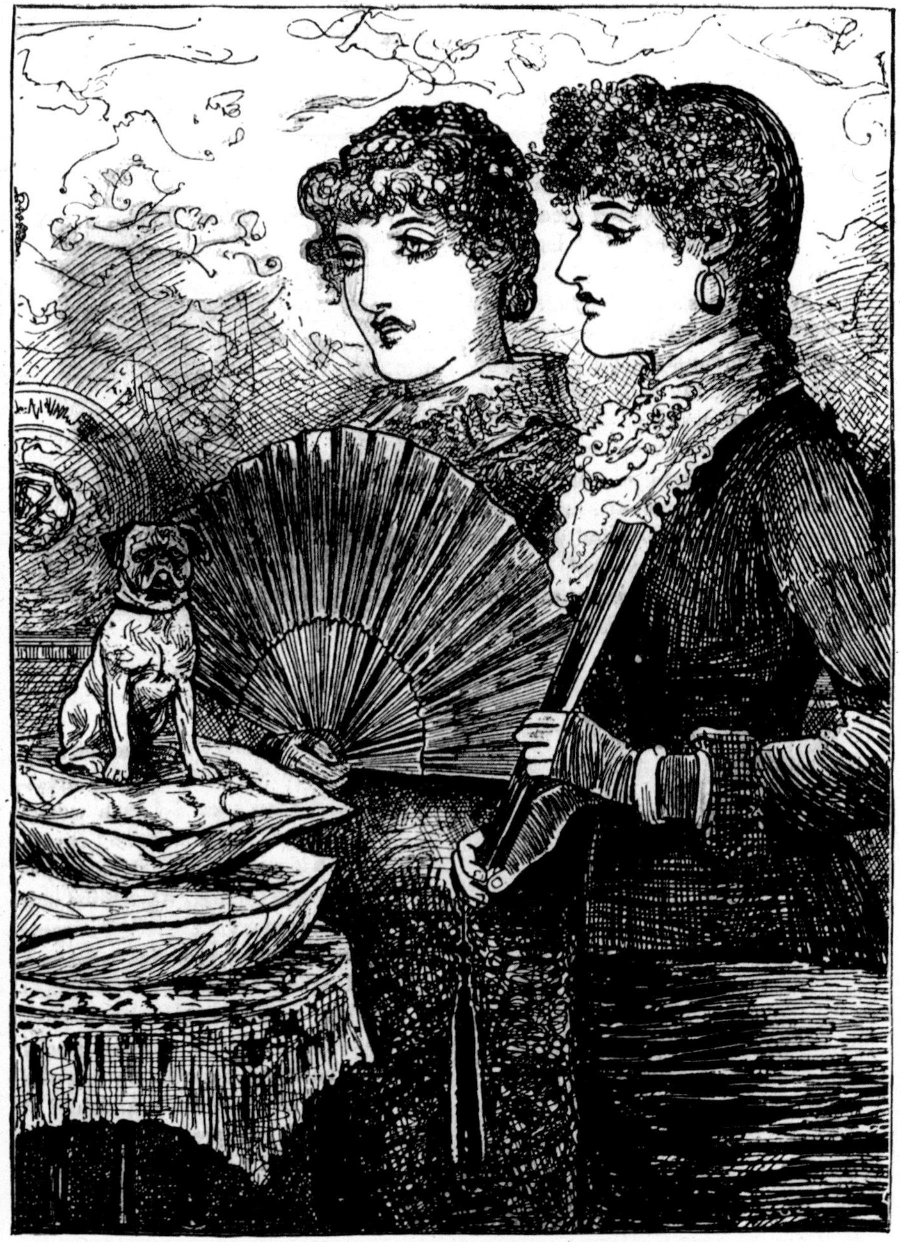

TWO CAPABLE CRITICS.

"What odd tastes they used to have."

scraps of doggerel verse recording their charms, written by a contemporary poetaster, and not worth quoting.

I have somewhere read (I suppose the man knew who wrote it) that a baby-girl is born in the world every hour of the twenty-four—when I come to think of it, is it not every minute the event takes place?—but never mind, there are many baby-girls born, that is certain, and many grow up good and beautiful. There have been, since the waves of Fashion first flowed Brightonwards, some thousands of Brighton Beauties, each succeeding generation more beautiful than their predecessors.

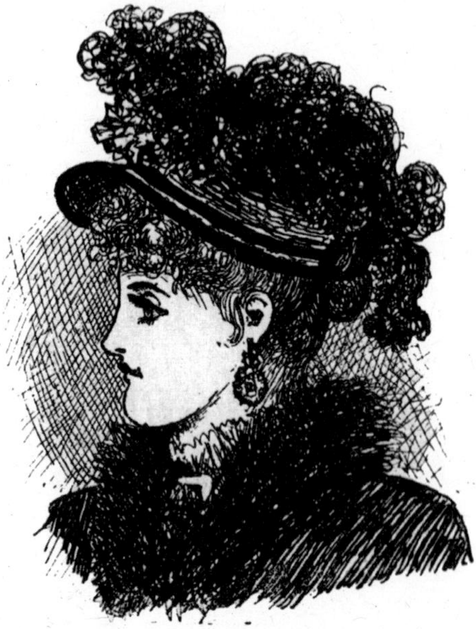

Last Season.

When I was a little boy no ladies wore black stockings, and only the poorest servants would have done so. During my early youth, when I began to notice such things, the dresses women wore were surely among the ugliest ever worn. Then came the hideous era of crinoline, of hoops of iron and wood, of beetle-crushing, flat-soled boots; but, Heavens! how pretty the women were in spite of it all, and how youth and beauty ever had the mastery over the milliner and dressmaker when they did their worst! The delightful slimness and clingyness that characterized the costumes of the first French Revolution and the gayest days of the Regency came in vogue, when crinoline went out, and many beautiful old-fashioned styles seem to be now-a-days mingled with the modern frocks and hats and bonnets, so that the costume of the pretty grandchild of 1881 and her pretty great grandmamma of 1780 are not so very far dissimilar.

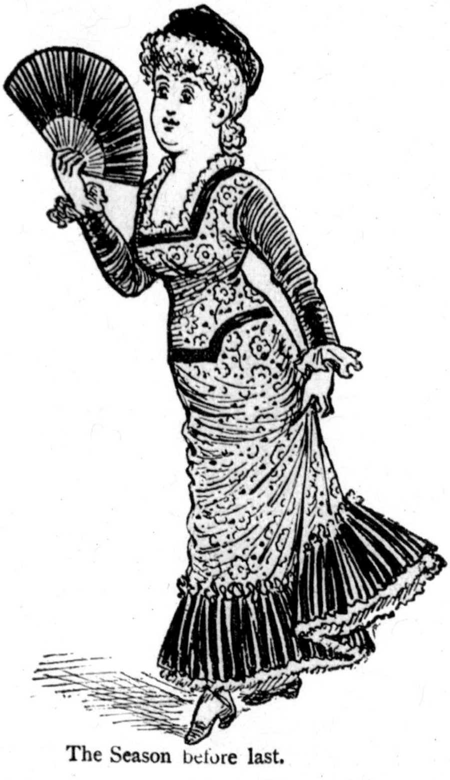

The Season before last.

I am just old enough to have seen more than one decade of Beauties sweep imperiously through the King's Road, and pass away as they came, leaving no trace behind. Read that list up, young lady, to your papa and mamma, and ask them if they have anything more to tell you of the owners ot the names than I have told, and I have told—absolutely nothing.

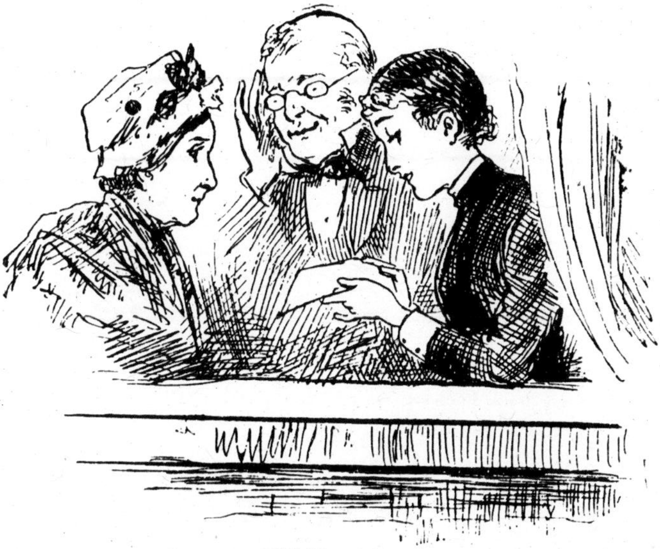

Old Memories.

THE LITTLE MISSES AND YOUNG GENTLEMEN.

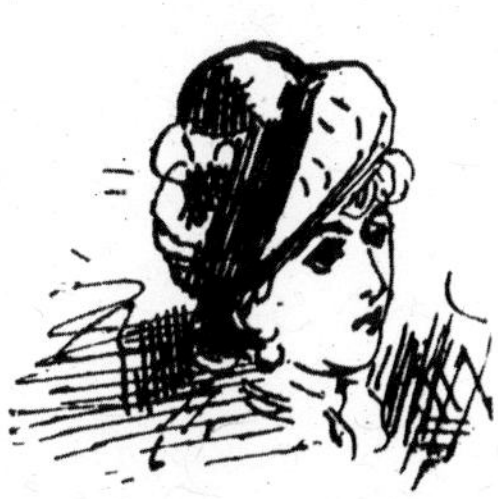

THE culture of the youthful mind is zealously pursued at London-super-Mare. There are set down in the "Directory" 77 establishments for young ladies, 70 academies for young gentlemen, and 45 day schools, which I am compelled, in default of further information, to classify as mixed. No wonder, when one takes one's walk during certain hours, one scarcely ever fails to encounter troop after troop of tender fledgelings primly pacing two by two. How good and gentle they all look, and, as a rule, what plump and rosy cheeks they have, which proves that Brighton breezes and thick bread and butter are beneficial to the growing girl; aud some of them, it must be allowed, have grown quite big ones. Stand aside, young sir, and let them pass. From time immemorial the young ladies' schools have had a right to the middle of the path, and it is a right they maintain, when there is occasion to assert it, with undaunted courage. There, I told you so! next time you give them more room.

What do they learn, I wonder? They are not crammed, I trust, as at Doctor Blimber's, where little Paul Dombey was a pupil. When I was a little boy I hated school awfully; but I don't think schools now are much like those there were then. However, by the way, Blimber's had their moments of gaiety—at breaking-up time—for don't you remember how, "Though Miss Blimber's head showed a graceful bunch of plaited hair on each temple, she seemed to have her own little curls in paper underneath, and in a playbill, too; for little Paul Dombey read 'Theatre Royal over one of her sparkling spectacles, and 'Brighton' over the other."

I don't think that, now-a-days, the Blimber tribe exist in large numbers; nor is education conducted entirely upon the principles laid down by Miss Pinkerton of Chiswick Mall. I fancy that at young ladies' schools as well as at young gentlemen's, the sanitary tub is an important item, and gymnastics have, to a great measure, superseded the back-board. I don't happen to be a father of girls—a fader o' shes, as Mr. Toole puts it—and my views as to young ladies' education may be erroneous and impracticable, but I would have them fed plentifully, and not obliged to eat anything they did not like. They should learn to ride, and to swim, and to perform on the trapeze, and to cook pies and puddings, and make stews, and boil potatoes, and they should also learn some lessons. If, after a course of this kind, they did not all turn out pretty, straight and graceful, and awfully clever, I think they ought to be smacked—hard.

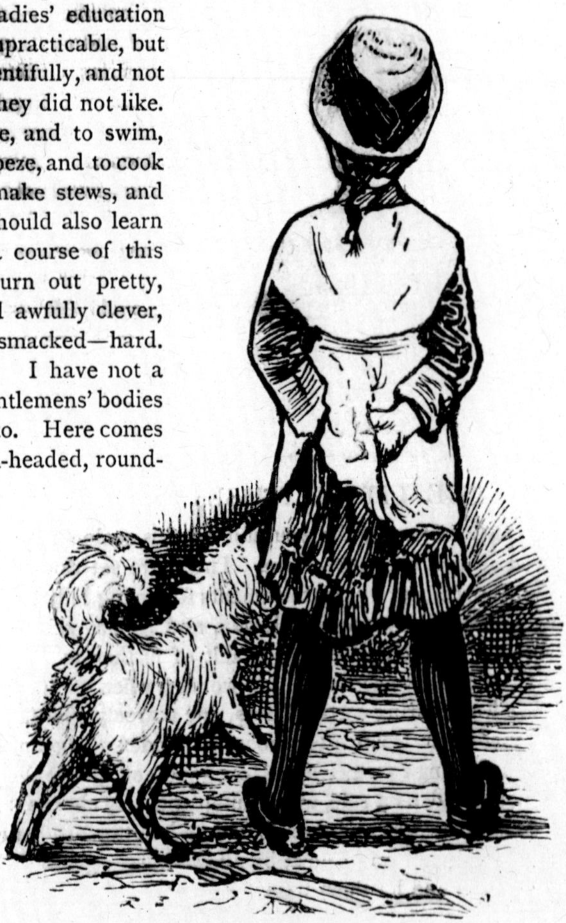

The Bold and Resolute Epoch.

And the boys' schools. I have not a doubt that these young gentlemens' bodies and brains are well seen to. Here comes a long procession of round-headed, round-jacketed little boys in astonishingly tall hats—most conservative of costumes, that has lasted in its unadulterated ugliness since my own school-days. There goes another with an odd kind of regimental cap, giving them something of the look of a highly respectable juvenile German band. How the little fellows stare into the pastry-cooks' windows; and see here, another detachment coming from the opposite direction, all wearing high hard hats. But what ails them? A chuckle runs through their ranks, and, gazing upwards, o the terrace of the Aquarium I descry another boy in a high hard hat sitting at a table with a sister or a cousin, or maybe a very young aunt indeed, and—HE IS SMOKING!

Oh, days of my youth! how this brings them back to my recollection. How I longed to go home "for good" and be my own master, smoke as much as I liked, and——. But we were comparatively slow boys in those days. I was myself but a very poor smoker at eleven.

MRS. PIPCHIN.

WHERE did Charles Dickens's Mrs. Pipchin live? I have searched in vain for a street in Brighton answering to this description:—

"This celebrated Mrs. Pipchin was a marvellous ill-favoured, ill-conditioned old lady, of a stooping figure, with a mottled face, like bad marble, a hook nose, and a hard grey eye, that looked as if it might have been hammered at on an anvil without sustaining injury. The castle of this ogress and child-queller was in a steep bye-street at Brighton; where the soil was more than usually chalky, flinty, and sterile, and the houses were more than usually brittle and thin; where the small front gardens had the uncomfortable property of producing nothing but marigolds, whatever was sown in them; and where snails were constantly discovered holding on to the street doors, and other public places they were not expected to ornament, with the tenacity of cupping-glasses. In the winter-time the air couldn't be got out of the castle, and in the summer-time it couldn't be got in. There was such a continual reverberation of wind in it, that it sounded like a great shell, which the inhabitants were obliged to hold to their ears night and day whether they liked it or no."

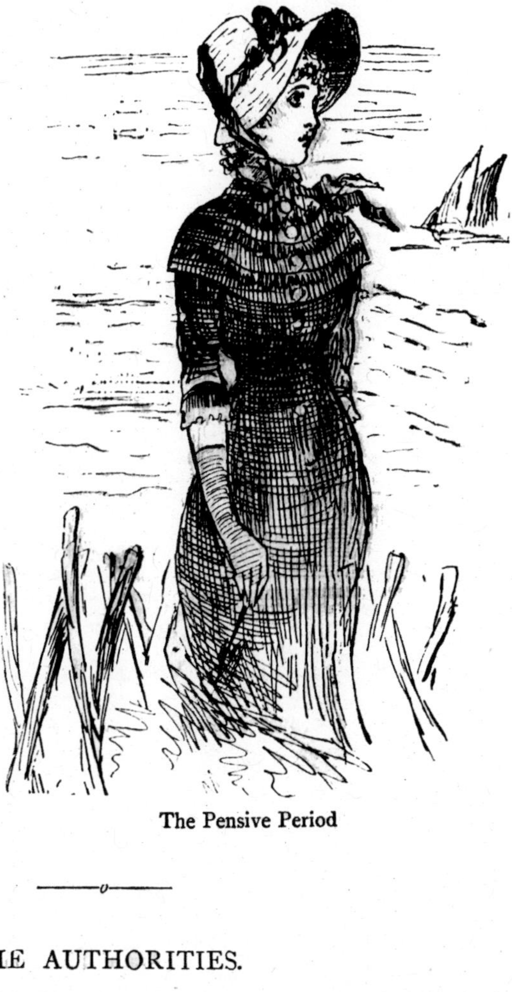

The Pensive Period

THE AUTHORITIES.

ONE of the things that first strikes the stranger in Brighton is the odd way in which the architect engaged to design its public buildings, streets, squares, and places has utilized, or failed to utilize, the space at his command. How came Pool Valley as it is, and why? I have walked backwards and forwards through Pool Valley, and I give it up. In the ordinary course of nature such a thing might have happened after a landslip or an earthquake, but it didn't. It has simply come about in consequence of two or three resolute builders turning their backs to one another, as drapers sometimes cut silk, "on the cross."

In a sort of twisted neck or passage, leading to the Pool, there are several good shops, and one little one in the pastry line is to be found round the corner; but in the actual Pool itself, there is only to be found a royal dairy, lonely and forlorn, and Simpsonless—seemingly drying up for want of another flood.

But the situation of the Town Hall is the most remarkable. Several of our London Police Courts have a shy look about them, but here we find the head-

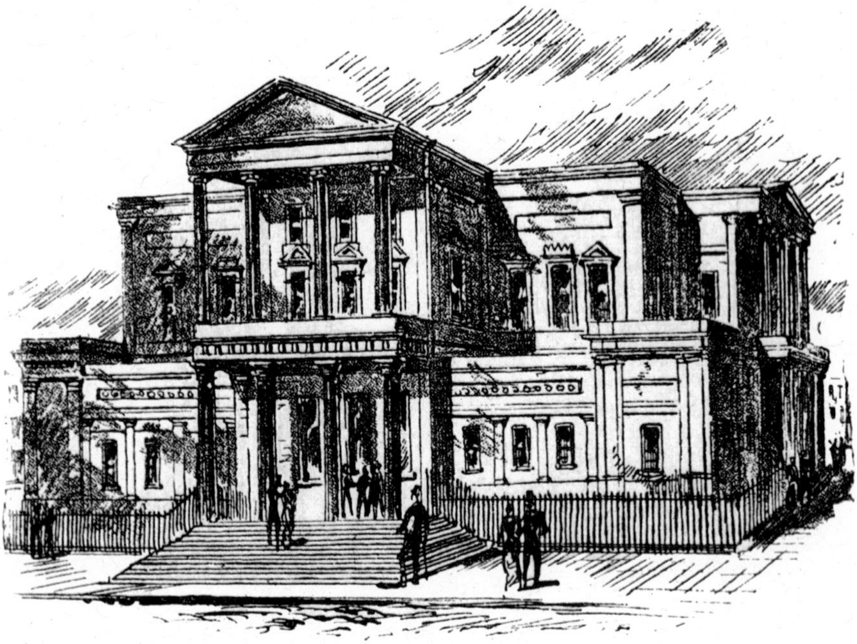

TOWN HALL.

quarters of justice crowded into a corner in the most shamefaced fashion imaginable. However, there is not much trouble in finding out the portion devoted to police cases—particularly during the race week; and many persons are said to have found themselves there quite contrary to their desire.

In an office, on the right-hand side of the building, is on view an extensive and interesting collection of bracelets, or darbies (some call them handcuffs) ancient and modern.

Oddly enough, until lately I had no idea that there were as many wicked people in Brighton as there are; but when I pick up the Brighton newspapers and read of outrages on the beach, rowdy ruffians in the streets, and of the "unenviable notoriety of the Brighton rough," I feel glad there is a mayor, and that there are also magistrates, judges, and assizes, and police constables—of whom there possibly might be more.

Jemmy Botting, a hangman, once lived at Brighton, and had busy times, it seems, among the playful residents in Petty France, Bunker's Hill, and such localities; and it is said that when one day set upon and unmercifully blackguarded, he was urged to retaliate, he replied, "No, no; I never quarrel with my customers." Three months later, as luck would have it, he had the tying up of his principal assailant. Townshend, the famous Bow Street Runner, once lived at the corner of Duke's Street; and a few doors off, Ings, the butcher, one of

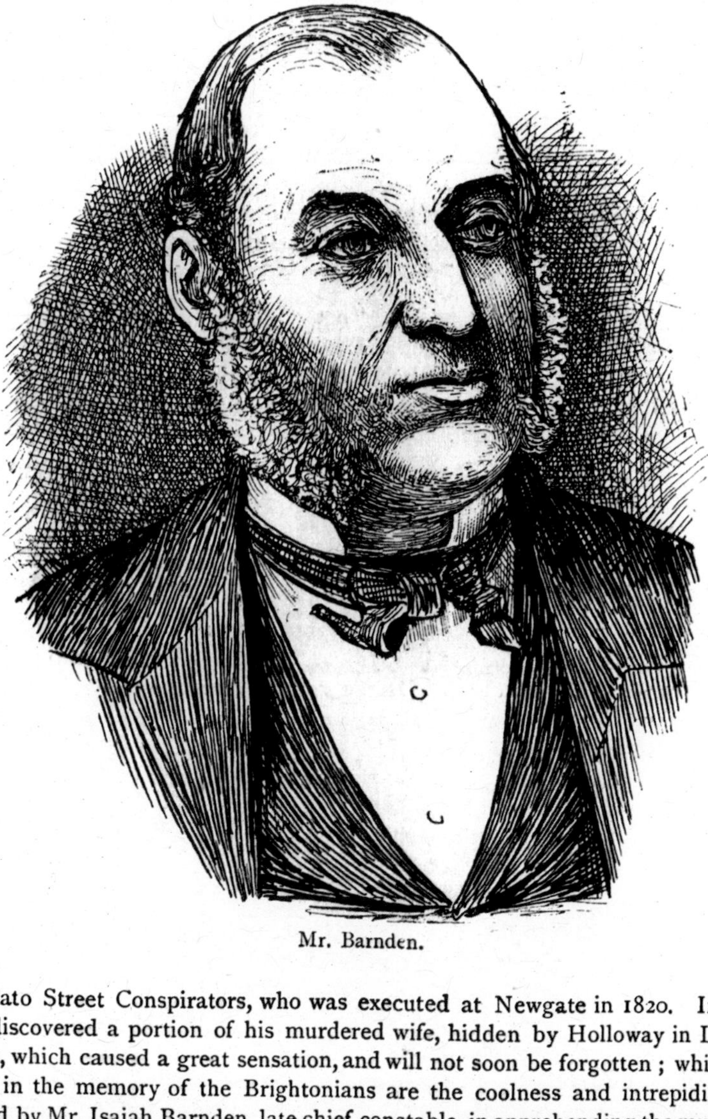

Mr. Barnden.

the Cato Street Conspirators, who was executed at Newgate in 1820. In 1830 was discovered a portion of his murdered wife, hidden by Holloway in Lovers' Walk, which caused a great sensation, and will not soon be forgotten; whilst yet fresh in the memory of the Brightonians are the coolness and intrepidity displayed by Mr. Isaiah Barnden, late chief constable, in apprehending the murderer Leigh, who pointed a revolver at him, the ball cutting through the braiding of his uniform; an act of bravery afterwards recognized by a public testimonial of a substantial character.

THE CHALYBEATE.

"IN those diseases where tonic remedies are required," says Doctor Henderson, writing of this spring about eighty years ago, "it promises under due regulation to be useful."

The Chalybeate Spring is at Wick, about half a mile from the town, where a pump-room is erected. The spring is cold, and according to the analysis of sixteen ounces of the water, by Dr. Marcet, it contains :—

	Oz.	*Gr.*
Muriate of soda	3	0
Muriate of magnesia	0	27
Sulphate of zinc	4	0
Oxide of iron	1	4
Silica	0	14
	9	29
Cubic inches of carbonic acid gas in 100 cubic inches of water	7	62

Dr. Henderson describes the taste as "not unpleasant, and something like that upon a knife after it has been used in cutting lemons." I myself have no doubt it is very good in its way, but I should draw the line short of eight quarts. As much as that might make you write libels, or might "crowd" you, as the American young lady expressed it.

THE GROWTH OF BRIGHTON, HOVE, AND CLIFTONVILLE.

FOR the parish of Brighton the census returns for 1881 give the number of inhabitants as 99,049, against 90,011 in 1871—an increase of 9,038. The numbers apply only to the municipal district. In the Parliamentary borough are included the township of Hove and part of the parish of Preston. The Preston returns, recently issued, give a population of 8,454.

Hove, which still retains nearly its ancient name, being written in the Domesday Book *How*, is termed the younger sister of Brighton, and has continued to grow by her side from an infant-like village into a large, prosperous, and fashionable town. "A few years since," I read, "a person might have stood in the field which then ran from the top of Brunswick Place to Chatfield's Farm, and looking towards the west, have seen at a distance of a mile or two the neat and unpretending church, with the village lying to the southward of old Hove. All between were green fields, dotted here and there with a house or farm, &c., but which offered little interruption to the view of the spectator. At the present time the aspect and condition of this vast area is entirely changed. From the village has sprung a town—a town of magnificence—inhabited by the wealthy of the land. The population of Hove at the beginning of the century was 100; in the year 1831, 1360; and ten years later it had increased to 2,509. In 1878 the population stood at 17,587, the number of houses being 2,432, and the rateable value £144,058."

THE "PRETTY FISHING VILLAGE"—THE FISHERMEN, THE SHRIMPS, AND THE FRESH BUTTER.

IN a book now lying open before me, entitled "A Tour through the Whole Island of Great Britain," and described as being "originally begun by the celebrated Daniel Defoe, continued by the late Mr. Richardson, author of 'Clarissa,' and brought down to the Present Time by a Gentleman of Eminence in the Literary World," I find Brighthelmstone described as it appeared in 1769. "The town," says our tourist, "stands upon a rising ground open to the S.E., and sheltered to the north by hills that are easy of ascent and command a pleasant prospect. To the west it is bounded by a large corn-field, which forms a gradual descent from the beach to the banks of the sea; and on the east by a fine lawn, called the Steyne, which is the resort of the company for walking in an evening, and which runs winding up into the country to the distance of some miles. The town is built in a quadrangular form, and the streets are at right angles with each other: they are six in number, besides many lanes and squares. Many of the houses are of flint, and the windows and doors frequently of brickwork. Brighthelmstone is now become a polite place, by the annual resort of the gentry in the summer season, as being the nearest seaport to London, and very convenient for sea-bathing; for the accommodation of whom there have been two handsome ball-rooms built and several machines for bathing. The gentry may also have the use of two circulating libraries, by which means the inhabitants have of late been greatly benefited, and the provisions in that neighbourhood greatly advanced in their price." I don't quite follow that last bit, but doubtless the reader will. To continue: "The principal inns in this town are the Castle and the two Ships. The men of this town are wholly employed in fishing and the women in making their nets, so that it is an excellent nursery for seamen."

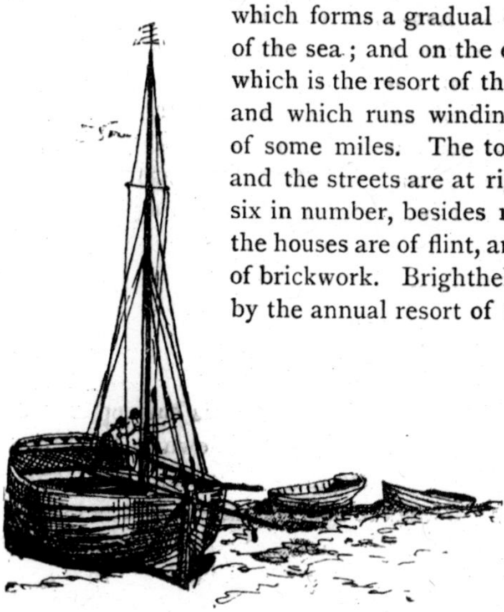

On the Beach.

Ah! where are all the brave old fishermen gone to now? There are a few about, to be sure. One may, indeed, occasionally meet with an uncouth figure carrying a net high and dry on land at the north end of the town, and doubtless there are a score or two any fine day dozing their life away upon the sunny shingle under the sea-wall, but it is only one in a thousand of Brighton visitors who goes near the shingle, and I vow you may pass a week at the Queen of Watering-places and never once set eyes upon a seafaring person. I take it, the greater part of the descendants of the old original fishermen have taken up another business: got married, most likely, and, whilst their good ladies let lodgings and wait upon the lodgers, they themselves stroll round and smoke pipes.

As to the fish itself, the supply appears to be very limited, and the best kind quite as dear as it need be. It is true that sometimes you may hear men crying mackerel in the streets twenty-four for a shilling, but the same day a small red mullet is selling in the shops for half a crown. Even the "plebeian shrimp" has a fancy price, and I think eightpence a pint is quite as much as shrimps are worth. I see here and there live, or, rather, half-live, shrimps may be bought and boiled by the buyer, but I mistrust the home boiling. I am inclined to think that there are almost as few cooks in the world who can boil a shrimp properly as there are who can well cook a potato. You may buy some delicious potted shrimps at a little shop in Little East Street, for which they told me, when I bought some, there was so great a demand I must give my order the day before. I suppose the shrimps which are here potted are not natives of the Brighton coast. I have found the Brighton shrimp to be much inferior to his Gravesend relation.

Reverting to the high prices at Brighton, I have, in an old book, just come across an instance of what I think to be most unreasonable grumbling. Here 's a man, in 1771, complaining of butter costing him eightpence a pound, he stating that thirty years before it had only cost fourpence. The stingy old curmudgeon! Why, what I had for breakfast this morning I paid two and twopence a pound for.

THE "LADIES OF THE BATH."

"My morning business," writes the Rev. Mr. Clarke, in 1736, "is bathing in the sea." All the world, including Dr. Johnson, once on a time went down to Brighton to bathe in the sea, or to drink of it. Says Dr. Awsiter, in 1768: "There are many constitutions too delicate and stomachs too weak to bear the nausea and sickness sea-water-drinking produces;" and he therefore recommends an admixture of milk. "United with milk," says he, "it becomes a noble medicine." In 1750 there were only seven bathing machines for the whole town, and furious scuffles occurred every morning among the visitors to obtain possession of one. The ladies were enthusiastic bathers. Mrs. Thrale and the three Misses Thrale, and Miss Fanny Burney, got up at six one November morning, and bathed by the pale blink of the moon, returning home to dress by candlelight. "It was cold but pleasant," says the vivacious authoress. In the *Lewes Journal*, in 1766, a gentleman (probably young) wrote a set of verses about the water-nymphs, in which he says, among a host of other pretty things:

> " * * Here so many queens of love we see
> Caress the waves and wanton in the sea."

Another gentleman of the same epoch, however, thought differently. "Observe them," says he, "at the instant of bathing. How humiliating! They appear more deplorable than so many corpses in shrouds!" What a dreadful person to say such awful things! As though ever—I mean "hardly ever——" But, there, I 'll say no more. I hate rows.

* * * * * *

I read in a New York fashion-book that they make "figures" of fine wire netted in long meshes, perfectly pliable, and much superior to nature.

* * * * * *

In writing about Brighton bathing, do what one will, it is next to impossible to avoid coming to one's Martha, the greatest of great Gunns. In spite of her popularity during her life and the immortality she has since achieved, it would appear that Mrs. Gunn was not the first among bathing women—or "dippers," I should say (the men who bathed the gentlemen were distinguished by the name of "bathers," the gentlemen were called "bathees"—therefore some nice distinction, of which no record remains, evidently lies in the "dip.") There was a Mrs. or Miss Mary Cobby I find much quoted, and a Mary Howell, whose address is now

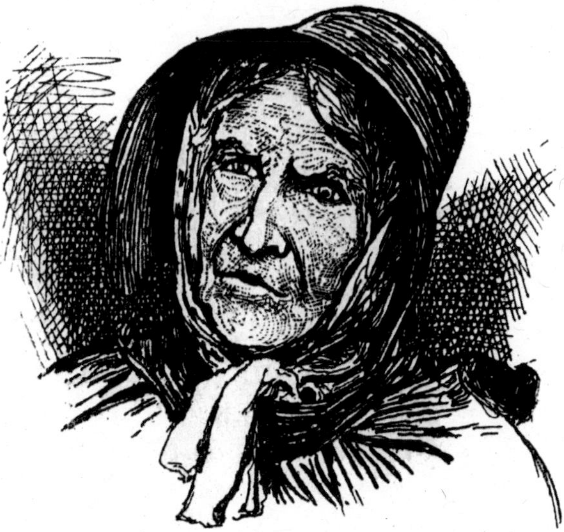

A Dipper.

historical (No. 3 East Street). There are jewellers there now by the name of Marx, knowing more of hall-marks than water-marks, I should imagine. I also, during my researches, have come many times upon an Ann Smith (late Ann Cherry), a cherrybobber, we may presume, if ladies in the water behaved then as now.

But Martha was the popular one. "Brighton would not look like itself without you, Martha," said the author of a "Donkey Tour," in 1815. "Oh, I don't know. It's like to do without me some day" (she was eighty-eight years old at the time). "But I ought to feel proud, for I've as many bows from man, woman, and child as the Prince himself. Ay, I do believe the very dogs in the town know me." "I left her," he says, "hobbling to the side of the London coach to deliver cards from the repository of her poor, withered, sea-freckled bosom, for, like a woman of fashion, her bosom was her pocket."

Brave old Martha! the chubbiest girl-baby and lithest rosy girlette you dipped must be, alas! an old woman now. How remorselessly Time eats up men and things! Those Brighton dogs' descendants are still bow-wowing lustily, in spite of laws and bye-laws. Martha's successors continue to dip more chubbiness and rosy litheness, and the same old sea keeps on the same old rumble-jumble, rumble-jumble, and will when you who read and I who write are but invisible dust. She died in her eighty-ninth year, and "the whole town was in motion to witness her funeral. About forty of her relatives and friends followed her to the grave."

"Public bathing at Brighton," says my good guide book for 1803, "is exposed to some interruptions, as well as danger, from the violence of the north-west winds, which produce a heavy swell. The ladies generally resort to the water on the east side of the town, and the gentlemen on the west. Thus public decency is preserved, without which no society can long exist."

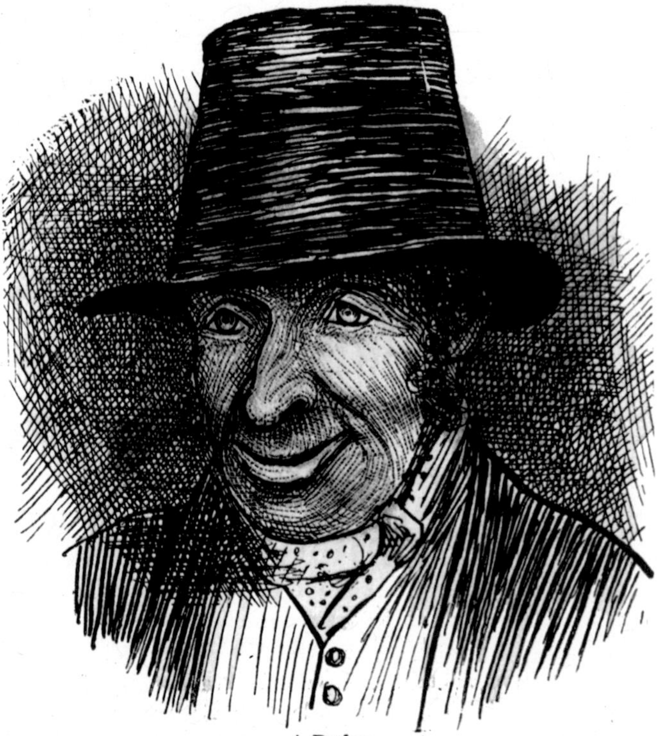

A Bather.

There are now at least two hundred and fifty bathing machines in use at Brighton irrespective of those at Hove, and the following facts may be found of service to the reader :—

For those who prefer the open sea, bathing is allowed from the head of the West Pier every morning, from 6 to 10 o'clock, weather permitting. A single bath ticket, including admission to the Pier, 6*d.* ; book of twelve tickets, 5*s.* Boat and experienced men always in attendance.

BATHING MACHINES.

For every person bathing and occupying a machine for less than half an hour—gentlemen, 6*d.* ; ladies, 9*d.* ; two ladies, 1*s.* For every additional half-hour or portion thereof, 6*d.* each person. Children under 14 years of age (if more than one bathe at the same time from one machine), 4*d.* each.

BATHS.

The principal Baths are Brill's Shampooing, Hot Air, Vapour, Douche, Warm, and Shower Baths for Ladies and Gentlemen ; First-class Swimming Bath, Warm, and Shower for Gentlemen, 77 East Street; Brill's Swimming Baths, Warm, and Shower, for Ladies, 78 East Street; Hobden's Royal Hot, Cold, Vapour, Douche, and Shower Baths, for Ladies and Gentlemen; also Hobden's Royal Tepid Swimming Baths for Gentlemen, adjoining the Grand Hotel, King's Road; the Brunswick Baths, Western Street, near Brunswick Terrace; the Brighton Turkish Baths Company, for Ladies and Gentlemen, 59 West Street; the Public Baths and Washhouses, North Road; and Brake's Magnetic and Electro-Chemical Baths 11 York Place.

———o———

THE DOCTORS AND THE DEAR OLD LADIES.

As early as 1800, according to my trusty guide book, it was suggested that a statue should be raised to the memory of Dr. Russel, "who is venerated by the natives as the first person who brought Brighton into public repute." But I don't think the business was ever gone on with. Brighton, indeed, is not prolific in statues. There is the statue to Sir John Cordy Burrows, three times mayor, in the Pavilion Garden, and the statue to his Gracious Majesty George the

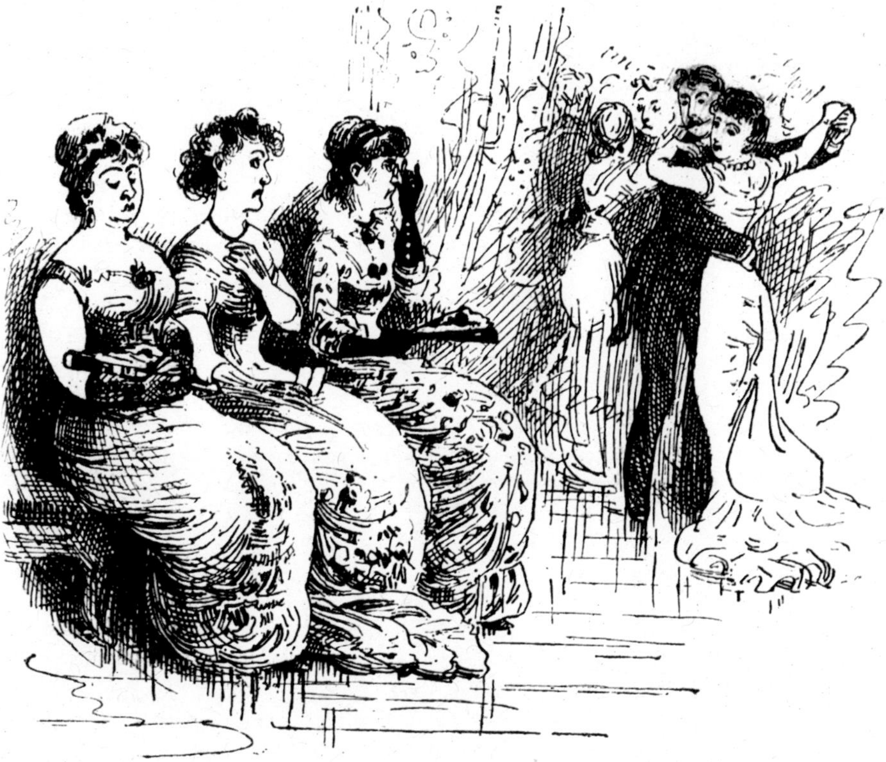

"Canst thou minister?"

Fourth, which Chantrey stipulated to produce for 3,000 guineas, and which cost him 6,000, he sustaining a great portion of the loss:—I daresay if he had laid out another thousand or two he might have made it weather-proof.

As far as I can ascertain, the natives named a street after the Doctor, and

some one (possibly the Doctor, at his own expense) had a portrait painted of him by Zoffany, which now hangs in the card-room of the Old Ship. A good guide book of 1803 says it is in the ball-room, but possibly, when the latter apartment came to be used for auctions, the picture was moved, lest somehow in the hurry of business it might have been inadvertently "knocked down."

There is a Russell Square, but I fancy this has no connection with Dr. Russel, firstly, because the name is spelt with two l's; and secondly, because there is also a Bedford Square close to it. To a person accustomed to the sober grandeur of Russell Square, W.C., Russell Square, Brighton, is disappointing. Approached by a narrow passage, rendered narrower still by two obstructive posts—a narrow passage in a corner, squeezed up against a public house—the aspect of the square is not imposing, though, by-the-way, it is only fair to say that there are other and broader ways into it at the other corners. Russell Square will be found to be three-sided,—one side, which has a grander look about it, being Canon Place. To make up for this, however, Russell Square begins its early numbers up a side street, in the general line, also selling pastry and new-laid eggs. Bedford Square, on the contrary, is of much nobler proportions, and enjoys an imposing sea-view. I expect Bedford Square was an afterthought, or most likely it would have been called Russell Square.

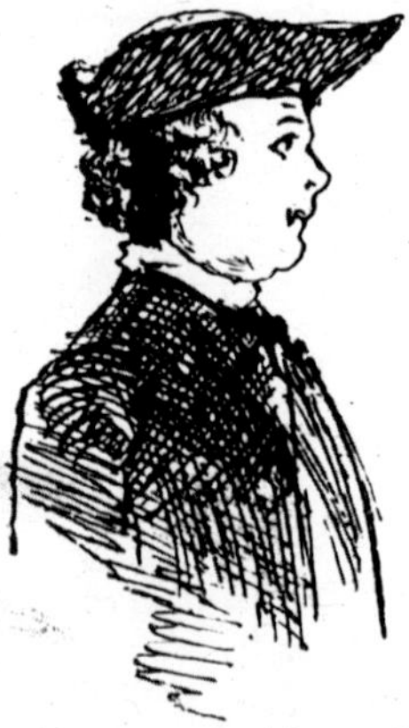
A young practitioner a long while ago.

In 1800, as shown by the Directory, there were but thirteen doctors and apothecaries in the town, but there are over two hundred now. There was then only one undertaker, and he made such a poor living out of it that he had to keep a hosier's shop to keep life in him betweenwhiles. There are twenty-five undertakers now, and probably everybody who dies in Brighton is not buried there. Now, as in Russel's days, "silken folly and bloated disease" come down to Brighton, and the doctors have a gay old time of it. Many—very many learned and accomplished physicians and surgeons are there, of whom nothing but words of the highest praise can be uttered, and there are quacks and charlatans not a few, and brisk is the business done in patent medicines, salves and ointments, and harmless messes, highly testimonialized.

What shovelsfull of gold pass from the pockets of the dear old ladies to those of the sons of Æsculapius, and the hangers-on and free-lances attached to the great schools of medicine, even unto the descendants of the immortal Rawkins, with his "*Pilula Humbugensis* of yellow soap and liquorice-water," good for all diseases under the sun—ay, even the spots on that. Dear old ladies, without throwing the least doubt on the medical skill of the faculty generally, I venture to assert that good old breezy Doctor Brighton himself does more real good than all the rest put together. And after him I would beg to recommend a trial of a young beginner, for whose ability I can conscientiously speak. His charges are extremely moderate—in no case exceeding a shilling. Many dear old ladies have made wills in favour of far less deserving persons, but I know for a fact that he would strongly object to such a proceeding as regards himself. What he says is—"There are people who, whilst living, would hesitate to give others money, and people who would hesitate to take it otherwise than in the form of a legacy. But both are wrong. I would have all the dear old ladies now living, live on for ever—or as long as they liked. If any one of them thinks she owes me a happy hour—that I have anyhow, in chasing away sad thoughts and alleviating pain, got a claim on her gratitude, which she is of opinion should take a negotiable shape, I have only to say that now is the time, and Heaven bless her!" The name of this worthy though yet struggling young physician may be found upon the title-page and cover of this entertaining volume, is monosyllabic, and begins with R. His "permanent" town address, as actors say, is No. 99 Shoe Lane. An addressed envelope (which need not be stamped) will procure all further particulars desired.

THE POOR PEOPLE AND THE PAWNBROKERS.

BRIGHTON has unquestionably a wealthy look about it. When I have feasted my eyes with dazzling jewels and costly furs, I open the visitors' list and count up my noblemen and ladies. Everybody here is rolling in wealth, and presently I shall roll too. The post comes in Saturday evening, bringing me a cheque on a London Branch of the London and County. The bank here closes at two, and at one minute to ten on Monday I am standing outside the Brighton Branch. I walk at a feverish rate twice (or nearly) round the town to pass the minute, and then ascertain that on Wednesday morning I can draw the cash. My landlady says, "Oh, my butcher would have done it in a moment if you had only asked me." I had not absolutely asked point-blank. I just said, "I have a cheque on the London and County, which I wish I could cash, as I am awfully short, and don't know whom to ask. I wish to goodness I did, for I am absolutely penniless." That was all I said to her.

Some people are better at giving hints than other people are. I am a bad one—I am so backward.

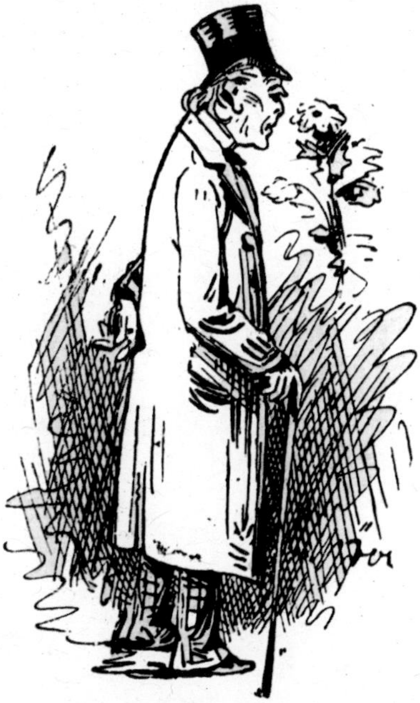

Toddling along.

* * * * * *

After all, perhaps I was wrong about there being no poor people here. Yesterday, I remember, I for the first time saw the new workhouse—which, by-the-way, commands a cheerful view of the cemeteries; and this very morning a stalwart man, out of work, begged me, for the love of Heaven, to buy a pencil of him. I asked how much they were each; he said what I chose. I took a pencil and gave him a penny, asking how much profit accrued to him by the transaction. With a wounded look upon him, he said, "A blessed farthin'." I gave him another penny, and he brightened up. When I met him he had but two pencils in his hand, and I left him with one. The one I took would not mark.

For the benefit of those whose supplies run short, but who carry watches, or are adorned with costly gems, it may be casually mentioned that the town of Brighton owns nine pawnbrokers. In my travels I have only happened to notice one; and if the rest in any way resemble it, I fancy it must require a good deal of pluck to cross the threshold. It stands in a conspicuous position in Ship Street; it has a portico and a flight of steps. There has never been the faintest sign of life, or bustle, or business about it when I have passed by. It is a fear-inspiring place; an abode of mystery—dark, silent, and inscrutable.

SUNDAY.

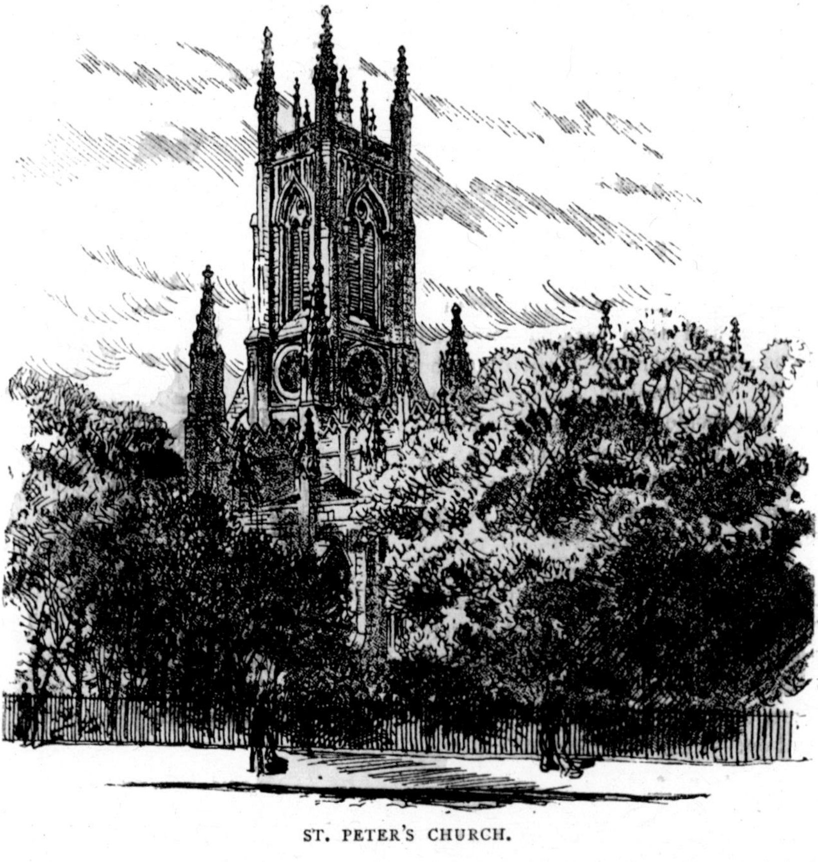

ST. PETER'S CHURCH.

LIKE London, Brighton is at its worst on Sunday. The townspeople, between church-times, ramble through the King's Road, and the shop-boy smokes his cigar, and the shop-girl wears tight boots, the West Pier band plays hymn tunes,

EACH OF

Judy's Shilling Books

CONTAINS HUNDREDS OF COMIC PICTURES.

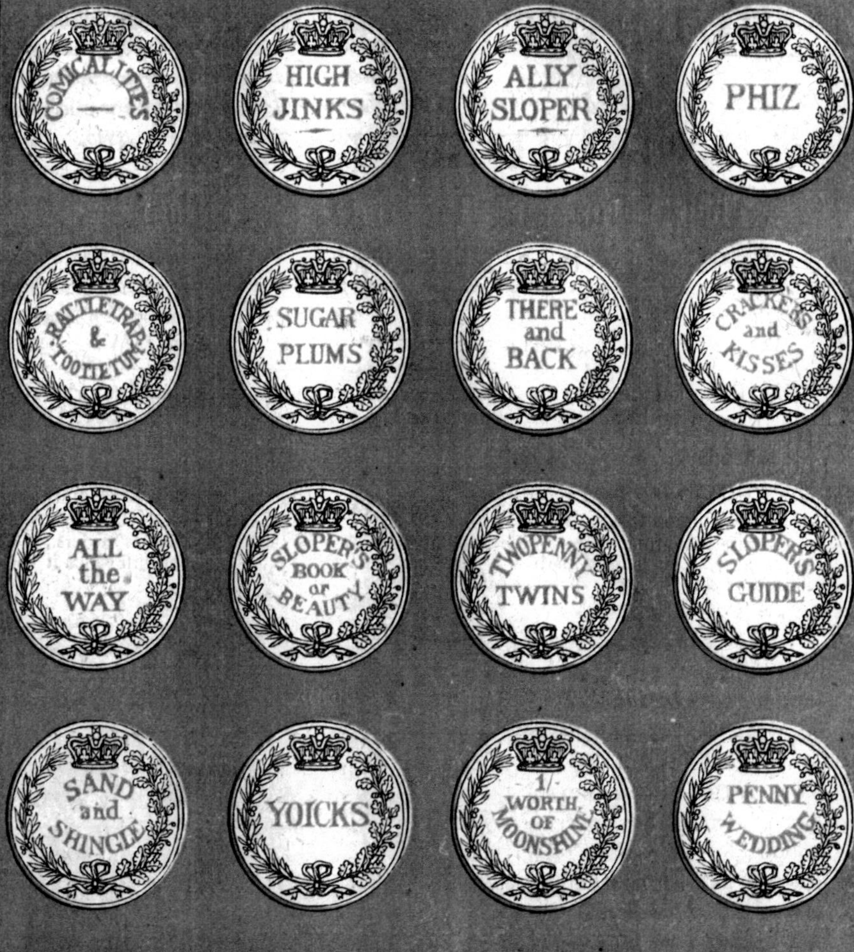

TWENTY VOLUMES. TWENTY SHILLINGS.

"The cheapest pound's worth ever issued."

"Judy" Office, 99 Shoe Lane, Fleet Street, E.C.

A "Programme of Processions" is here before me, "for the celebration of the Gunpowder Plot of November 5th, 1605; the landing of William of Orange's forces at Torbay in the Protestant cause on November 5th, 1688; and the Battle of Inkerman, November 5th, 1854." The programmist would appear to be a little foggy in the opening of his sentence; few except Nihilists desire to celebrate the Gunpowder Plot itself. He could not have meant that.

Of all mournful things, I take an empty squib-case after the squib has gone off to be one of the mournfulest. In the half-minute of his short-lived

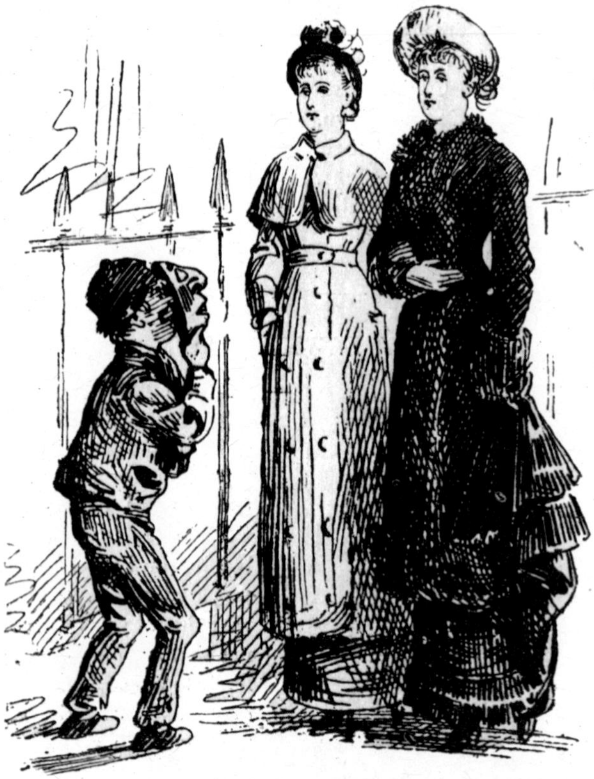

"Ain't ye frightened?"

triumph the halfpenny squib (fourpence per dozen if taken in large quantities) is but a poor spluttering creature, ending with a feeble wheeze or gasp. There is nothing of the rowdy nature of the cracker about him—here, there, and everywhere in a moment. Like the cracker, he is hard to set light to, but when lighted he is, alone and unsupported, a poor, mean, miserable little show, and so soon over. And burst up, exhausted—what a hopeless thing! But yet thus lying here trodden in the earth he is, when I come to reflect, on about a par with the soaring rocket. All fireworks are vanity and vexation, and burnt-out bonfires the deadest of dead ashes.

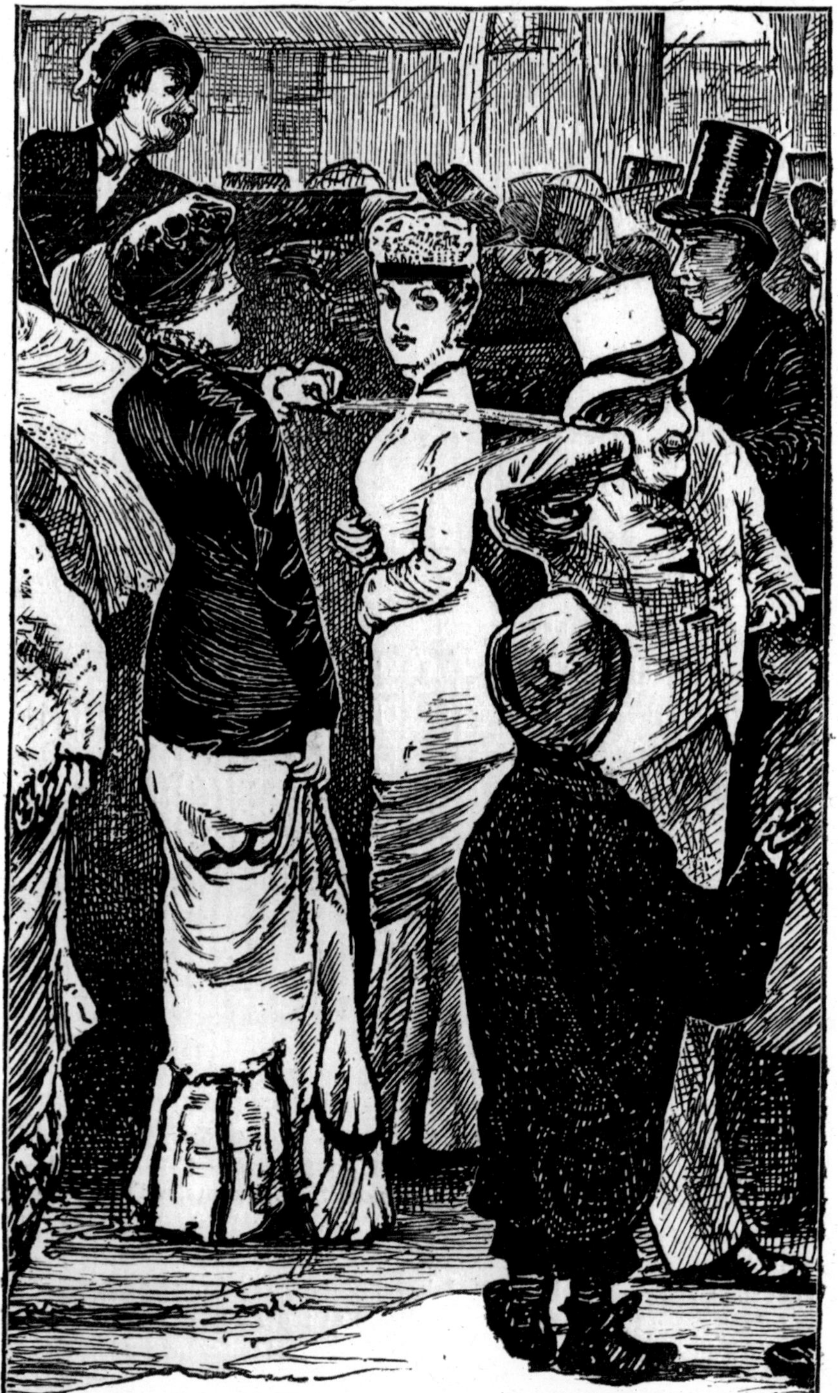

Guy Fawkes Day.

THE ACCOMMODATION.

IN the guide book for 1803 there are only three inns and two taverns mentioned where can be found "good entertainment and accommodation either for a short or a longer space." These are the Castle Tavern,* the Old Ship Tavern, the New Ship Inn, the New Inn,† and the White Horse.‡ There are now 48 hotels, 401 public houses, and 167 beer-houses, making in all a total of 616 houses of entertainment, so that with pence in poke an honest wayfarer surely need not long go hungry and athirst.

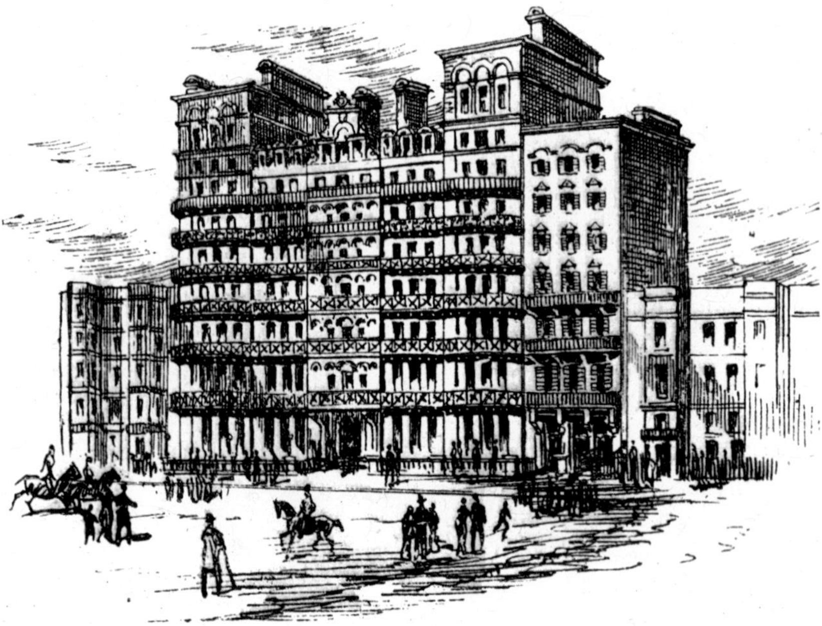

The Grand.

There are among the signs: 4 Black Lions, 1 White Lion, 1 Lion, 1 Lion and Unicorn, 3 Black Horses, 2 White Horses, 2 Running Horses, 3 Horse and Grooms, 1 Waggon and Horse, 1 Nag's Head, 2 Eagles, 1 White Eagle, 2 Dolphins, 3 Foxes, 2 White Harts, 1 Green Dragon, 1 Greyhound, 1 Lamb, 1 Unicorn, 1 Swan, 2 Stags, 1 Nightingale, and 2 Sea-Serpents, a Traveller's Joy, Mazeppa, Flying Dutchman, Olive-Branch, Traveller's Rest, Barley Mow, and Blue Anchor.

What shall I say of the hotels? I have, now and again, been at several of them for a "space." I have been numbered at the Lofty, and lifted sky-high —the lower floors are not for the likes of me. I have felt somewhat lonely, and as though recently in trouble, and for the time being only out on a ticket-of-leave. As I have crossed the hall the head waiter's eye has seemed to pierce

* Pulled down. † Now the Clarence. ‡ Pulled down.

me through and through, as though its owner said, "What ! you again, No. Two Thousand and Two, wearing out the mat with those boots of yours ! Have a care, sir, have a care !" Yet, again, have I formed one of a joyous dinner-party, at which one of the Chosen has been host, and the wine has flowed, and the diamonds sparkled, and we did enjoy ourselves, believe me.

Of the Duke's an amusing writer recently said, "If you are only a commoner you are apt to starve until the Duke has done his breakfast, to be ignorant until the Duchess has done with the newspapers, and to be bedless until his Sereneness's valet has departed." Possibly there is some exaggeration in this, but the Duke's is assuredly solemn and somewhat sad in its chill grandeur.

The Old Hull has a reputation for coziness and comfort, which has endured over a century and a half. A curious rambling old place, it is full of nooks and corners, and unexpected steps leading up and down from passage to room and room to passage.

But as the inside pages of this book are not intended to be advertisements, I must leave you to pick upon your own inn to take your ease in ; or, if your taste lies that way, you may find some sixty-odd boarding establishments, mansions, and houses, at which you may take up your quarters. For my own part, I fancy a boarding-house is rather too much like a school ; but, of course, tastes differ, and they are the earthly Paradise of warriors on half-pay, and mature maidens with little independencies.

Of the Brighton lodging-houses what can I say? Some of course are very bad, and some very good. You make your choice and pay your money, and trust to fate. Some people are luckier than others. As to the situation, you must choose that also, and if you want a sea-view you must prepare to pay well for that luxury. I read that, in 1809, of Devonshire Place, that "the situation is unexceptionable, for it is unconfined, salubrious, and fashionable ;" that the houses in Russell Street are "occupied by our fashionable visitants," and that Dorset Gardens "is an elegant range of buildings which are constructed in a uniform, light, and elegant manner !" Mr. Bishop says, "Nothing shows more clearly the rapid rise of the middle classes in England than the contrast of the accommodation which suited the citizens of London seventy or eighty years ago, and that now demanded by their sons and grandsons. Middle Street and Russell Street sufficed for the one, Brunswick Square and Terrace, Palmeira Square, and the palatial mansions of West Brighton can scarcely suffice for the other !"

Of the Restaurants I cannot speak with unqualified praise: indeed as far as my experience goes there are not any that I can say are quite what they should be, although some are sufficiently expensive. There is, however, a vast amount of eating and drinking going on, particularly at luncheon-time, and, for instance, it is a sight to see the solid food put away by the ladies who frequent Booth's decorous establishment in East Street. I should think a new restaurant, conducted with spirit, ought to be a great success.

Of refreshment-rooms and eating houses of the second and third class there are plenty, which will be found to be cheap enough and good enough for the not over-particular, and at certain of the hotels and inns there is a *table d'hôte* or "ordinary" that might be recommended, only this is not my province.

As to the poor old sandwich, an English institution to which railway refreshment-room contractors have wellnigh dealt th death-blow, I may mention that a variety, and many of them very good in their way, may be found at the Bodega, an establishment hidden round a corner up Ship Street, which I should think might be made better known than it is at present with advantage to its proprietors.

They sell a very pleasant liqueur at Mutton's that, for reasons of their own, they call *White* Curaçoa, at only sixpence a glass, and with which the nicest possible young ladies serve you. In one respect, however, Mutton's may possibly be looked upon as a snare, if not a delusion; at least I found it so one day during the race week. Upon the tables at many restaurants one is accustomed to meet with an assortment of glasses, including the hock, sherry, and champagne; but when I, in all my lamblikeness, and with loveliness on either arm, crossed the Muttonian threshold, I found the champagne itself in pint bottles set out upon the table. I fell—not under the table—I speak figuratively when I say it, but I did fall heavily.

THE THEATRE ROYAL.

"THE stage, when properly conducted," says a right-down regularly good guide-bookist, "is almost universally allowed to rank among the most rational amusements; and, in regard to the Brighton Theatre, this praise may fairly be allowed it."

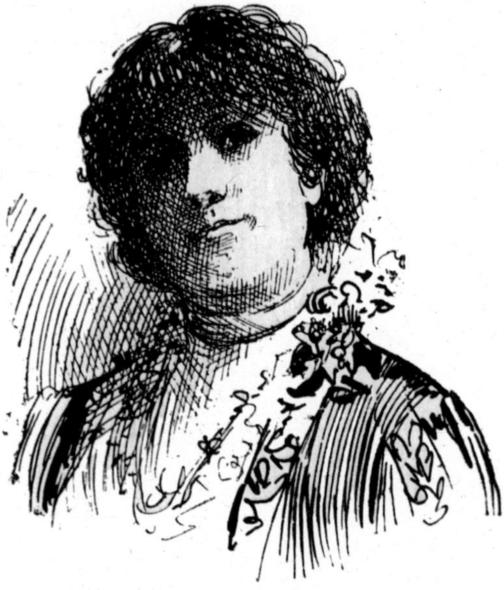

A popular Manageress.

This sentiment, I must confess, does honour to the heart and head of the compiler of the foregoing information. He is not describing the theatre now existing, and so ably managed by Mrs. Nye Chart; the one he speaks of was situated at the upper end of Duke Street, and was "neither ill built, nor inelegantly fitted up," whilst the "scenes" were "well executed," and the "dresses and decorations" were "very decent."

It opened at that time (1801) at the beginning of July, and closed the latter end of October. The nights of performing were Tuesdays, Wednesdays, Fridays, and Saturdays; and the "regular actors and actresses," who were "respectable for provincial boards," were occasionally reinforced by some "first-rate performers from London," who made a "trading voyage to this place."

Our author thus concludes:—"In short, the Brighton Theatre better deserves encouragement than many places which are more frequented. The evening can nowhere be so cheaply and so creditably spent."

After the glories of King George's day, until within the last twenty years or so, things do not appear to have gone too well with the Theatre Royal, for I find it written that it was "usually in a condition trembling between the sere and yellow leaf of disregard and the catastrophe of utter collapse."

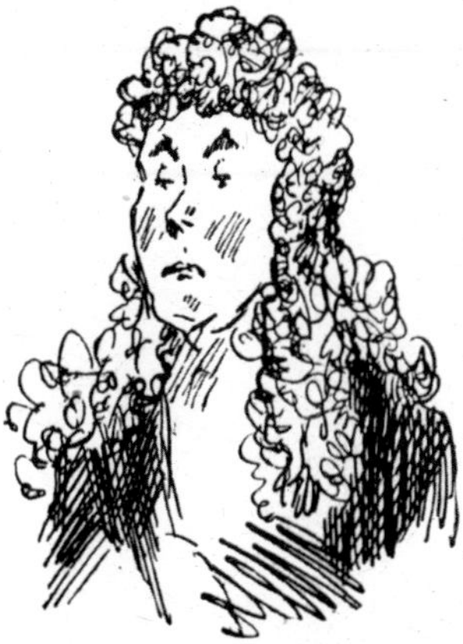

The palmy days.

But the boards of the old Brighton Theatres have been trodden by the "great Sarah," the stately Siddons; Mrs. Glover, with "a handsome expressive face and noble figure," as Hamlet; beautiful and unhappy Dorothy Bland, *alias* Mrs. Jordan, favourite of King William IV. and mother of the first Earl of Munster; Harriet Mellon—Mrs. Coutts, and afterwards Duchess of St. Albans—the lady whose parties, Sir Walter Scott says, it was "the fashion to attend and to abuse her," the great benefactress of the Brighton tradesmen and the beloved of the Brighton poor, who died worth £1,800,000. But I could easily swell the list to fill half a dozen pages. All the celebrities came down to Brighton during the season, even to that notorious mountebank, whose sex was the subject of wagers and actions at law, the Chevalier d'Eon, who wore petticoats, and was "the first fencer in the world." Some people said he was the lover of Queen Charlotte, but that story has been very clearly proved to be false by Mr. Thoms; some said he was mad, but, if so, there was much method in this madness of his, and his case was wholly unlike that of Du Moret, who passed as Mademoiselle Rosette or the Abbé de Choisy, Comtesse des Barres, whose delectable histories have been respectively written by Sir Lascelles Wraxall and Monsieur, or rather Madame "Marc de Montifaud."

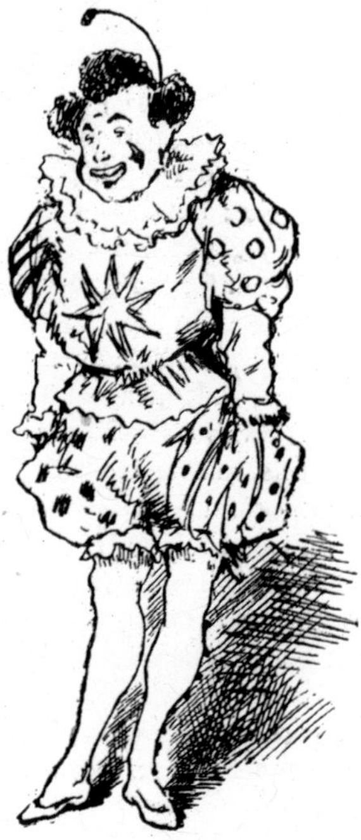

At the present time all the great actors and actresses in turn come to Mrs. Chart's theatre, where all plays are most carefully placed upon the stage, and at which, at Christmas-time, Mr. Frank Green's clever pantomimes are as well mounted as a like entertainment at the best London theatre.

PLEASURE GARDENS AND RUNNING GIRLS.

DOCTOR JOHNSON complained that Brighton was without trees, and in the guide book for 1803 it says: "The plantation at the Pavilion could not be forced to grow." But some portion of the famous Promenade Grove, I believe, forms part of the Pavilion grounds; and it was here that the Prince and his Court breakfasted in public, picnicked and promenaded. The price of admission, including refreshments, was a shilling. The effect of the music in the grove, says a writer of the time, "was most enchanting." Later on we read of a "public tea-drinking, with music; then fireworks, by Signor Hengler, artist and engineer in fireworks to H.R.H. the Prince of Wales and the Duke ot Clarence;" and "original pony races," and presently a rural *fête*, a Dutch fair, country dances, and a balloon ascent.

Elsewhere we have young women running races (Sussex loveliness is, as a rule, said to be long-legged) "for a Holland smock, with ribbon, value 30*s*.," the winner to have the smock; the second to have a pair of cotton stockings, value 5*s*.; the third a pair of pumps; and the fourth a flannel petticoat." The advertisement concludes with this notice: "The young women may depend on protection from any insults from the country people, as proper care is and will be taken by hiring persons for that purpose."

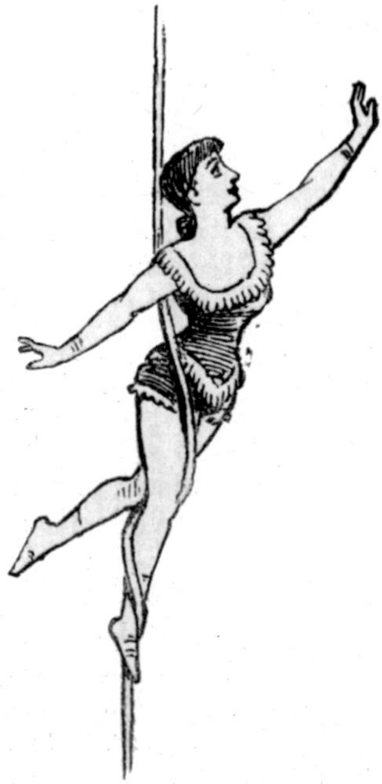

Her rope and pride.

In what costume the young women ran does not appear; but a fashionable beauty, after some races by gentlemen on the Steyne, challenged one to run for ten guineas, and is said to have gone home "to breech and otherwise equip herself for the conflict;" she, however, did not turn up again, and the spectators were sold.

The Swiss Gardens at Shoreham—now under the able management of Mr. George Reeves Smith—form a favourite pleasure resort. They are about twelve acres in extent, and are well timbered. Besides the attraction in summer for boating and fishing, the lakes, which are spanned by ornamental rustic bridges, are much resorted to by skaters in the winter-time. Walks shaded by trees skirt the southern lake, and among the fish are some enormous carp. The Swiss Cottage, which stands at the head of the lakes, was erected when the gardens were first laid out, and is built entirely of Stockholm timber. For many years this Cottage has been acknowledged as the finest example, both interior and exterior, in the kingdom. A *bijou* theatre, capable of holding about 1,500 people, is open during the season, dramatic and other performances being given three times daily. Besides these attractions is a ball-room 200 feet long by 70 feet wide, probably the finest in Sussex. An excellent band plays at frequent intervals daily during the season. The Gardens are situated midway between Worthing and Brighton; they are about a quarter of an hour distant by rail from either place, by road about half an hour's drive.

THE PRESS.

THERE are quite enough newspapers in Brighton: two morning papers, and an evening paper with special editions, one published twice a week, and one three times, and several weeklies, including two of a partly humorous, partly society journal style, all very creditably and in most cases ably conducted. There was even, until lately, an avowedly "comic" paper, called "Toby," edited by a Mr. Ross, who is, however, in no way connected with the person named upon the title-page of this instructive work. It may, indeed, be casually mentioned that there are Rosses and Rosses; for instance, there are nine set down in the "Brighton Directory."

ODDS AND ENDS.

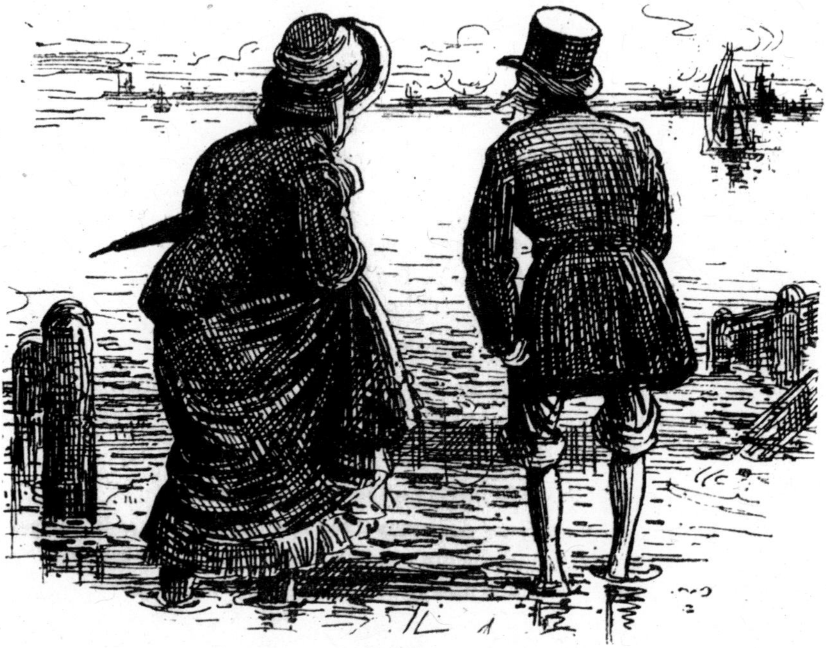

Paddlers.

BATHING AND BATHS.

THE paddlers who elsewhere, at Ramsgate, Margate, and so on, do so much towards enhancing the picturesque, are but rarely met with, save on a balmy Bank holiday, maybe, upon the beach. Perhaps the shingle is somewhat uncongenial to the toe, or there may be some other reason I know not of. "Brighton being on the sea" said a sprightly writer in *Sketch*, "no one ever bathes there—no man, that is to say; all the ladies bathe in the sea; and lest any should be swept away by the under-tow and drowned, hundreds of fine athletic young Englishmen stand as near the ladies' machines as possible, so as to be able to render assistance in the possible hour of need. This sight warms the blood in a man's heart, and if his wife or sister be bathing, makes him proud to reflect he is an Englishman. All the men at Brighton bathe at ——'s. Bathing at ——'s is very nice, though if you dive in the shallow part, under the impression that it is the deep, you are apt to think the world hollow, and all systems of philosophy, from Aristotle's down to Herbert Spencer's, mistakes. The bathing here is very nice and quiet, providing there are not more than six boarding schools in the bath at the same time; when there are nine or ten you cease to pity your grandmother's deafness, and respect the memory of that much-abused ruler Herod."

WHAT WAS GEORGE LIKE?

Those accustomed only to George the Fourth's portrait handed down to us by amiable caricaturists who depicted him in his declining days, should go and see the full-length picture of him by Owen after Hoppner at Hampton Court, in some of the grand robes now in the glass case at Madame Tussaud's. It is the portrait of a handsome, opened-faced, bright-eyed, genial-looking gentleman, and the robes themselves are wonderful to behold. See No. 356 in the catologue.

WHAT IT WAS TO BE A MILITIA MAN EIGHTY-ODD YEARS AGO.

On the 4th May, 1795, a court-martial was opened at the Old Ship, for the trial of thirteen men of the Oxford Militia, charged with mutiny at East Blatchington. The trial lasted nine days, and three of the men were condemned to be shot, which sentence was carried out upon two of them, Cook and Parish, in Goldstone Bottom, on the 12th June, the other, Haddocks, being pardoned "on condition of being transported to Botany Bay for ten years." Six others were sentenced to be flogged, one to receive 500 lashes, one 1,500, and the rest 100 each. The remaining four got off, and, let us hope, felt glad.

THE SOUTH DOWNS.

The beautiful greensward on the Downs is in most parts intermixed with thyme and other aromatic herbs, to which has been ascribed the sweet flavour of the mutton, for which this part of Sussex is celebrated.

THE HEALTHIEST PART OF BRIGHTON.

It has been said that Brighton possesses three distinct climates. In the east the air is bracing and dry, and for the most part free from the saline particles impregnating the air in the lower part of the town. In the west the air is much milder and more humid, in consequence of the south-west winds. The air ot the central portion of Brighton is said to "differ very little from that of any inland town in a low situation, and possesses no bracing properties whatever," but this statement I can hardly believe. The healthiest portion of the town, it has been "generally agreed, is that lying between Western Road on the south, Hove on the west, through Clifton Street to the workhouse on the north, and the eastern extremity of Western Road on the east." The workhouse is healthy too.

THE OLD STORY.

On the 10th September, the Chevalier Maupeau, the son of a French gentleman, took apartments at the New Ship; and on the evening of the following day shot himself under a hedge of a field to the west of the town. It would appear, as usual, to have been "all along of Eliza," and he had twice before attempted to drown himself on his passage to England. Among his effects were three miniatures of a lady set in gold, a large sum in gold and silver, and two diamond crosses of the Order of the Knights of Malta. On the outside of the packet containing these was written in pencil in a trembling hand, "J'en meurt innocent, j'en atteste le ciel."

RINKOMANIA.

I don't believe much in rinks or roller-skating, and I should fancy a good many unfortunates who madly invested capital a few years ago are by this time of my way of thinking. The Brighton Rink, in West Street, has, however, signs

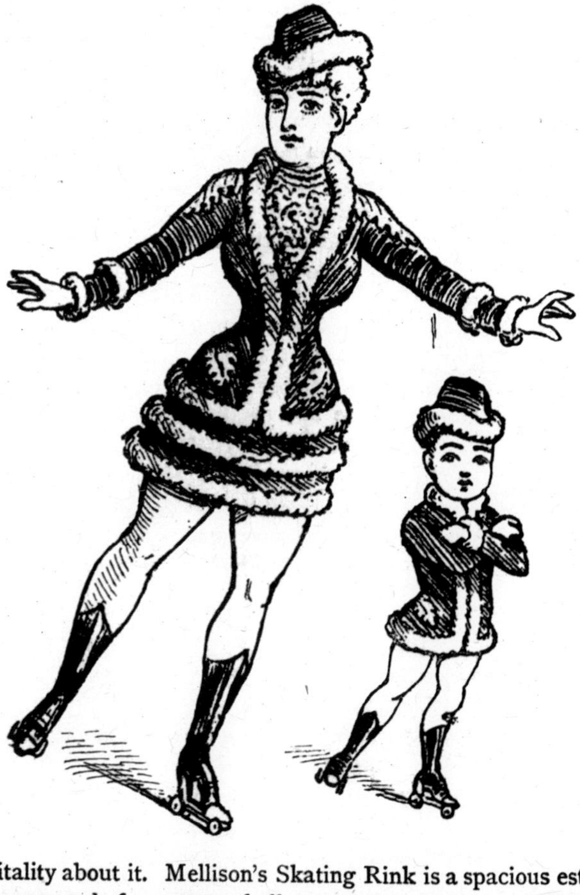

of unusual vitality about it. Mellison's Skating Rink is a spacious establishment, originally constructed for concert hall purposes. It has a well-laid asphalte floor, forming as near an approach to ice as possible. An orchestral band plays several times daily, and occasionally there are special *réunions*, when a regimental or other favourite band is engaged. On either side of thc Rink is a balcony, at the western end a gallery, and at the eastern a large orchestra, containing a good organ. The Rink is not wholly devoted to purposes of roller-skating, occasionally there are other amusements given within its spacious area.

It may be mentioned that the foregoing illustration does not represent the ordinary costume of the lady visitors to the Rink. Were I to say it was I should be deceiving the reader, though I am of opinion that the dress is vastly becoming, and you may see it for yourself, as I have done, at a theatre or a music hall—if you ever go to such naughty places! Pray let us be accurate and—correct.

LADY HUNTINGDON.

According to the Rev. Mr. Toplady, a gentlewoman who lived in the vicinity of Brighton dreamed that a tall lady, whose dress she particularly noted, would come to that town and be an instrument of doing much good. About three years after this dream Lady Huntingdon was induced to visit Brighton in consequence of the illness of her son, for whom sea-bathing had been recommended, but who died here. A few days after the Countess's arrival, the gentlewoman above alluded to met her ladyship in the street, and, instantly she saw her, said, "Oh, madam, you are come!" Lady Huntingdon, naturally surprised, asked, "What do you know of me?" Upon which the other replied, "I saw you in a dream three years ago dressed as you *now appear*," and proceeded in the relation of her dream. Now I would not for a moment cast a doubt upon this story, but it proves one of two things: either that round-about 1757 fashions were slow to change, or the Countess did not follow them.

THE BRAIN OF BRIGHTON.

The good guide book informs me that Brighton has never "produced, at least as far as we can learn, any one person of extraordinary talent. The one exception to this rule may be made, perhaps, in the case of one John Grover, who was born here about the middle of the last century, and distinguished himself in mathematical science under the most adverse circumstances, never having had the least instruction therein, but working his way by sheer labour and indefatigable diligence." I hardly know whether it is much of a recommendation to mention it, but a good many celebrated people have died here, an event which, upon occasion, may be more easily regulated by the person most concerned.

THE MERRY FISHERMEN.

It is surprising how from the beginning of time the native of a seaside resort has "set his back up" against the visitor who is the making of him. In a guide for 1800, I read, "One inconvenience is universally felt, because it might be easily removed. The Brighton fishermen spread their nets to dry on the Steyne where the company walk, by which means they are often in danger of being caught. Where so much benefit is derived to native individuals from strangers resorting thither, surely every compliment should be paid to them, and every accommodation furnished." Surely indeed!

THE FISH MARKET.

This is, weather permitting, held upon the beach, and is a curious sight for those who care to get up at six in the morning to enjoy. The Dutch auctions are conducted by fish salesmen, who put up mixed collections of fish on the Cheap Jack principle, at a much higher price than they expect to get for them, and gradually reduce it till a spectator clenches the bargain with a "Have 'em," and bears away the spoil.

COCK-FIGHTING.

It is not, as a rule, the fashion to give Oliver Cromwell his due, but he was the first in power in England to prohibit cock-fighting. Not that the prohibition would seem to have much interfered with sport. At Brighton as late as 1811 you may find an advertisement of a "main of cocks" to be fought at the King's Arms Yard, George Street, five guineas the battle, and twenty guineas the main; but before this date the practice of throwing at cocks would appear to have been highly popular at Brighton and Lewes, the custom being to tie the poor bird to a stake and throw a cudgel at him until the last gasp of life was beaten out of him. The White Lion used to be, in the beginning of the present century, the head centre of cock-fighting in Brighton; it was, in fact, the great sporting house.

LADY BILLIARD-PLAYERS.

The ladies played billiards in the public rooms on the Steyne in 1769; "and when I beheld them—oh, how I did stare! They handled the sticks with a grace and an air," lispeth a poet of the period.

THE MUCH-ABUSED PAVILION.

The writer of "My Holiday: Where shall I spend it?" says: "The music-room has a noble Saxon simplicity, the whole is in exquisite taste. Sir Walter Scott is said to have considered it an eyesore. It is in vain to attempt to please every one." Now which do you think is right, Sir Walter Scott or the anonymous writer? Shall I tell you? Sir Walter, for once in his life, talked about what he did not understand.

THE PRODDERS.

Says a writer on the Aquarium, "Tanks in the form of octagon tables are exhibited, where the rarer marine zoophytes and smaller and more valuable fish do well, when not interfered with by the foul and forbidding finger of too deeply interested English impertinence." There is something in this. A zoophyte I interviewed upon the subiect said there was a very great deal in it indeed.

THE NOBLE ART.

Six prize fights were appointed to take place on the Brighton Racecourse one day in May, 1788, but at the end of the third, one of the combatants, Earl, a shoemaker, having been punched to death, the sport concluded. The Prince of Wales hearing of the matter next day, settled an annuity upon the dead man's mother for life. In 1800, a fight for a sovereign took place on the Race Hill, before about 4,000 spectators, in which Daniel Watts killed James Smith: the former, committed to Horsham Gaol on a charge of manslaughter, died a few days afterwards of the injuries he himself had received during the battle. In 1811, in a large room at the back of the Unicorn, an exhibition of sparring took place, which was honoured by the presence of the Duke of Cumberland. After a show by Molineux the black, two subordinate professors set to "in imitation of the old school. His Royal Highness laughed heartily, and said he could do as well himself."

THE ROOKS IN THE PAVILION GARDEN.

I am told that they are not to be found there all the year round, but that they build their nests and hatch their eggs there, and go away again. How old is the oldest I wonder—the aged King of the little settlement that caws so bravely in the tall trees? Does he remember these trees when they formed part of the Promenade Grove, where rank and fashion strolled and frivolled eighty years ago? Why not? or if he doesn't, his father or grandfather did for certain, and handed down the long stories of what was said and done by the fine ladies and pretty gentlemen of that now far-distant time. I hold it that these rooks are the last connecting-link between Brighton "as it was and as it is." I reverence rooks: their age, their sagacity, their solemnity:—they are almost human. When young they make middling good pies.

JOHN AND MARY.

A MATTER-OF-FACT NARRATION.

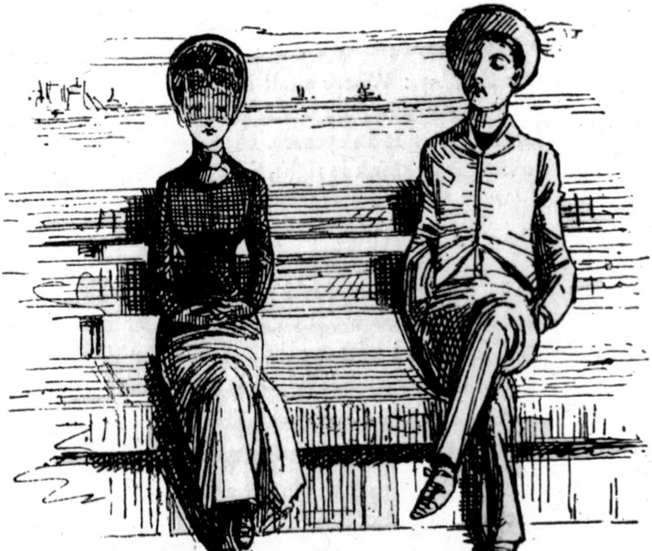

Jemima and James (another couple).

IT was the pier that they were on,
  A situation light and airy;
The Christian name of one was John,
  The other one was christened Mary.

She was a wee thing,—*toute petite*,—
  He majestic towered above her;
A long lank male of many feet
  Was pretty little Mary's lover.

Her eyes were grey, her hair was brown.
  Upon her forehead thick and curly.
Her cheeks were rosy;—out of town
  They go to bed and get up early.

His hair was red, *his* eyes were green,
  His cheeks ridiculously rosy,—
A thing which in a girl when seen,
  The poets liken to a posy.

Hers was quite the prettiest shoe,
And the glossiest black silk stocking,
Just now and then revealed to view
In manner the reverse of shocking.

His boots? A serviceable pair,
With serviceable feet inside 'em;
Too creaky, p'raps, the soles, and there
Are people who cannot abide 'em.

Her bonnet was what 's called a "poke;"
His hat what 's called a "butter-cooler;"
His tawny beard he 'd ofttimes stroke,
A way, when young, with Man the Ruler.

He had, in truth, a noble beard,
Out in the wind a trifle shaggy;
She secretly the same revered!
His trousers at the knees were baggy.

An awful patterned tourist suit
With that cheap look we know as sloppy;
A cane wherewith to slap his boot,
And in his buttonhole a poppy.

Her skirt was black, of course, and tight,
The body to her closely clinging;
She was, in fact, exactly right,
She of whose charms I 'm lamely singing.

* * * *

He loved, she loved, they loved:—'tis true,
And why the dickens should you doubt it?
And I?—I only wish I knew—
Well, just a little more about it.

All 's true I 've said of her and John,—
His name *was* John, her name *was* Mary,
It *was* a pier they walked upon;
And who dare say to the contrairy?

But when I'd got as far as this,
A sudden change came o'er the weather,
"John, it is going to rain," said Miss.
He gave his arm,—they left together.

I watched them till clean out of sight,—
Her wee hand on his coat-sleeve resting,
He looking down,—she, pretty mite!
Up looking. It was interesting!

The rain comes quickly pit-a-pat,
Home to my lunch my way I 'm wending;
I 'm growing old, I 'm growing fat,

* * * *

Here ends this tale without an ending!

THIRTEEN HOURS AT THE AQUARIUM.

It came about in this way:—

There is a vagueness about that sex which it has become a figure of speech to call Adorable, a want of punctuality and a want of consideration for the feelings of others. SHE had simply said, "Meet me at the Aquarium." I shall be as careful as possible in setting down the few facts you will find below to say no more than is absolutely necessary. Therefore I have no intention of telling you why SHE wished me to meet her at the Aquarium. The note, in its entirety, ran thus: "I *must* see you to-morrow. Meet me at the Aquarium."

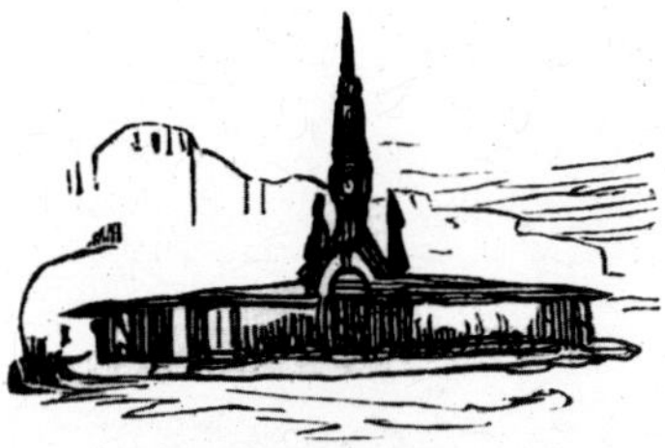

The Outside.

The note bore the Brighton post-mark (she had been staying there some time). I received it in the afternoon, just in time to catch the five-o'clock express; went to a concert at the Dome, in the hope of seeing her; then wandered desolately in the wild night wind past the Bedford, where she was staying; and at last drowned my sorrows in the smoking-room of the Old Ship, and betook myself to bed to await the morrow.

I didn't then know at what hour the Aquarium opened its doors, but I was there very shortly after ten, when the bear in the left-hand corner, at the bottom of the steps, immediately began to beg for buns. I gave him instead a peppermint lozenge I myself had had given me, and had long carried about. He ate it in a supercilious style, and begged no more. You noticed, I presume, that SHE named no time, but between ten and twelve seemed to me to be the most probable, and it is not a very hard thing to spend two hours at the Aquarium.

Wishing to be near to the entrance, I took my seat at the table almost facing the door, and had a good long read at the newspapers. Then yielding to the solicitations of the youth in charge, I was weighed, and with the voucher in my pocket, went back to the newspapers. The door now and again opened and closed, but she came not. I thought I would go for a walk round.

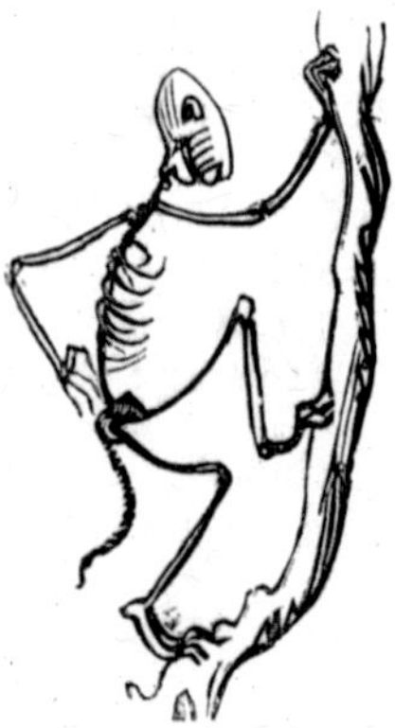

The Ring-tailed Rooster.

The skeleton of a monkey is an improving spectacle, as is also the human skeleton when obtainable. A deuce of a fellow who thinks a lot of himself cannot do better than go and look at another deuce of a fellow's bones, and reflect upon his own osteology. If another fellow's bones are not handy, a monkey's come quite near enough to point a moral and adorn a tail.

When it struck twelve I determined to give the tanks a turn. SHE would be sure to come up the passage; and I devoted an hour to a thoughtful contemplation of the monsters of the deep, lulled by the dulcet strains of the instrumental concert taking place close by. Fish are queer things, as you possibly may have noticed yourself. How they drink, too, and all the while pretend it is only their way of breathing. The worst one they call a toper, and the morning I was there he appeared to have the jumps. The herring, when fresh, is restless, and, flocking with his kind, swims round and round his tank, seemingly without aim or end, unless it be to find a way out. The octopus quiescent looks something like a large tobacco-pouch, but if you dive and take it in your hand, I am informed that it becomes quite lively. The varied formations of the finny tribe are marvellous, but I think any ordinary shoemaker, with a leather portmanteau and a pair of jack-boots to work on, might improve on the manatee. The gurnards put me in mind ot imps and elves, and you may find a row of them all day long staring through the glass, evidently in the hope that Mrs. Nye Chart will engage them for her next pantomime. I should have liked to have had a hermit-crab's opinion on the law of eviction, and I should have liked to know whether among skates

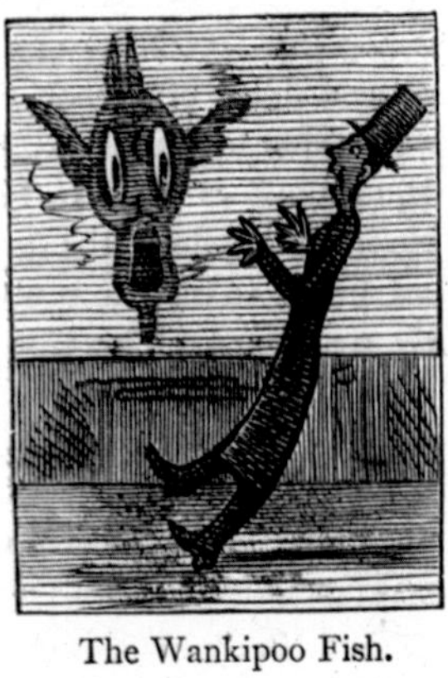

The Wankipoo Fish.

the gentlemen think the ladies pretty, but the glass of the tank divided us, and I passed reluctantly on.

I have heard a lot of unkind things said about fish. They are one and all cannibals. They are one and all cruel and rapacious. They are always hungry. Their quickest sense is that of sight, yet they can't contract the iris of the eye, and there isn't a wink in a sea full of them. They cannot hear much, and they can't smell, and have no taste at all, so that winkle or whale-flesh is alike to them. I have it on authority that they possess a blunted nervous energy, which renders them almost insensible to any infliction; and a fishmonger tells me that instead of the crimping of a cod, the skinning of an eel, or the slow boiling of a lobster hurting the stupid things, they regularly enjoy it. There is no doubt about it, there is something wanting in fish, and yet how I do enjoy a red mullet cooked woodcock fashion in a well-buttered curl-paper!

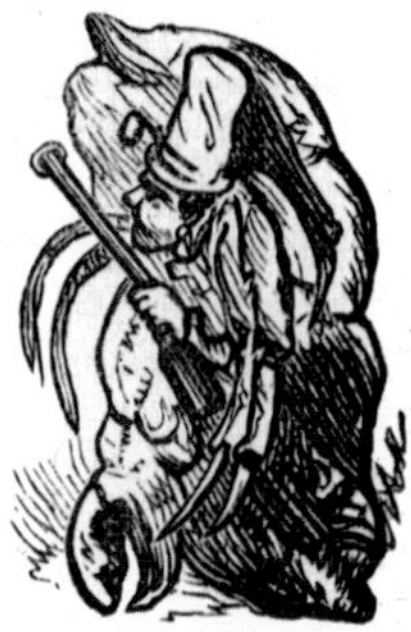
The Hermit-Crab (of Irish extraction).

But SHE did not come, and now it was two o'clock. "Will it be unmanly of me to lunch alone?" I asked myself. "Had I not better allay the pangs of famine with a few wine biscuits and support sinking nature with cold Scotch?"

They feed the seals at three, and I saw them fed. The seal is the only fish (if he be a fish by-the-bye) that can sit down. Even he does not look as though he were shaped for it, but a seal near the fernery frequently sits and seems to like it.

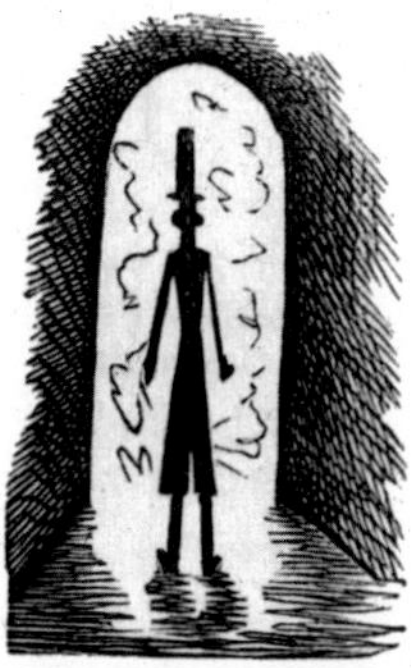
On the Way to the Fernery.

From three to five the band plays again. I heard every piece, saw the sea lions fed, and then I did break down, and went and had my dinner. You can get a very nice little dinner at a very reasonable rate at the Aquarium; but what *chef* can minister to a mind diseased, or what viands tickle the palate of one who has every other moment to thrust his head round a pillar to look after a passing form which might belong to one long waited for? And yet a cigar and a cup of black coffee have at most times something of a soothing effect, and they had then when taken on the gallery overlooking the skating-rink, where, in the orchestra, the Guards' band played, whilst the moon lit up the old Chain Pier and the sea beyond. "But," said I to myself, "perhaps SHE is down below. I suppose I had better go and look." About half-past eight I went to look, but did not find her. I found instead an entertainment of some kind, at which, for a while forgetting my sorrows, I sat and laughed, and then somehow, with a stroll down to the bar, the time passed, the clock struck eleven, the lights were put out, and I walked silently home to my hotel.

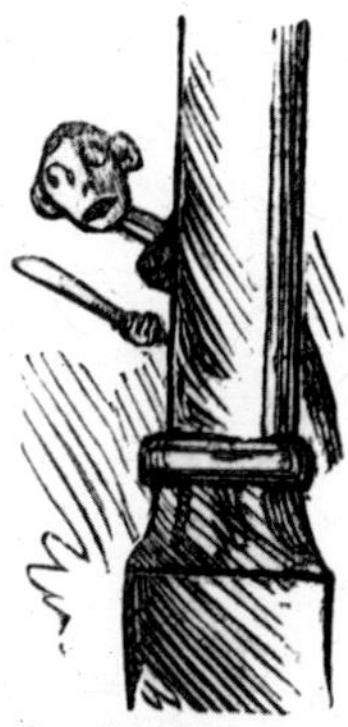
On the Look-out.

When I got a letter it was to say that all was at an end, and to ask for the return of her photograph. All day SHE, too, had been waiting—at another Aquarium, —at Westminster.

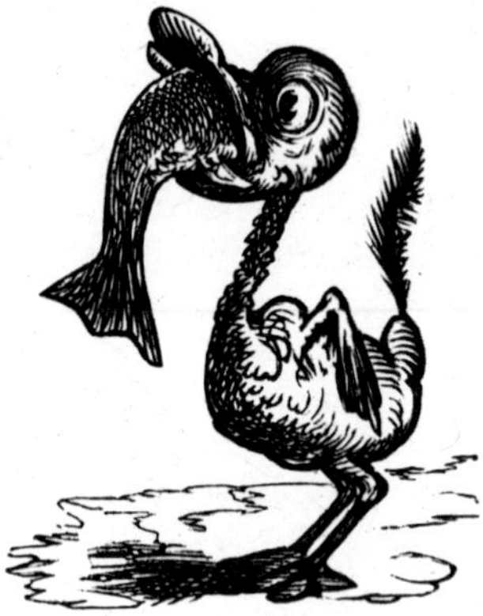

Tailpiece.

THE POST.

CHIEF OFFICE, SHIP STREET.

☞ *The Index Letters—A, B, C, D, E, F and G—next to the times for closing the Box for dispatch of Mails from the Chief Office and the Railway Terminus, agree with those under the words "Collections in Brighton," which denote the corresponding times at which Letters and Papers can be posted at the Pillar and Wall Boxes, and at the Receiving Houses.*

LETTERS FOR LONDON,

Posted at Chief Office or at Railway Wall Box up to the time of closing the Box at			FROM TO		Posted at Receiving House) and Pillar Boxes (as belows FROM TO	MARKED
7 30 a.m.	are delivered	in the City	10 0...12 0;	in other districts	12 0...1 0 p.m.	......*A*
10 30 ,,	ditto	ditto	1 0... 2 0;	ditto	3 0...4 0 ,,	......*B*
1 0 p.m.	ditto	ditto	4 0... 5 0;	ditto	5 0...6 0 ,,	......*C*
3 0 ,,	ditto	ditto	6 0... 7 0;	ditto	7 0...8 30 ,,	....
4 15 ,,	ditto	ditto	8 0... 9 0;	ditto	8 0...9 30 ,,	......*D*
5 30 & 7 30	ditto	ditto	following morning		....	*E*
10 0 ,,	ditto	ditto	7 30 to 9 30 the following morn. (in all districts)...			*F*

On *Sundays* the Box closes at 8.30 p.m. (*G*), and Letters are delivered the following morning.

On Saturdays, *London* Letters posted after 4.15 p.m. (*D*), are not delivered till first post on Monday. *Towns beyond London*, for early morning deliveries, 4.15 (*D*), or for day deliveries, 10 p.m. (*E & F*).

The Colonial and Foreign Mail is dispatched at 4.15 (*D*), and 10 p.m. (*F*); Sundays, 8.30 p.m. (*G*).

LETTERS FOR BRIGHTON,

Posted at the Chief Office or

Railway Wall Box	by	5 50 a.m.	are sent out	by delivery,	commencing at	7 0 a.m.*	... *A & F*†
ditto	ditto	7 30 ,,	ditto	ditto	ditto	9 30 ,,	....
ditto	ditto	10 30 ,,	ditto	ditto	ditto	11 30 ,, *†	... *B*
ditto	ditto	3 30 p.m.	ditto	ditto	ditto	4 30 ,,	... *C & D*
ditto	ditto	6 15 ,,	ditto	ditto	ditto	7 0 ,, ‡	... *E*

On Sundays there is but one delivery, commencing at 7 a.m. (*F*).*

* Including Ovingdean, Patcham, Preston, and Rottingdean. † Including Portslade and Southwick. ‡ Including Preston.

LETTERS FOR THE COUNTRY,

FOR	Posted at the Chief Office or Railway Station,			
Day Delivery,	at Hayward's Heath, Hurstpierpoint, Worthing, and Eastbourne	received up to	7 30 a.m.	*A*
ditto,	at Shoreham and Arundel............................	ditto	9 40 ,,	*A*
ditto,	at Lewes, Uckfield, Hastings, Worthing, Bognor, Chichester	ditto	10 30 ,,	*B*
Evening Delivery,	at Portsmouth, Southampton, and Ryde, Isle of Wight	ditto	12 30 p.m.	*C*
ditto,	at Tunbridge Wells	ditto	1 0 ,,	*C*
ditto,	at Shoreham, Eastbourne, Hastings, Dorking, Redhill, Reigate	ditto	3 0 ,,	*C*
ditto,	at Lewes	ditto	4 0 ,,	*D*
ditto,	at Worthing, Horsham, and Burgess Hill.........	ditto	4 15 ,,	*D*
Following Morning Delivery,	at Shoreham, Worthing, Arundel, Littlehampton, Bognor, Chichester, Hurst, Burgess Hill, Lewes, Eastbourne, Hastings, Hayward's Heath, Cuckfield, East Grinstead, Redhill, Reigate, Croydon, and Crawley	ditto	10 0 ,, *Sun:* 8 30 ,,	*F* *G*
ditto,	at Horsham, Pulborough, Petworth, and Dorking [*Sunday Letters* delivered by first day mail on Monday]	ditto	10 0 ,, *Sun:* 8 30 ,,	*F* *G*
ditto,	at Portsmouth, Godalming, Guildford, Southampton, Isle of Wight, and towns between Bishopstoke and London	ditto	7 30 ,, *Sun:* 8 0 ,,	*E & G*
ditto,	For places not mentioned above, in East Sussex and Kent	ditto	7 30 ,, *Sun:* 7 0 ,,	*E & G*

COLLECTIONS IN BRIGHTON.

AT THE PILLAR AND WALL BOXES:	A	B	C	D	E	F	F	
Aberdeen Road	5 30	9 20	11 20	2 45	5 25	7 45	9 0	*Sundays at 6 p.m. only.*
Arundel Terrace	...	9 25	11 25	2 50	5 25	7 45	9 0	
Baker Street	5 30	9 15	11 20	2 40	5 20	7 45	9 0	
Blatchington Road	...	9 15	11 15	2 25	5 10	8 0	9 0	
Brill's Baths	...	9 45	11 45	3 10	5 40	7 45	9 0	
Castle Square	5 30	9 40	11 35	3 0	5 35	7 45	9 0	
Cavendish Place	5 30	9 40	11 40	3 0	5 40	7 45	9 0	
Crown Street	5 30	9 45	11 45	3 10	5 45	7 45	9 0	
Co. Hospital	5 30	9 15	11 15	2 40	5 15	7 45	9 0	

8—2

COLLECTIONS IN BRIGHTON (*continued*).

At the Pillar and Wall Boxes:	A	B	C	D	E	F	
Devonshire Place	5 30	9 40	11 35	3 0	5 35	7 45	9 0
Ditchling Terrace	5 45	9 30	11 30	2 50	5 30	7 45	9 0
¶Ditchling Rise	...	9 15	11 30	3 15	5 15	8 30	...
Dyke Road	5 30	9 35	11 35	2 55	5 35	7 45	9 0
Egremont Place	5 30	9 15	11 0	2 40	5 15	7 45	9 0
Grand Parade	5 30	9 15	11 0	2 40	5 15	7 45	9 0
Holland Road	5 30	9 25	11 25	2 40	5 25	8 0	9 0
Islingword Road	...	8 45	...	2 15	...	7 45	...
Kemp Town, R.S.*	5 30	9 15	11 15	2 40	5 15	7 45	9 0
Lansdowne Place	5 30	9 15	11 15	2 30	5 15	8 0	9 0
Lansdowne Road	5 30	9 15	11 15	2 15	5 30	8 0	9 0
¶Lovers' Walk	...	9 15	11 30	3 0	5 15	8 30	...
Marine Square	5 30	9 30	11 30	3 0	5 30	7 45	9 0
Medina Villas	5 30	9 20	11 20	2 35	5 20	8 0	9 0
Montpelier Road	5 30	9 40	11 40	3 0	5 40	7 45	9 0
North Street	5 30	9 45	11 45	3 10	5 45	7 45	9 0
Old Steyne, P.B.	5 30	9 40	11 35	3 0	5 35	8 0	9 0
*Old Steyne, W.B.	5 30	9 40	11 35	3 0	5 35	7 45	9 0
Park Crescent	5 30	9 20	11 20	2 45	5 25	7 45	9 0
Percival Terrace	5 30	9 25	11 25	2 50	5 25	7 45	9 0
Prestonville	5 30	9 30	11 30	2 55	5 35	7 45	9 0
St. John's Terrace	5 30	9 15	11 15	2 30	5 15	7 45	9 0
St. Katherine Terrace	5 30	9 20	11 20	2 35	5 20	8 0	9 0
St. Michael's Place	5 30	9 35	11 35	3 0	5 45	7 45	9 0
Sussex Square	5 30	9 25	11 25	2 50	5 25	7 45	9 0
West Street	5 30	9 45	11 50	3 15	5 45	7 45	9 0
¶Preston	...	10 0	...	3 0	6 0	8 0	...

Sundays at 6 p.m. only.

* Telegraph Offices.

¶ Patcham (B) 9.30. (E) 5.30; Ovingdean (B) 8.0, (E) 5.15; Southwick (C) 12.25, (F) 8.15; Portslade-by-Sea (C) 11.0, (F) 8.0; Portslade Station (C) 12.30, (F) 8.20; Portslade (C) 10.55, (F) 8.0.

At the Receiving Houses:							
5 Alma Terrace	...	9 20	11 20	2 35	5 20	8 0	...
10 Blatchington Road	...	9 20	11 20	2 35	5 15	8 0	...
19 Bedford Street	...	9 40	11 35	3 0	5 35	8 0	...
1 Oxford Terrace	...	9 20	11 20	2 35	5 20	8 0	...
45 Dyke Road	...	9 25	11 25	2 50	5 30	8 0	...
7 Belgrave Terrace*	...	9 30	11 30	2 55	5 30	8 0	...
6 Lewes Road	...	9 20	11 20	2 45	5 25	8 0	...
19 North Road	...	9 10	10 55	2 35	5 10	8 0	...
Lewes Road, North	...	9 20	11 20	2 45	5 25	8 0	...
1 Preston Road	...	9 20	11 20	2 45	5 25	8 0	...
30 Preston Street	...	9 40	11 40	3 0	5 40	8 0	...
50 Queen's Road*	...	9 40	11 40	3 5	5 45	8 0	...
109 St. James's Street	...	9 40	11 35	3 0	5 35	8 0	...
101 Southover Street	...	9 0	...	2 30	...	7 45	...
Victoria Road*	...	9 30	11 30	2 55	5 35	8 0	...
65 Waterloo Street	...	9 30	11 30	2 45	5 30	8 0	...
West Pier	...	9 40	11 40	3 0	5 40	8 0	...
22 Western Road, Hove* ...	...	9 10	11 10	2 25	5 10	8 0	...
1 York Place	...	9 15	11 20	2 40	5 20	8 0	...
Preston	...	10 0	...	3 0	6 0	8 0	...
¶Rottingdean	...	9 50	...	...	5 0	...	...

No Sunday Collection.

* Telegraph Offices.

¶ *Sundays*, 5.30 p.m. at Ditchling Rise, Lovers' Walk, and Preston; and at Patcham, 9.30 a.m.; Ovingdean, 11.15 a.m.; Rottingdean, 11 a.m.; Southwick, Portslade-by-Sea, Portslade Station, and Portslade, 5 p.m.

RATES OF POSTAGE.

Letters not exceeding 1 oz., 1d.; 2 oz., 1½d., and ½d. extra for every additional 2 oz. up to 12 oz.; exceeding 12 oz. charged 1d. per oz. To France or America, under ½ oz., 2½d.

BOOK POST.—½d. for every 2 oz., but not to exceed 5 lbs. in weight, nor 1 ft. 6 in. long and 9 in. in width. *POST OFFICE ORDERS.*—Under 10s., 2d.; for 10s. and under £2, 3d.; for £2, and every £ up to £10, 1d. extra. *LETTERS REGISTERED* on payment of 2d. Special envelopes for this purpose can be purchased at 2½d. each.

TELEGRAMS.

The Chief Office is open for transmission of Telegrams day and night on week days, and on Sundays from 7 a.m. till 8 p.m.; and at the Receiving Houses marked with on asterisk (*) from 8 a.m. to 8 p.m. on week days only.—20 words, 1s.: every 5 words after, 3d.

OMNIBUSES.

From Castle Square, *viâ* Western Road, for Church Street, Hove.—Fare, 2d.

MORNING.

8 57	9 27	9 42	10 4	10 19	10 34	10 50	11 4	11 19	11 34	11 5
9 19	9 34	9 57	10 12	10 27	10 42	10 57	11 12	11 27	11 42	11 5

AFTERNOON.

12 4	12 42	1 19	1 57	2 34	3 12	3 50	4 27	5 4	5 42	6 19	6 57	7 34	8 12	8 50	9 27	*Saturdays*
12 12	12 50	1 27	2 4	2 42	3 19	3 57	4 34	5 12	5 50	6 27	7 4	7 42	8 19	8 57	9 34	*only*
12 19	12 57	1 34	2 12	2 50	3 27	4 4	4 42	5 19	5 57	6 34	7 12	7 50	8 27	9 4	9 42	10 34
12 27	1 4	1 42	2 19	2 57	3 34	4 12	4 50	5 27	6 4	6 42	7 19	7 57	8 34	9 12	9 50	10 42
12 34	1 12	1 50	2 27	3 4	3 42	4 19	4 57	5 34	6 12	6 50	7 27	8 4	8 42	9 19	9 57	10 50

From Church Street, Hove, *viâ* Western Road, for Castle Square.—Fare, 2d.

MORNING.

8 30	9 0	9 37	9 52	10 7	10 23	10 37	10 52	11 7	11 23	11 37	11 52
8 52	9 30	9 45	10 0	10 15	10 30	10 45	11 0	11 15	11 30	11 45	...

AFTERNOON.

12 0	12 45	1 30	2 15	3 0	3 45	4 30	5 15	6 0	6 45	7 30	8 15	9 0	9 45
12 7	12 52	1 37	2 23	3 7	3 52	4 37	5 23	6 7	6 52	7 37	8 23	9 7	*Satdys*
12 15	1 0	1 45	2 30	3 15	4 0	4 45	5 30	6 15	7 0	7 45	8 30	9 15	9 52
12 23	1 7	1 52	2 37	3 23	4 7	4 52	5 37	6 23	7 7	7 52	8 37	9 23	10 7
12 30	1 15	2 0	2 45	3 30	4 15	5 0	5 45	6 30	7 15	8 0	8 45	9 30	10 15
12 37	1 23	2 7	2 52	3 37	4 23	5 7	5 52	6 37	7 23	8 7	8 52	9 37	10 23

From Pavilion Buildings, Castle Square, for London Road and Preston.—Fare to Viaduct, 2d.; to Preston, 3d.

9 0	9 40	10 20	11 0	11 40	12 20	1 0	1 40	2 20	3 0	3 40	4 20	5 0	5 40	6 20	7 0	7 40
9 20	10 0	10 40	11 20	12 0	12 40	1 20	2 0	2 40	3 20	4 0	4 40	5 20	6 0	6 40	7 20	8 0

From Glebe Side, Preston, for Pavilion Buildings, Castle Square.—Fare to St. Peter's Church, 2d.; to Castle Square, 3d.

9 20	10 0	10 40	11 20	12 0	12 40	1 20	2 0	2 40	3 20	4 0	4 40	5 20	6 0	6 40	7 20	8 0
9 40	10 20	11 0	11 40	12 20	1 0	1 40	2 20	3 0	3 40	4 20	5 0	5 40	6 20	7 0	7 40	8 20

And on *SUNDAYS*, to and from the Aquarium, at short intervals, commencing at 2.30 p.m., till dusk.

From New Road (North Street end) for Cemeteries, Lewes Road.—Fare, 2d.

10 0	11 0	12 0	1 0	2 0	3 0	4 0	5 0	6 0	7 0	8 0	9 0
10 30	11 30	12 30	1 30	2 30	3 30	4 30	5 30	6 30	7 30	8 30	9 30

From Cemeteries, Lewes Road, for New Road (North Street end).—Fare, 2d.

9 40	10 40	11 40	12 40	1 40	2 40	3 40	4 40	5 40	6 40	7 40	8 40
10 10	11 10	12 10	1 10	2 10	3 10	4 10	5 10	6 10	7 10	8 10	9 10

And on *SUNDAYS*, to and from the Aquarium, at intervals of a quarter of an hour, from 2.0 p.m. till dusk.

From Castle Square, *viâ* St. James's Street, for Rock Street, Kemp Town.—Fare, 2d.

...	9 27	10 27	11 27	12 27	1 27	2 27	3 27	4 27	5 27	6 27	27	8 27	9 27
8 57	9 57	10 57	11 57	12 57	1 57	2 57	3 57	4 57	5 57	6 57	7 57	8 57	9 57

From Rock Street, Kemp Town, for Castle Square.—Fare, 2d.

...	9 0	10 0	11 0	12 0	1 0	2 0	3 0	4 0	5 0	6 0	7 0	8 0
8 30	9 30	10 30	11 30	12 30	1 30	2 30	3 30	4 30	5 30	6 30	7 30	8 30

Brighton, Portslade, Fishersgate, Southwick, Shoreham, &c.

An Omnibus leaves the Unicorn Stables, North Street, *daily*, at 12.0 noon, and 6.0 p.m., and the King and Queen Hotel, Marlborough Place, at 12 noon and 5.30 p.m., for Shoreham, *viâ* Portslade, Fishersgate, Southwick, and Kingston.—Fare, to Southwick, 5d.; Kingston and Shoreham, 6d. Leaves the Royal George Hotel, Shoreham, for Brighton, *daily*, at 9.0 a.m. and 2.0 p.m.

Brighton, Patcham, Pyecombe, Hurstpierpoint, Albourne, Henfield, &c.

On *Tuesdays, Thursdays, and Saturdays only*, an Omnibus leaves the Clarence Yard, North Street, at 4 p.m. for Hurstpierpoint, *viâ* Patcham, Pyecombe, Newtimber, and Albourne. (Leaves White Horste Hurst, at 9 a.m., for Brighton.) Fares, to Patcham, 6d.; Pyecombe, 9d.; Albourne, 1s.—Also from the Union Yard, North Street, for Henfield, *viâ* Patcham and Woodmancote, at 4 p.m. (Leaves Henfield a 9 a.m., for Brighton.) Fare, 1s.

Brighton and Rottingdean.

Omnibuses leave Brighton Terminus at 11.50 a.m., 12.30, 5.20, and 5.50 p.m. for Rottingdean, calling at Castle Square on the journey. From Rottingdean to Brighton Terminus at 9.50 and 10.30 a.m., and 2.0 and 2.30 p.m. Fares, 6d. each way.

CAB FARES, &c.

CAB, HAND-CHAIR, AND GOAT-CHAISE FARES.

First-Class Hackney Carriages are constructed to carry Four Adults; Second-Class vehicles carry Two Adults; Third-Class Carriages consist of Bath Chairs drawn by hand, constructed to carry One Adult—or Chaises drawn by mules, donkeys, or goats, and constructed to carry Four Children; and Fourth-Class Carriages are Chaises drawn by a goat or goats, and allowed to carry not more than Two Children. The fixed tariffs for hiring are as under:—

		s.	*d.*
	FIRST-CLASS CARRIAGE.		
By Time.			
	Any time not exceeding one hour	3	0
	Every additional half-hour or portion of a half-hour	1	6
By Distance.			
	Any distance not exceeding one mile	1	0
	Every additional half-mile or portion of a half-mile	0	6
	SECOND-CLASS CARRIAGE.		
By Time.			
	Any time not exceeding one hour	2	0
	Every additional half-hour or portion of a half-hour	1	0
By Distance.			
	Any distance not exceeding one mile and a half	1	0
	Every additional half-mile or portion of a half-mile	0	4
	THIRD-CLASS CARRIAGE.		
By Time.			
	Any time not exceeding one hour	1	0
	Every additional half-hour or portion of a half-hour	0	6
By Distance.			
	Any distance not exceeding one mile	0	8
	Every additional half-mile or portion of a half-mile	0	4
	FOURTH-CLASS CARRIAGE.		
By Time.			
	Any time not exceeding one hour	0	6
	Every additional half-hour or portion of a half-hour	0	3
By Distance.			
	Any distance not exceeding one mile	0	6
	Every additional half-mile or portion of a half-mile	0	3

After twelve o'clock at night, and until two o'clock in the morning, all fares are increased one-half; and after two o'clock until six o'clock in the morning, the ordinary fares are doubled.

Every Hackney Carriage Driver standing at any of the stands or in any street, who refuses, without reasonable excuse, to drive such carriage to any distance not exceeding five miles from the Town Hall, Brighton, is liable to a penalty of Forty Shillings. Misconduct on the part of any Driver should be reported to the Inspector of Hackney Carriages, whose office is at the Town Hall.

FARES TO SOME OF THE PRINCIPAL PARTS FROM THE RAILWAY STATION.

One Mile Fare.—The Town Hall, the Theatre, Pavilion, Aquarium, Old Ship Hotel, Markwell's Hotel, bottom of West Street (opposite the Sea), Grand Hotel, Regency Square, Powis Square, Montpellier Road, London Road, the Viaduct, the Circus (Lewes Road).

One Mile and a Half.—West corner of Marine Square, County Hospital, Brunswick Square, Adelaide Crescent, and Cavalry Barracks.

Two Miles.—Lewes Crescent, Sussex Square, and Cliftonville (Medina Villas, Albany Villas, Ventnor Villas, &c.).

Luggage.—A reasonable quantity of Luggage may be carried in or upon every Hackney Carriage without any additional charge; but when two persons or more are carried in any Hackney Carriage with more luggage than can be carried inside, a sum of 3d. for every package carried outside is to be paid.

Dalziel Brothers, Camden Press, London, N.W.

WRITING, BOOK-KEEPING, &c.

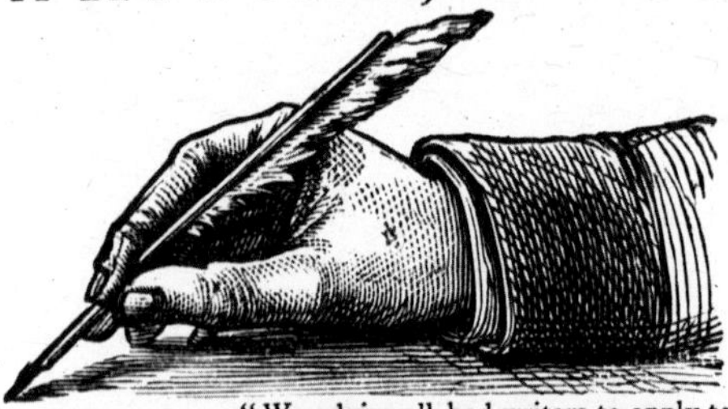

PERSONS of any age, however bad their writing, may, in EIGHT to TWELVE easy LESSONS, acquire permanently an elegant and flowing style of PENMANSHIP, adapted either to professional pursuits or private correspondence.

ARITHMETIC on a method requiring only one-third the time usually requisite.

BOOK-KEEPING, as practised in the Government, Banking, and Merchants' Offices; Shorthand, &c. For Terms, &c., apply to Mr. SMART, at the Institution, Quadrant, Regent Street.

"We advise all bad writers to apply to Mr. Smart."—*Evening Star.*

⁂ CAUTION.—No connection with any parties teaching in the Provinces or elsewhere assuming the Name, copying the Advertisements, &c., of Mr. WILLIAM SMART, whose Sole Address is 97B, QUADRANT, REGENT STREET, W.

N.B.—Agent to the West of England Fire and Life Insurance Company.

GOODALL'S HOUSEHOLD SPECIALITIES.

A Single Trial solicited from those who have not yet tried these Splendid Preparations.

GOODALL'S YORKSHIRE RELISH.

The most Delicious Sauce in the World.

This cheap and excellent Sauce makes the plainest viands palatable, and the daintiest dishes more delicious. To Chops, Steaks, Fish, &c., it is incomparable. *In Bottles at 6d., 1s., and 2s. each.*

GOODALL'S BAKING POWDER.

The Best in the World.

Makes delicious puddings without eggs, pastry without butter, and beautiful light bread without yeast. In 1d. Packets, 6d., 1s., 2s., and 5s. Tins.

GOODALL'S QUININE WINE.

The Best and most Agreeable Tonic yet introduced.

The best remedy known for Indigestion, Loss of Appetite, General Debility, &c. Restores delicate individuals to health. *At 1s. 1½d. and 2s. 3d. each Bottle.*

GOODALL'S CUSTARD POWDER.

For making Delicious Custards without Eggs, in less time and at half the price.

The Proprietors can recommend it to Housekeepers generally as a useful agent in the preparation of a good Custard. GIVE IT A TRIAL. *Sold in Boxes, 6d and 1s. each.*

GOODALL'S GINGER BEER POWDER.

Makes Three Gallons of the Best Ginger Beer in the World for 3d.

The most valuable preparation for the production of a delicious and invigorating beverage. It is easily made, and is by far the cheapest and best Ginger Beer Powder ever offered to the public. *Sold in Packets, 3d. and 6d. each.*

GOODALL'S EGG POWDER.

Its action in Cakes, Puddings, &c., &c., resembles that of the egg in every particular. One penny packet will go as far as four eggs! and one sixpenny tin as far as twenty-eight! Sold everywhere, in 1d. packets; 6d. and 1s. Tins.

GOODALL'S BLANC MANGE POWDER.

Making delicious Blanc Manges in a few minutes. In Boxes, 6d. and 1s. each.

GOODALL'S BRUNSWICK BLACK.

For Painting Stoves, Grates, Iron, Tin, &c. In Bottles, 6d. and 1s. each.

All the above-named Preparations may be had of all Grocers, Chemists, Patent Medicine Dealers, and Oilmen.

Manufacturers:—GOODALL, BACKHOUSE, & Co., White Horse St., LEEDS.

VOSE'S PATENT HYDROPULT.

The best Portable Garden and Fire Engine made. Weighs but 8 lbs., and will throw water 50 feet. Also

LOYSEL'S PATENT HYDROSTATIC TEA AND COFFEE PERCOLATORS.

(Block Tin and Copper Bronzed.)

These Urns, of which more than 200,000 are now in use, are, without exception, the simplest and the most efficient ones yet introduced. They produce quickly, and with very little trouble, beautifully clear and fine-flavoured Tea or Coffee, and effect a considerable saving by extracting all the strength.

THE ABOVE ARE SOLD BY ALL RESPECTABLE IRONMONGERS.

Manufacturers—GRIFFITHS & BROWETT, Birmingham; 21 Moorgate Street, London; and 47 Avenue Parmentier, Paris.

BERTIN,

(Artiste de Paris),

PHOTOGRAPHER

By Appointment to the Theatre Royal and Opera House,

88 KING'S ROAD, BRIGHTON.

The Studio, which contains some of the finest specimens of Photography, is open to the Public from 9 a.m. to 6 p.m.

NOTE THE ADDRESS,—88 KING'S ROAD, BRIGHTON.

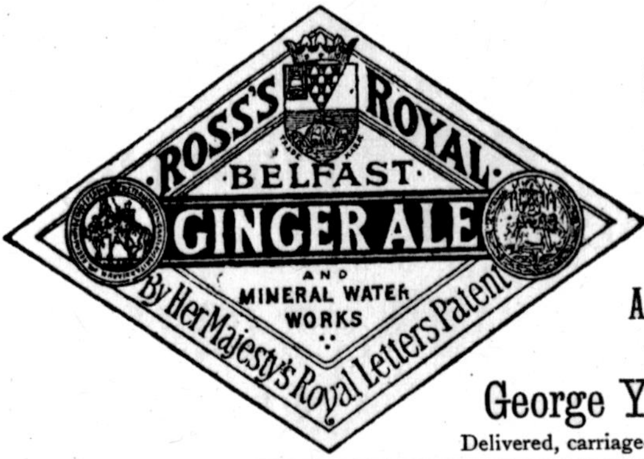

CAUTION.

BELFAST GINGER ALE.

W. A. ROSS, the Original Patentee and Maker of this celebrated Drink, cautions the public that the "Genuine" can only be had at

Ross's Royal Ginger Ale

AND

Aerated Water Works, Belfast.

LONDON OFFICE:

George Yard, Aldermanbury.

Delivered, carriage-free, within Fifteen Miles of London.

ESTABLISHED 1851.

BIRKBECK BANK,

Southampton Buildings, Chancery Lane.

Current Accounts opened according to the usual practice of other Bankers, and Interest allowed on the Minimum Monthly Balances when not drawn below £25. No commission charged for keeping Accounts, excepting under very special circumstances.

The Bank also receives money on Deposit at Three per cent. Interest, repayable on demand.

The Bank undertakes for its Customers, free of charge, the Custody of Deeds, Writings, and other Securities and Valuables; the collection of Bills of Exchange, Dividends, and Coupons; the granting of Annuities; and the purchase and sale of Stocks and Shares.

Letters of Credit and Circular Notes issued.

A Pamphlet, with full particulars, on application.

31*st March*, 1880. FRANCIS RAVENSCROFT, *Manager.*

The BIRKBECK BUILDING SOCIETY'S Annual Receipts exceed Four Millions.

HOW TO PURCHASE A HOUSE FOR TWO GUINEAS PER MONTH,

With Immediate Possession and No Rent to pay. Apply at the Office of the BIRKBECK BUILDING SOCIETY.

HOW TO PURCHASE A PLOT OF LAND FOR FIVE SHILLINGS PER MONTH,

With Immediate Possession, either for Building or Gardening Purposes. Apply at the Office of the BIRKBECK FREEHOLD LAND SOCIETY. A Pamphlet, with full particulars, on application.

FRANCIS RAVENSCROFT, *Manager.*

Southampton Buildings, Chancery Lane.

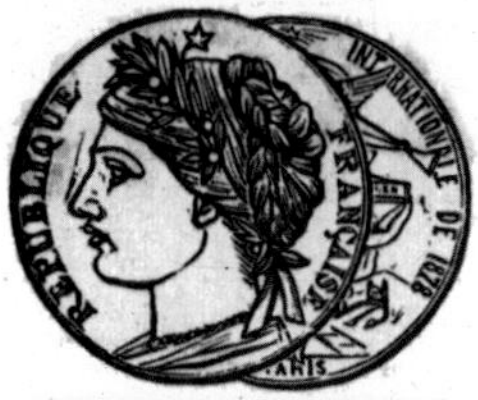
REPUBLIQUE FRANÇAISE
INTERNATIONALE DE 1878
PARIS

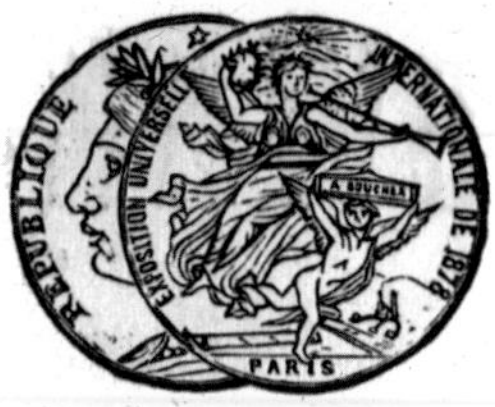
REPUBLIQUE
EXPOSITION UNIVERSELLE
INTERNATIONALE DE 1878
A. BOUCHER
PARIS

SWANBILL CORSETS

(REGISTERED).

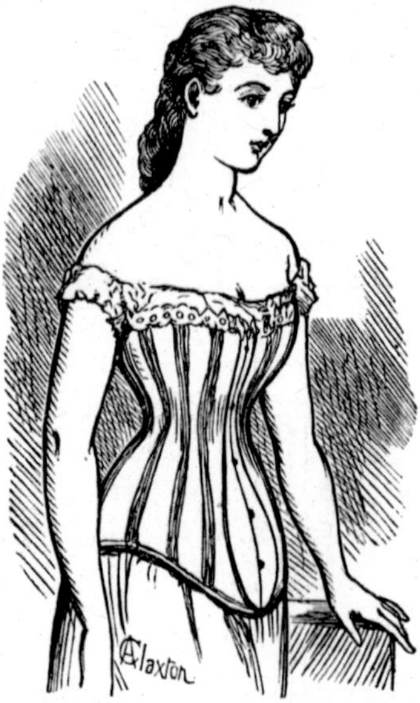

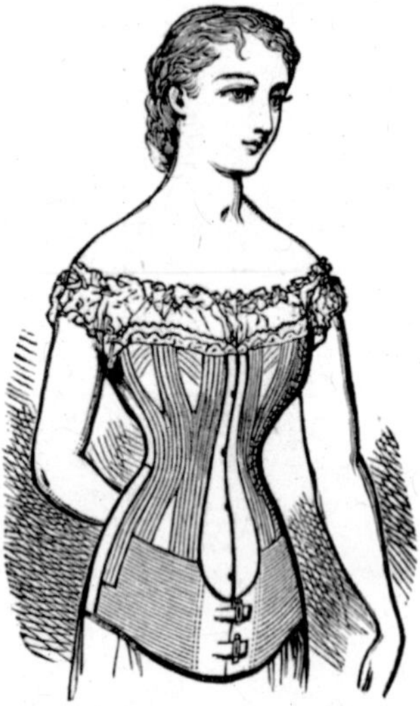

SWANBILL CORSETS,
14s. 6d.
For Medium Figures, 17s. 6d.
For Tall Figures, 18s. 6d.
For Short Figures, 14s. 6d.

Swanbill Belt Corset, 21s.,
31s. 6d.
In Black or Scarlet, 42s.
Descriptive Key of Forty Different Corsets, Post-free.

Send Size of Waist, with P.O. Order, to prevent delay and inconvenience.

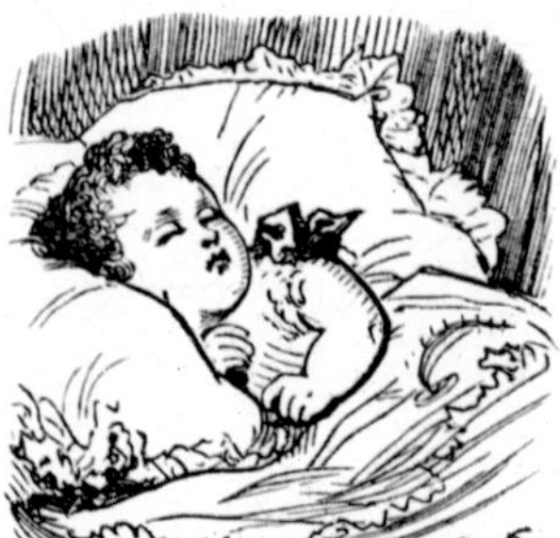

LAYETTES.

	£	s.	d.
List No. 1	5	5	0
,, 2	11	2	3
,, 3	25	11	8
,, 4	47	6	9

Full particulars post-free.

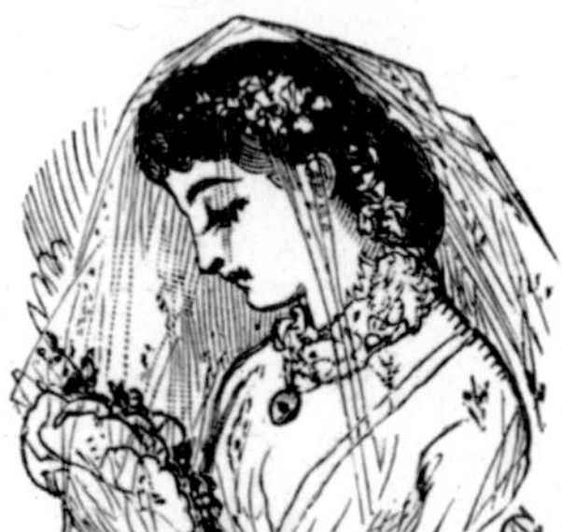

TROUSSEAUX.

	£	s.	d.
List No. 1	25	6	3
,, 2	35	12	0
,, 3	51	6	0
,, 4	70	4	6

Full particulars post-free.

MRS. ADDLEY BOURNE,

37 PICCADILLY (OPPOSITE St. JAMES'S CHURCH), LONDON.

This book is a reprint of a guide first published in *1881*.
It is reproduced here with minor amendments
to aid legibility and clarity.

Published by
QueenSpark Books
a charity and not-for-profit company which, for 45 years, has
helped the good people of Brighton & Hove to tell their stories.

www.queensparkbooks.org.uk
www.photosbrightonandhove.org.uk

Charity number: 1172938
Company number: 02404473

ISBN: 978-1-9996699-1-1

A catalogue record of this book is available from the **British Library**

Printed by **One Digital**

Re-formatted and laid out by Timothy Pilcher, Esq.
with much gracious assistance from Ms. Julie Weir.

Acknowledgements

Deepest gratitude to **THE KEEP** (*www.thekeep.info*),
and particularly Andrew Bennett, for their help
in the retrieval and scanning of this book.

QueenSpark Books acknowledges the continued support from,
and our collaboration with, Brighton & Hove City Council
and the University of Brighton.

Brighton & Hove City Council

QueenSpark Books

University of Brighton

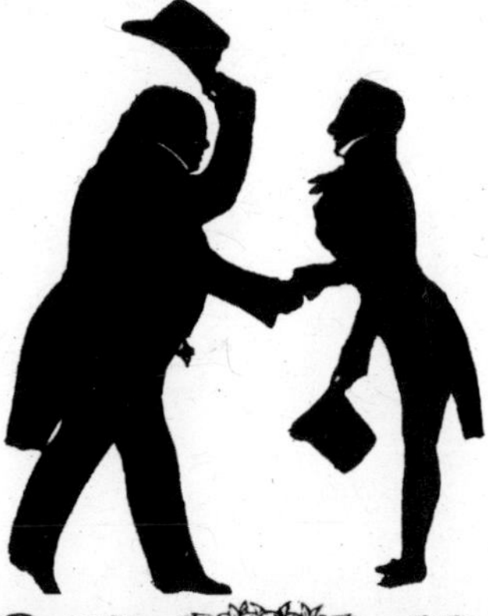